MERCHANT OF TERROR

General Sherman and Total War

MERCHANT
of
TERROR

General Sherman
and Total War

JOHN BENNETT WALTERS

THE BOBBS-MERRILL COMPANY, INC.
INDIANAPOLIS   NEW YORK

The Bobbs-Merrill Company, Inc.
Indianapolis   New York
Copyright © 1973 by John Bennett Walters
All rights reserved
ISBN 0-672-51782-2
Library of Congress catalog card number 72-89711
Designed by Jack Jaget

This book is dedicated
to my wife,
MARTHA PATTERSON WALTERS

Contents

Acknowledgments

A book like this one can be written only with the cooperation of many people. From the outset, the author realizes that he cannot express his appreciation to each one who had a part in the final work. However, recognition should be given to those who had a direct influence on the writer and who had a part in producing the manuscript.

The late Frank L. Owsley, Sr., eminent Southern historian, teacher and close friend at Vanderbilt University, continually encouraged me in the collection of materials for the book. His conviction that the study was worthwhile kept me from giving it up. My sincere appreciation is extended to Hartwell T. Bynum, Colonel, U.S.A. (Retired), for his insistence that I have the book published and he personally recommended the work to Bobbs-Merrill Company.

Mrs. Lena N. Jeter worked long and patiently in the preparation of the manuscript, and her efficiency and sense of humor carried us over some trying times. I deeply appreciate the welcome assistance of Mrs. Corinne Miller in the typing of the manuscript.

I wish I could personally thank, individually, the many librarians and their assistants for their help while the research was being done.

J.B.W.

Montevallo, Alabama
Spring, 1972

Preface

Within recent years the term "total war" has been so definitely accepted as a part of the everyday vocabulary that there is danger of losing sight of the fact that the concept has not always prevailed in its twentieth-century form. In a measure, of course, all wars have involved more than the clash between armed forces, but with the development of the modern state, war became an instrument of national policy waged by specially organized units, either recruits or mercenaries, according to more or less generally recognized rules. By the nineteenth century the laws of land warfare, established by long usage, had begun to take form as a definite body of international jurisprudence, violations of which were subject to diplomatic protest and to reprisal. Prominent among the problems which received cognizance in the course of this development were those dealing with the status and the rights of that part of the population of a belligerent state who did not participate in the hostilities. Although effective sanction was not always present, it was generally understood that the noncombatant or civilian population should be free from all violence or constraint other than that required by military necessity. In the case of the American Civil War, for example, the federal government officially recognized the distinction between combatants and noncombatants in the Confederacy by incorporating in its famous "Instructions for the Government of Armies of the United States in the Field" (General Orders No. 100) specific provisions concerning the treatment of the civilian population in the zones of military operations. "As civilization has advanced during the last centuries," stated Article 22 of those instructions, "so has likewise steadily advanced, especially in war on land, the distinction between the private individual belonging to a hostile country and the hostile country itself, with its men in arms. The principle has been more and more acknowledged that the unarmed citizen is to be spared in person, property, and honor as much as the exigencies of war will admit." Succeeding articles proceeded to explain that in contrast with the practice of barbarous armies, where "the private individual of the hostile country is destined to suffer every privation of liberty and protection, and every disruption of family ties," in modern civilized warfare "protection of the inoffensive citizen of the hostile country is the rule; privation and disturbance of private relations are the exceptions." Article 44 then specified that "all wanton violence committed against persons in the invaded country, all destruction of property not commanded by the authorized officer, all robbery, all pillage or sacking, even after taking a place by main force, all rape, wounding, maiming, or killing of such inhabitants, are prohibited under the penalty of death, or such other severe punishment as may seem adequate for the gravity of the offense."[1]

Paradoxically, it was in that same conflict that a Union general, William Tecumseh Sherman, gradually evolved his own personal philosophy of war along lines which were clearly at variance with the official pronouncements, and in his practical application of that philosophy became one of the first of the modern generals to revert to the idea of the use of military force against the civilian population of the enemy. While this represents only a part of the present concept of total war, its significance lies in Sherman's demonstration of the effectiveness of a plan of action which would destroy the enemy's economic system and terrify and demoralize the civilian population. By paralyzing the economy, Sherman destroyed the Confederacy's ability to supply its armies; and by despoiling and scattering the families of the soldiers in the opposing armies, he undermined the morale of their military forces.

Sherman's conduct, reflected in the actions of his men, demonstrated a strange hatred—one without parallel even in World War II. Even as brutal as the Japanese were to prisoners and to civilians who came under their bayonets, there was no demand in United States newspapers for the burning, sacking and pillaging of towns. Nor was there any public sentiment for the humiliation of civilians.

No efforts are made here to show that Sherman's program of terror was original with him. It is evident that he was willing to proceed in the face of official pronouncements to the contrary to apply the terrifying force of an uncontrolled soldiery against noncombatants. It is likewise evident that he would not have dared do so without the tacit approval of Abraham Lincoln and General Grant. Sherman pleaded that he could not control his troops in the face of their righteous indignation against those who would rebel against a benign government. The pages of recent history reveal that this plea was reiterated by both Japanese and German generals as they mounted the steps of scaffolds to which they were condemned by international tribunals.

There were extreme and unnecessary cruelties involving civilians in the Korean action. However, it was in the highly dramatic court martial of Lieutenant Calley that the army undertook to point up the brutal attack upon civilians in the village of My Lai, South Vietnam. The nation and the world were shocked at the pictures and detailed accounts of witnesses which placed upon the consciences of people everywhere the details of the massacre of the inhabitants, including women and children, of My Lai.

Because the lessons which Sherman's philosophy taught were not likely to be ignored in the conduct of future wars, the process by which his plan was developed, applied and rationalized is perhaps worthy of special examination. There can be little doubt that Sherman's actions toward a proud and almost defenseless people left a heritage of hate which lasted far longer than it might otherwise have lasted.

Introduction

The early life of William Tecumseh Sherman is familiar to most of those who have interested themselves in his career, and there is comparatively little variation in the major details; but a brief sketch of his background and early life is necessary to a proper evaluation of the man and a clearer understanding of his later actions.

William Tecumseh Sherman was born at Lancaster, Ohio, on February 8, 1820, the third son and sixth child of Charles and Mary Hoyt Sherman. Charles Sherman, a graduate of Dartmouth College, came of a long line of distinguished jurists and lawyers. The Sherman family had come over from England in the latter part of the seventeenth century and settled in Connecticut. Charles Sherman went west from Connecticut in 1810 and was so at-tracted by the natural beauty and the advantages of the little frontier town of Lancaster, Ohio, that he returned to Connecticut and moved his family to that place in 1811. In Lancaster he devoted himself to the practice of law until 1813, when he was appointed Collector of Internal Revenue by President Madison. In 1817 the government refused to accept local banknotes, and Charles Sherman was left with the obligation to make good to the government funds collected by his deputies in local notes. He spent the remainder of his life in the discharge of this debt.

The Sherman home in Lancaster during the young Tecumseh's early years was a center of education and society. His parents entertained Governor DeWitt Clinton and the Duke of Saxe-Weimar in their home in 1825.

Charles Sherman was appointed a judge of the Ohio Supreme Court in 1823, a position which he filled with ability and dignity until his untimely death in 1829. Judge Sherman left little in the way of an estate for the support of his widow and her 11 children. In order to assure support for her large family, Mary Hoyt Sherman found it necessary to distribute her children among friends and relatives. The nine-year-old Tecumseh was turned over to his family's close friends and neighbors, the Ewings. Thomas Ewing, a United States senator and later Secretary of the Interior, a department which he had helped to institute while in Congress, had been one of Judge Charles Sherman's closest friends, and Tecumseh was accepted as a member of the Ewing family. Although Thomas Ewing never did legally adopt him, Sherman always considered him as a father. Senator Ewing profoundly influenced General Sherman's life, not only in Sherman's boyhood, but throughout his adult years. This is clearly shown by the exchange of correspondence between them through the years. Sherman nearly always sought Mr. Ewing's advice when he had an important decision to make, and he was ever anxious to merit his foster father's approval.

The young Sherman interrupted his local education to accept an appointment to West Point, which Senator Ewing had secured for him. In 1840 he was graduated, sixth in his class, and was commissioned as a second lieutenant of artillery. Sherman's first orders, after his graduation, sent him to Florida to take part in the army's efforts to round up Seminole Indians who still resisted the government's removal policy. Later he did tours of duty at Charleston, where he was stationed at Fort Moultrie, and at Marietta, Georgia, where he handled claims of volunteers for losses in Florida. It was while at Marietta, and on a later trip to the Augusta Arsenal, that Sherman said he familiarized himself with Georgia topography—the Etowah and Chattahoochee River country, and the ground around Allatoona Pass.

With the outbreak of the Mexican War, Sherman was shipped out around the Horn for California in high hopes that he would see action. His hopes on that score, however, were short-lived, as he was stationed with occupation forces. The inactivity and the knowledge that many of his classmates at West Point received recognition and promotion resulting from their actions under fire depressed Sherman. His discouragement and disappointment finally led him to submit his resignation from the army, but he was persuaded to remain as General Persifor F. Smith's adjutant. In the latter part of 1850 he was called to Washington as the bearer of dispatches from California.

In May 1851, Sherman was married to Ellen Ewing, the daughter of his guardian, in a wedding that was a social event of note in Washington. Shortly after his wedding, Sherman was promoted to the rank of captain and ordered to St. Louis to take charge of the Army Commissary—a place which soon became monotonous for him. In 1853 he was offered a position as manager of Lucas & Symonds bank in San Francisco, and he secured a six months' leave of absence from the army to investigate it. The bank made such an attractive offer that Sherman resigned his commission and moved to San Francisco to take up his duties in 1853.

The financial crisis of 1854–1855 caught Sherman's bank along with others in California, and although Lucas & Symonds came through with smaller loss than some of the others, it was forced to close. Sherman had at the insistence of his friends and fellow officers invested over 100,000 dollars of their money in California securities, and he found himself compelled to refund it. This obligation he eventually discharged in full.

After the San Francisco failure the bank transferred Sherman to its New York office, where shortly after his arrival it, too, was forced to close its doors—this time, however, without loss. After assisting Lucas & Symonds in closing out its affairs at New York and in California, Sherman returned to Lancaster without any prospects of employment and much depressed in mind over his unfortunate business ventures. Thomas Ewing urged him to take over the management of the Ewing Salt Works, a part of his extensive holdings, but Sherman chose instead to go out to Kansas to look over lands owned there by Mr. Ewing. During the time in Kansas he was keenly aware of his failures and humiliated by his dependence on his father-in-law, and after several months he again tried to establish himself. His brothers-in-law, Tom and Hugh Ewing, had established a law office in Leavenworth, Kansas, and Sherman joined the firm after "reading" law and being admitted to the bar without examination. Again he was forced to admit failure, as his legal career was of short duration, and he lost the only case he tried.

A letter which Sherman wrote to Ellen Sherman from Kansas was indicative of his frame of mind during this time: "I am doomed to be a vagabond, and shall no longer struggle against my fate. . . . I look upon myself as a dead cock in the pit, not worthy of further notice and will take the chances as they come."[1] The next few months saw Sherman unsuccessfully try to get back into the army as he cast about to secure employment which would permit him to provide for his family, who had accepted the Ewing hospitality far longer than he thought proper. Through a friend in the army he was informed that the board of trustees of a newly founded seminary and military school in Louisiana needed a superintendent. In response to his application, Sherman was advised that he had been appointed head of the new Louisiana State Seminary and Military Academy. In October 1859, he left his family at Lancaster and started for Louisiana to assume his new duties.

MERCHANT OF TERROR
General Sherman and Total War

Part I

TOTAL WAR
A Rehearsal

I

⟨⟨⟨⟨ ⟨⟨⟨⟨ ⟨⟨⟨⟨ ⟨⟨⟨⟨

Louisiana to Bull Run

Without doubt Sherman was successful as the head of the Louisiana State Seminary (eventually renamed the Louisiana State University), and his industry in the organization of that institution was approved by its board. That he was popular with both cadets and faculty is testified to by David French Boyd, Sherman's Professor of Ancient Languages, who said, "Often have I seen his private rooms nearly full of boys, listening to his stories of army or western life which he loved so well to tell them. Nor could he appear on the grounds at recreational hour without the cadets one by one gathering around him for a talk."[1] He was a visitor in the comfortable homes on the rivers and bayous, and was said to have been a great favorite with the young society of the community. It seemed that here in the deep South Sherman had at last found a place of contentment, in which he could forget the failures in his military and business careers.

In this happy beginning there was one discordant note. An air of sectionalism, surrounding the exciting presidential campaign of 1860, permeated the whole country. Sherman continued about his business of putting the seminary on a sounder footing and attended the state legislature at the request of the seminary's board

of supervisors to urge personally the passage of a bill favorabl
to that institution. It was necessary in the winter of 1860 for him
to go to Baton Rouge several times in the interests of the seminary
and there he became friendly with such men as Governor Thoma
O. Moore and Braxton Bragg, who was a member of the board o
public works.

There was apparently no effort on Sherman's part to evade th
issues of the day, and he did not hesitate to make his positio
clear at the very outset. He expressed himself to Boyd in the firs
days of their acquaintanceship when Boyd, thinking Sherman t
be a Georgian, asked his position on the question of secession.
Along with this question Boyd also inquired whether Sherma
was related to the well-known John Sherman, then a candidate fo
speaker of the House of Representatives. Sherman replied in hi
abrupt manner:

> "Only a brother, and I don't care who knows it," and from
> that time on, he and I had it up and down on politics. He
> believed that the Union was supreme and secession treason;
> I believed the states supreme, and secession a reserved right.
> For two long years in Louisiana before secession became an
> attempted fact, this was the burden of his political talk, with
> no concealment whatever. We all knew what he thought, and
> what he would do if war came.[3]

Sherman was well aware that his brother John was considere
an abolitionist of the darkest hue by those in the South, and h
recounts that many people in Louisiana looked on him with sus
picion and questioned the propriety of his occupying the super
intendency of an important state institution. It was not strang
that the members of the state senate and house should regard th
brother of a well-known "abolitionist" with a questioning eye. A
a dinner party at the governor's home, at which there wer
present several members of the state legislature, Sherman agai
was felt out as to his views. Governor Moore turned to Sherma
and said: "Colonel Sherman, you can readily understand that
with your brother the abolitionist candidate for Speaker, some o
our people wonder that you should be here at the head of a

important state institution. Now you are at my table, and I assure you of my confidence. Won't you speak your mind freely on this question of slavery, that so agitates the land?"[4]

In reply, Sherman denied that his brother John was considered an abolitionist at home, and he continued that, although John preferred free institutions to those of slavery, he did not advocate the taking away either by force or law of any property, even slaves. Sherman then spoke freely of his own stand on the issue, a position which he maintained throughout the war. This was, in essence, that the South had inherited slavery and it represented a heavy capital investment to the South. The Negro could not abruptly be given his liberty and turned loose in a society which was not prepared for him and for which he certainly was not prepared, and would not be for years to come. Sherman's correspondence throughout, with his wife, his brother, and even with the government in Washington, supports his views as he expressed them in Louisiana, and his attitude on the slavery question is not a point of dispute among those who have studied his career. In the face of the mounting tension and excitement prevailing in Louisiana, Sherman managed to hold his place well. Secession was in the air. It was the main topic of conversation. Individuals felt the force of impending events, and all appeared to be poised, awaiting a signal.

There appears to be no reason to doubt that Sherman was completely sincere in his deep affection for the Union. Such regard for the Union, rising above that of devotion to the individual state, had come to him early in his boyhood, as he sat at the knee of his foster father, Senator Thomas Ewing. He had heard the Union upheld and revered, and its supremacy had become a part of his thinking in his impressionable years. As was the case with many Westerners, the national government and the union of states, essential to its efficient operation, were of far greater importance to Sherman than the individual states. The Ohio of Sherman's boyhood was the frontier, and the older Eastern states were often in conflict with what the West felt was its best interests. The West had looked to the government at Washington from the earliest days for protection from the menace of marauding and murdering Indians, for an advantageous land policy and credit system, and for assistance in road building and river transportation. Tens of thousands, seeking new opportunities and new homes, built the Western states, which existed largely as creations of the national government, and owed to it their equal footing with the older Eastern states.

It is reasonable to assume that being a son of the West and living under the influence of a staunch old Whig such as Thomas Ewing, Sherman would support the Constitution as he understood it. Had not the young Sherman heard Senator Ewing rise above his Whig sentiments and enthusiastically applaud and support a Democrat, Andrew Jackson, as President when Jackson had taken his stand for the indissoluble Union against the nullificationist John C. Calhoun in South Carolina?

It is not strange then to find Sherman in Louisiana stating his position on the question of secession, even though he found the position rather difficult. Boyd said of Sherman at this time that "his moral courage, his free outspoken thought commanded the respect of the people of Louisiana. Besides, he was so singularly efficient as chief of the State Seminary and Military Academy, and so universally popular, that there was no feeling against him on account of his political views—only a regret that so good and true a man differed from us."[5]

Sherman was concerned over his position under the peculiar circumstances of the time, and his letter written to Mrs. Sherman on November 26, 1860, shows that he had reached a decision. He wrote: "For myself, I will not go with the South in a disunion movement, and as my position at the head of a State Military College would necessarily infer fidelity and allegiance to the State as against the United States, my duty will be on the positive act of disunion to give notice of my purpose."[6]

On December 10, 1860, Governor Moore issued a call for the legislature to convene for the purpose of calling a convention—a convention to consider the right of the state to secede, and further to make the momentous decision as to whether Louisiana should now withdraw from the Union.

Sherman's position was daily becoming more untenable, and

he informed Mrs. Sherman in his letter of December 16 of his reaction to the Louisiana governor's actions in seizing the forts at the mouth of the Mississippi River and the occupation of them by New Orleans volunteers. State forces had also forced the surrender of the United States arsenal at Baton Rouge. Sherman was outspoken in recognizing just what this meant, as he wrote: "All of these are acts of hostility and war. The news will cause intense feeling in the North and West. They were entirely too precipitate, and Governor Moore is even censured here; still the fact is manifest that the people of the South are in open rebellion against the government of the United States."[7]

The arms and munitions which were stored in the arsenal at Baton Rouge were taken over by the New Orleans militia and distributed. In the distribution, part of them were consigned to the central arsenal at the State Academy, where Colonel Sherman commanded; and they were accompanied by orders from Governor Moore that the superintendent should receive them and give his receipt for them. Sherman was placed in an embarrassing position, and he described his predicament: "Thus I was made receiver of stolen goods, and these goods the property of the United States. This grated hard on my feelings as an ex-army officer, and on accounting the arms I noticed that they were packed in the old familiar boxes, with the 'U.S.' simply scratched off."[8]

The arsenal had been seized at Baton Rouge on January 10, 1861, and the secession ordinance was not to be passed until the latter part of that month, but as early as January 18 Sherman wrote Governor Moore, informing the governor that he had accepted his position, a quasimilitary one, under the laws of the state and at a time when Louisiana was a state of the Union, and he added:

Recent events foreshadow a great change, and it becomes all men to choose. If Louisiana withdraws from the Federal Union, I prefer to maintain my allegiance to the Constitution, as long as a fragment of it survives; and my longer stay here would be wrong in every sense of the word.

In that event, I beg you will send or appoint some authorized agent to take charge of the arms and munitions of war belonging to the state, or advise me what dispositions to make of them.[9]

In this letter Sherman also included a request to the governor, in his capacity of president of the board of supervisors, to relieve him as superintendent the moment the secession ordinance passed, "for on no earthly account will I do any act or think any thought hostile to or in defiance of the old Government of the United States."[10]

There was no question in Sherman's mind that his time in Louisiana was drawing to a close, and it was not an easy matter for him to leave a position in which he enjoyed both a certain amount of prestige and the friendship and high esteem of influential men. Sherman had intended to settle there, with his family once again together under the same roof. He had a free home on the campus, even then under construction, and an excellent salary. He had felt a new security against the fear which had beset his earlier years—the constant fear that he could not support his family. He had written Ellen Sherman from Alexandria in a jocular vein on February 13, 1860, that "if Louisiana will endow this college properly, and is fool enough to give me $5,000 a year, we will drive our tent pins, and pick out a magnolia under which to sleep the long sleep."[11]

Now his undertaking in Louisiana, begun so auspiciously and with such promise for future independence, must be left behind him. The time was short as events moved rapidly. Fort Sumter was besieged and South Carolina had already warned Washington that any attempt to relieve or reinforce the fort would bring direct action. In Louisiana, Sherman was outraged at the vacillation shown by the President, and he summed up his reactions as he wrote on February 1, 1861, to Mrs. Sherman in the intense, exaggerated style which characterized his expressions throughout his correspondence: "If the government be a reality it should defend its flag, property and servants. Anderson should be reinforced if it costs ten thousand lives and every habitation in Charleston."[12]

When the news of South Carolina's secession came it visibly

shook Sherman, and Professor Boyd, who was with him at the time, described Sherman's shock and his emotional nature:

> I happened to be with him in his private room when the mail came telling us of the actual passage of the ordinance of Secession of South Carolina. Sherman burst out crying, and began, in his nervous way, pacing the floor and deprecating the step which he feared might bring destruction on the whole country. For an hour or more this went on. Every now and then he would stop, and addressing himself to me, he would exclaim, as if broken-hearted, "You, you people of the south, believe that there can be peaceable secession. If you will have it, the North must fight you for its own preservation. Yes, South Carolina has by this act of secession precipitated war. Other Southern States will follow out of sympathy. This country will be drenched in blood. God only knows how it will end. Perhaps the liberties of the whole country, of every section and every man will be destroyed, and yet you know that within the Union no man's liberty or property in all the South is endangered. Then why should any Southern State leave the Union? Oh, it is all folly, madness, a crime against civilization!"[13]

Sherman's departure was now imminent as matters drew rapidly to a head, and although his openly expressed antipathy toward secession was well known, the influential men who supported the seminary were loathe to let him go. Braxton Bragg, Pierre G. T. Beauregard and Governor Thomas Moore wrote urging him to remain in Louisiana, and in their persuasive efforts they went so far as to assure him that he would neither be asked nor expected to take up arms for the South. Sherman was decided in his course, and he took passage from Alexandria for New Orleans to meet Dr. S. A. Smith, the chairman of the board, for the purpose of settling his accounts in full and balancing the funds entrusted to him.

During the several days required to transact his business in New Orleans, Sherman called on Beauregard, to whose two sons he had given his personal attention at the seminary. He found Beauregard preparing to leave for Montgomery, where it was rumored he was to be commissioned a brigadier general by Jefferson Davis. Later, dining at the St. Louis Hotel with Colonel and Mrs. Braxton Bragg, Sherman caught a flash of the resentment Bragg felt toward Davis as a result of Beauregard's elevation. In the old army Bragg was Beauregard's senior in rank.[14]

Turning his back on Louisiana and all of the promises that it had held for his future, Sherman headed North about the first of March for Lancaster, via Cairo and Cincinnati. As he faced north, he left behind the security which he had so longed for—an office with a salary of 4,500 dollars a year[15] and a residence free of cost, the dignity of position and the friendship of high-placed men —all this he left to face his family, a far poorer man than he had been on coming to Louisiana.[16]

Again the ghost of past failures was raised, and doubts which had assailed him before now stalked him once more. Again he found himself subject to gloomy fears:

> I had managed to maintain my family comfortably at Lancaster, but was extremely anxious about the future. It looked like the end of my career, for I did not suppose that "civil war" could give me employment that would provide for the family.[17]

Traveling homeward, surrounded by an atmosphere of discouragement and keen disappointment, Sherman recalled that Major H. S. Turner, his friend who had put him into the banking business in California, had been in correspondence with him during the last days in Louisiana. Turner had written that he would assist his friend in securing employment in St. Louis, a city which Sherman thought had a future. In a letter to Mrs. Sherman, as early as 1858, Sherman had informed her that he liked St. Louis and thought it a good place to live. Said he in that letter, "I had such unbounded confidence in St. Louis, generally, that I would go to work with something like a conviction of success." With his San Francisco experience still fresh he could tell Ellen Sherman in his letter that no man could expect success in "a failing community such as San Francisco," where honesty and business ethics were not appreciated. St. Louis was different, he wrote, and he continued:

. . . but in a rising, growing, industrious community like St. Louis, all patient, prudent, honest men can thrive. This is why my thoughts revert to St. Louis, with its schools, libraries, places of diversion, amusement, etc.—all that we seek for, for ourselves and children.[18]

It was not strange that his thoughts should be on Major Turner's offer, and that, adrift again at forty-one years of age, he should say, as he turned toward Lancaster and his family: "I felt more disposed to look to St. Louis for a home, and to Major Turner to find me employment, than to the public service."[19]

Even as he said this, there is a good possibility that Sherman, with his peculiar inconsistency, was thinking of a letter he had received from his brother in Washington. John Sherman had not neglected his brother's interests, and his letter of January 6, 1861, indicates that Sherman had already put out feelers for a place in the public service. John Sherman's letter said in part: "I have spoken to General Scott, and he heartily seconds your desire to return to duty in the army. I am not at all sure but that if you were here you could get a position that would suit you."[20]

As he continued his journey northward, by rail and boat, he heard on all sides the hot discussion of politics and witnessed a situation which filled him with gloomy and extravagant opinions —opinions which he was later to express with his characteristic bluntness and with such vehemence that they would fill a part of his life with bitterness. Sherman passed from the South, where the people showed unanimity of purpose and a fierce, earnest determination in their hurried organization for action, into Illinois, Indiana, and Ohio, where there were no apparent signs of preparation, nor any too great concern over the trend of events. It appeared to him, in his disturbed state of mind, that the North would continue to argue and be apathetic, tamely submitting to the disruption of the Union. Sherman, who accepted no part of the lulling arguments of Southern orators, feared that the North was impressed with that group's assurance that there would be no war, and that "a lady's thimble would hold all the blood to be shed."[21]

Shortly after Sherman's arrival in Lancaster for a brief visit

with Mrs. Sherman and his children, two letters were received—
one from Major Turner, offering him the presidency of the Fifth
Street Railroad in St. Louis at a salary of 2,500 dollars a year;
the other from John Sherman, then Senator Sherman, urging him
to come to Washington. Acting with promptness, Sherman wrote
Major Turner his acceptance of the St. Louis job and made ready
to set out for Washington to see his brother and to discover how
matters stood in the capital.

The alacrity with which he responded to John Sherman's call
to Washington shows that Sherman still nurtured hopes of appointment to high place and that he felt that his knowledge of
conditions in the South should be recognized by those who would
need it in this critical time. The very fact that he went to Washington points to his having accepted Major Turner's offer with
mental reservations, doing so only for the purpose of having something sure to fall back on in the event that the Washington trip
resulted in failure.

In Washington, Sherman, fresh from the belligerent atmosphere
and the warlike preparations in the South, was shocked to note
the carefree air and lack of preparation on every side. Even
around the War Department there was open talk, which to him,
in his conviction that the South intended to fight if interfered
with, amounted almost to open treason. Senator Sherman took his
brother to see President Lincoln, assuring the President that
Colonel Sherman was just up from Louisiana and might furnish
information of value to the government. The President turned to
Colonel Sherman and apparently out of politeness asked: "Ah,
how are they getting along down there?" Sherman informed
Lincoln with deep seriousness that the people in the South were
preparing for war. To which Lincoln replied: "Oh well, I guess
we will manage to keep house."[22]

Of a sensitive nature, always quick to resent a slight, either
real or fancied, and just as easily offended by indignity, Sherman
was cut to the quick by the President's rebuff. Added to his
resentment was his disappointment that nothing had come of his
contact with the President. Not only had the President not offered
him a place, but he had treated with indifference the valuable
information which Sherman felt the government should have. The

casual attitude of the Chief Executive toward the portentous events shaping up caused Sherman to rail out to Senator Sherman against all politicians, and as they left the President's office he damned them all, severally and individually. He appeared to be strengthened in his conviction that he alone knew the real situation, and that the stupid fools would not heed.[23] Sherman was plainly disappointed, as he had expected more. John Sherman had aroused hopes in praising his brother's abilities and had built up in his mind a feeling that he was needed. Now in frustration and obvious anger, he struck out at John: "You have got things in a hell of a fix, and you may get them out as best you can." His government would have to do without his valuable services and extricate itself from what Sherman felt was an explosive situation. He washed his hands of a country "sitting on a volcano which might burst forth at any minute," as he expressed it. So far as he was concerned, he stormed, the politicians with their stupidity could have it; he was going to St. Louis as president of the St. Louis Railway—and go he did, in spite of Senator Sherman's begging him to be patient. He removed his family and household goods to that city on March 27, 1861.[24]

His new job, the duties of which he assumed April 1, was a far cry from the shaded campus in Louisiana, not only in the surroundings, but from the standpoint of income. In St. Louis, as president of the street railway, his salary was 40 dollars a week, and Ellen took in boarders to help defray expenses. Sherman experienced no great difficulties in his new place, since the road was in good order and required only sound economic administration. He was moody, and the flow of events around him served to aggravate his emotional condition. He was restless and irritable, as only one of his disposition could be; for he experienced a feeling of being left on the sidelines, while others, less well qualified, played the game. To add to his sense of frustration and his awareness that he sat in a quiet backwater, John Sherman, still trying to find something for him, wrote a letter which disturbed Sherman. Writing on April 12, John said:

> I have spent much of the day talking about you. There is an earnest desire that you go into the War Department, but

I said this was impossible. Chase is especially desirous that you accept, saying that you would be virtually Secretary of War, and could easily step into any military position that offers.

It is well for you to seriously consider your conclusion, although my opinion is that you ought not to accept. You ought to hold yourself in reserve. If troops are called for, as they surely will be in a few days, organize a regiment or brigade, either in St. Louis or Ohio, and you will then get into the army in such a way as to secure promotion. By all means take advantage of the present disturbances to get into the army, where you will at once put yourself in high position for life.[25]

John Sherman appears to have recognized that his brother took the St. Louis job largely out of resentment and possibly as a "stop-gap" until a place could be found for him which suited his dignity. How well this letter illustrates John Sherman's insight into Tecumseh's nature, and how well he counseled his brother not to have anything to do with the War Department job! John Sherman realized that a department of the government, so dominated by political maneuvering, would be ill-suited to one of Sherman's impetuous, outspoken nature, and his brother's ill-concealed contempt for politicians would cut short his career. Senator Sherman's knowledge of his brother's constant fear of insecurity permitted him to play effectively on him from that approach, and he urged him to get into the army "where you will at once put yourself in high position for life." John's letter continued:

I know that promotion and every facility for advancement will be cordially extended by the authorities. You are a favorite in the army, and have great strength in political circles. I urge you to avail yourself of these favorable circumstances to secure your position for life; for after all, your present employment is of uncertain tenure in these stirring times. . . . It [the government] will display energy and military power. The men who have confidence in it, and do their full duty by it may reap whatever there is of honor and profit in public life.[26]

Whether with studied intent or not, John Sherman had here employed almost every influence that he could bring to bear. His observation that Sherman's position was uncertain was a keen thrust. He left the unmistakable implication that now was the opportune moment for Sherman, who had made so many past failures, to recoup and redeem himself in his own estimation, as well as that of his family, his intimates and the world. If, in short, his brother wanted a shortcut to success—and at age forty-one such a shortcut was attractive—John urged that now was the time to seize opportunity by the forelock and wrest from the peculiar times the "secure position for life" and to "reap whatever there is of honor and profit in public life."

Two days later the news of the fall of Fort Sumter reached Washington, and on the same day, April 14, 1861, Senator Sherman again wrote to his brother in St. Louis, using the excitement of the moment to exert pressure on him. Again he urged Sherman to make his decision quickly, and said further:

> We are on the eve of a terrible war. Every man will have to choose his position. You fortunately have the military education, prominence and character that will enable you to play a high part in the tragedy. You can't avoid taking such a part. Neutrality and indifference are impossible. . . . If you want that place, you can have it, but you are not compelled to take it; but it seems to me that you will be compelled to take some position, and that speedily.[27]

There is a notable singleness of purpose in these letters John Sherman wrote to Tecumseh—self-advancement. No mention is made of selfless patriotism or service to country. The very practical tone of John's letters unquestionably had a far-reaching effect on the mind of the man sitting in the office of the St. Louis Railway Company. The sentiments expressed by his brother found ready accommodation in Sherman's thinking—he who had tasted the bitterness of failure, not once, but many times—and he appeared to reflect deeply on the suggestions offered by a brother who so zealously sought preferment for him. Sherman could see that the War Department would not only fret him, but, more important, would keep him out of the public eye and away from the field of action, where one had to be if he was to secure position and public acclaim. He was, as John had urged him, to hold himself in reserve, waiting and watching for the most advantageous and promising place.

There runs through General Sherman's correspondence, and very noticeably in his *Personal Memoirs,* an almost overbearing egotism and an overdeveloped sense of dignity, easily offended. Such emphasis on self, with attendant braggadocio, usually indicates pronounced egocentrism, and in many cases arises from a sense of inadequacy. It also causes the subject to indulge in self-pity and to keep ever fresh in his mind all his past failures and grievances. With self-pity comes great mental anguish, periods of gloom and despair, a tendency to exaggerate the difficulties of problems and to resort to rationalization in moments of strain and crisis. The egocentric is highly sensitive to criticism and can marshal facts to justify his actions, and so build a case in his own mind that it takes on the garb of truth, without regard for the actual truth. Or, in moments of impatience and anger, he may abandon whatever he attempts, convincing himself that he has not failed, but simply cannot convince those with less insight and vision. Thus the influence of John Sherman's letter of April 12 on Sherman's thinking cannot be overlooked.

In that letter he played upon the most sensitive side of his brother's nature, reminding him that venture after venture had ended unfortunately for him. Such a reminder spurred the sensitive Sherman and added fuel to a burning desire to "show the world" that he was a great man and merited the honor and praise of men. Under such impelling motives have men been driven to extreme actions when the means to do so once falls into their grasp. Under the impetus of driving ambition and constant fear of failure men are often tempted to abandon their ethical standards and throw overboard whatever scruples they might have had, comforting themselves with the belief that the ends justify the means. Sherman's ambition, supported and nourished by his brother down through the years of war ahead, and later intensified by public acclaim and recognition after Vicksburg, must go onto the scales in an effort to evaluate the forces which exerted themselves on his mind. These forces had a marked influence on the reasoning which presently led him to evolve his philosophy of total war—a philosophy foreign to the precedents and rules of war commonly accepted by the civilized nations of the world.

Later, in April, Sherman was offered the chief clerkship of the War Department by Montgomery Blair, Lincoln's Postmaster-General, but with Senator Sherman's sage advice in mind, he refused it. A few days later, Frank Blair, a political power in Missouri, called him to his home at night and offered him a brigadier generalship, commanding the Department of Missouri. Blair, the brother of the Postmaster-General, was, in effect, in charge of affairs in Missouri, and he distrusted General William S. Harney, then in command. Sherman, with his resentment toward the government still warm, refused, and he said:

> I told him that I had once offered my services, and they were declined; that I had made business engagements in St. Louis which I could not throw off at pleasure; that I had long deliberated on my course of action, and must decline his offer, however tempting and complimentary.[28]

A sound business proposition was still uppermost in his mind, and he was content to wait rather than take his chances with volunteer three-month troops. He expressed himself in a letter to Secretary of War Cameron on May 8, 1861—a letter written to clear up his attitude, as some of his associates had begun to wonder where he stood. He assured the Secretary:

> I hold myself now, as always, prepared to serve my country in the capacity for which I was trained. I did not and will not volunteer for *three months,* because I cannot throw my family on the cold charity of the world. But for the *three years* call, made by the President, an officer can prepare his command and do good service. I will not volunteer (as a soldier), because rightfully or wrongfully I feel unwilling to take a mere private's place, and having for many years lived in California and Louisiana, the men are not well enough acquainted with me to elect me to my appropriate place.[29]

Sherman, with John's advice still in mind to seek whatever profit and honor he might from the peculiar times, again put his personal interests above those of service to his flag. His ambition and his exalted ideas as to what should be his "appropriate place" were left, apparently, to the discretion of the Secretary of War. He certainly would not go into the army as a private, and he would not take his chances with a local militia outfit, which did not know him well enough, because of his having lived in other sections, to elect him commanding officer.

He was determined apparently not to fail again, and if it took time to look over the offerings, he felt that it would be time well spent. In April he had written John along these lines:

> The times will come in this country when professional knowledge will be appreciated, when men that can be trusted will be wanted, and I will bide my time. I may miss the chance: if so all right; but I cannot and will not mix myself in this present call.[30]

Sherman continued, pointing out to the Senator his reasons for not rushing into the army—that those first chosen for places of high responsibility would fall with the failure of the government's first moves, and he continued:

> A second or third set will arise, and among them I may be, but at present I will not volunteer as a soldier or anything else. If Congress meets, or if a National Convention be called and the regular army be put on a footing with the wants of the country, if I am offered a place that suits me, I may accept. But in the present call I will not volunteer.

Sherman was still resentful toward President Lincoln, not only because of the affront to his dignity, but also because Lincoln had failed to recognize and appreciate the knowledge which he was convinced was his alone and of great value to the government if it was not to underestimate the task ahead.[31] He reminded his brother, who had so urged his return to the army, that they were both present when Lincoln had asserted that he did not think he wanted military men, and he continued: "I was then free, uncommitted . . . and had I not committed myself to another duty, I would most willingly have responded to his call."[32]

Some three weeks later he did respond to the President's call by accepting a commission as a colonel of the Thirteenth Regular Infantry, undoubtedly secured through the indefatigable Senator Sherman's efforts and influence. Although his regiment was still to be formed, Sherman accepted his commission at once in preference to a brigadier-generalship of volunteers, as it had the advantages of being a permanent, regular army rank. In compliance with his orders he reported to Washington immediately where he was sworn in and ordered to inspection duty under the personal command of General Winfield Scott. This turn of events doubtless irked the new colonel, who, having previously expressed his opinion of all politicians, now found himself surrounded by them.[33]

Before leaving for Washington, Sherman had written his brother-in-law, Thomas Ewing, Jr., defending his refusal of the chief clerkship in the War Department. He stated that he had declined it simply because he did not want it, and he added: "I have seen enough of war not to be caught by its first glittering bait, and when I engage in this it must be with full consciousness of its true character."[34]

With the rank of colonel in the regular army and with the backing of such influential men as his senator brother and his foster father, Thomas Ewing, as well as the powerful Blairs in Washington, Sherman's prompt acceptance of his commission in the army indicated that he felt he could now find his "appropriate place." Writing again to the younger Thomas Ewing, on June 3, he said:

> After all the Mississippi River is the hardest and most important task of the war, and I know of no one competent unless it be McClellan. But as soon as real war begins, new men, heretofore unheard of, will emerge from obscurity, equal to any occasion.[35]

And though, later, whenever he mentioned it, he belittled promotion, it was apparent that he was determined to emerge from obscurity "equal to any occasion." Apparently Sherman did not see himself, or question his own motives as he wrote a few days later to Mrs. Sherman: "Some three or four hundred thousand people are now neglecting work and looking to war for a means of livelihood."[36]

Colonel Sherman remained on duty with General Scott for only ten days (June 20–30), and he was then placed in command of a brigade of McDowell's army. McDowell was preparing to move from the defenses of Washington to meet General Beauregard's forces at Manassas Junction. On July 16, the day the army was to begin its march, Sherman wrote to his wife:

> I still regard this as but the beginning of a long war, but I hope my judgment therein is wrong, and that the people of the South may see the folly of their unjust rebellion against the most mild and paternal government ever designed for men.[37]

The battle of Bull Run was joined on July 21, 1861, and Colonel Sherman's letters are filled with his mortification and shame at the disorderly rout of the Union Army. As the remnants of the army returned to Fort Corcoran, which had been thrown up to defend the approaches to Washington, Sherman and his staff labored at the job of collecting their men and shuffling them back into their respective companies and camps.

Sherman had often longed for fighting and had expressed his disappointment many times that he had had no opportunity to see action in the Mexican War. Now at Bull Run he had his baptism of fire. Writing to Mrs. Sherman, he expressed his reaction to shot and shell and scenes of blood and death:

> Then for the first time I saw the carnage of battle, men lying in every conceivable shape, and mangled in a horrid way; but this did not make a particle of impression on me, but horses running about, riderless, with blood streaming from their nostrils, lying on the ground hitched to guns, gnawing their sides in death.[38]

In the same letter he described the disgraceful actions of the volunteer troops, and he excused their actions only because they were volunteers. He made special reference to the habit each private had of thinking and acting on his own, asking permission of no man, simply taking anything he wanted; and to Sherman's consternation, he even burns the house of his enemy. Noting these actions on the part of the volunteer soldiery, he observed, with a peculiar insight, as he continued his letter:

> No curse could be greater than invasion by a volunteer army. No Goths or Vandals ever had less respect for the lives and property of friend and foes, and henceforth we should never hope for any friends in Virginia.[39]

Sherman summed up his reactions to the Battle of Bull Run by admitting that the disaster had had a serious effect on the Union Army, and the men were utterly discouraged. A letter of August 3 to his wife showed that he shared the discouragement of the troops. Indulging in his flair for prophecy—an accomplishment which he later admitted was peculiarly his own and in which he took increasing pride in the years ahead—he wrote:

> 'Tis folly to underestimate the task, and you see how far already the nation has miscalculated. The real war has not yet begun. The worst will be down the Mississippi, and in Alabama and Mississippi, provided, of course, we ever get that far. Already has the war lasted since December last, and we are still on the border, defeated and partly discouraged. I am less so than most people because I expected it.[40]

Nothing was ever to surprise Sherman, if his voluminous letters are dependable evidence. Through his correspondence he outlined policy for the administration, pointed out its errors, gave advice and counsel freely, not only to his subordinates, but to General Grant after Grant became his commanding officer. He had tried to advise President Lincoln and had been offended by Lincoln's failure to show the proper enthusiasm; and while occupying the chair of president of the St. Louis Railway, his mind had been busily engaged in defending the country, building forts, attacking and occupying positions, seizing and destroying strategic railroads. His letters of that period, outspoken in sharp criticism of the government where the government in its first efforts failed to follow his suggestions, illustrate his opinionated manner and his readiness to offer advice, without the redeeming quality of accepting criticism gracefully.[41] His later vindictiveness, approaching hatred, against the people of the South appeared to be founded, at least in part, on the grounds that they would not place credence in his arguments against their action, nor heed his warnings. He became more and more convinced that the South was either hardheaded or populated by those determined on a course of madness and folly. Either way, they must be convinced of the error of their ways; and what could be more fitting and proper than that he, who had warned them, should administer their punishment? It cannot be well denied that in the months ahead the "sacred duty" complex was to increase in intensity and Sherman was to continue to draw on it heavily to justify the harshness of his acts in his own mind, as well as to convince his troops that they were the instruments of justice and heavenly retribution.

With continued bitter criticism of his volunteer troops he again complained to Mrs. Sherman during August. These men, he declared, were constantly growling and complaining, leaving without official order, and above all were committing thievery and acts in violation of civilian and private property rights. He added, significantly:

> . . . and our soldiers are the most destructive men that I have ever known. It may be that other volunteers are just as bad, indeed the complaint is universal, and I see no alternative but to let it take its course. . . . now I suppose that there is not a man, woman or child but would prefer Jeff Davis or the Czar of Russia to govern them rather than an American Volunteer Army. My only hope now is that a common sense of decency may be inspired into the minds of this soldiery to respect life and property.[42]

Somewhere in the months ahead this praiseworthy hope for his men's improvement was to be dropped by the wayside, and the rank and file, in whom their commanding officer so fondly hoped to see develop a respect for life and property, were to be given free rein to follow unhindered a course of pillage and wanton destruction whose counterpart up to that time could be found only in the raids of barbarian tribesmen. Many of these same troops were later to be employed as rolling engines of devastation and manufacturers of despair and terror under the leadership of the officer who advanced after Bull Run, not only in rank, but to an entirely new viewpoint toward war. From the shame of that first battle to the applied terrorist program instituted at Memphis, Sherman evolved in his thinking from a former peacetime quartermaster, observing all of the niceties and precedents outlined in the regulations and adhered to by orthodox soldiers, to the calculating, self-appointed dispenser of heavenly justice, dedicated to the punishment of the South.

At the outset of the war it appears that Sherman's point of view was no different, fundamentally, from that of the average professional soldier of the United States Army of 1861. He was schooled in the rules of war and knew the niceties and obligations to be observed in his intercourse with the enemy. There is no reason to doubt that he shared with his brother officers of the regular army the more or less impersonal attitude of the professional soldier toward the enemy—an attitude marked by discussion of his opponent's methods and predictions as to the enemy's next move, based on a knowledge of military science and tactics. The professional soldier was, above all, interested in the game itself. The personalizing of the enemy or the emotional approach ordinarily did not have a place in the soldier's considerations, nor was it expected of him. Sherman measured up to the orthodox soldier's attitude right after Bull Run, as illustrated by his letters to Mrs. Sherman and to his brother John.[43] No personal enmity is reflected in this correspondence; rather he points out that the game went against them because of the nature of the terrain over which they fought, and also that the Southern forces were more familiar with the ground. He expressed surprise that his opponent, Beauregard, did not follow up his advantage, which to Sherman could not have been unobserved by the Confederate. There is none of the bitterness and the sense of personal insult which stands out in his utterances at Memphis in the summer and fall of 1862 and, more intensely, after the battle of Vicksburg. Even after the battle of Shiloh Sherman could still feel anxious and concerned that the forces under his command should observe proper conduct in the Mississippi Valley and in Tennessee. He went so far as to warn Brigadier General Hurlbut that he had reports that some of Hurlbut's troops had taken several horses and a pair of mules, and that such unwarranted acts hurt the Union cause and must be prevented.[44]

Thus, at the battle of Bull Run Sherman first experienced the blood and carnage that is war. Here he observed at first hand the suffering and destruction which men deal out when they resort to brute force, and he could not conceal his sense of shock at the actions of an undisciplined soldiery.

II

Kentucky Command — Specter
of Oblivion

Promotion came to Sherman in early August 1861, so shortly after the fiasco at Bull Run that he expressed surprise that his name was announced in general orders as a brigadier general of volunteers. His name appeared along with those of several other colonels, all of whom had shared in the unanimous retreat from the battlefield. Sherman's promotion was followed shortly by an assignment to accompany Brigadier General Robert Anderson to Kentucky. He was to assist Anderson, who as a captain had been young Lieutenant Sherman's commanding officer at Fort Moultrie, in recruiting a force in Kentucky sufficiently large to discourage any attempts at disunion, and to secure that state to the Union.[1]

Shortly after his arrival in Kentucky the General wrote Senator Sherman his estimate of the situation and assured him that unless Tennessee and Kentucky remained with the North the government might find it difficult to restore the old Union, and he added: "Slowly but surely the public is realizing what I knew all the time, the strong vindictive feeling of the whole South."[2]

The tendency here to judge the whole South on the basis of what he saw in Kentucky illustrates the beginning of Sherman's employment of generalization to support his contentions. This tendency is noted in numerous places and doubtless contributed to the exaggerated statements made in Kentucky. This tendency toward generalization later served Sherman well in the application of his program of vindictive retaliation.

In October 1861 General Anderson resigned because of ill health, and General Sherman assumed the command—a position which he did not relish. Full command weighed heavily on him, and the day he took over from General Anderson he wrote to Garrett Davis, a citizen of Paris, Kentucky, who was soon to become United States senator, that "I am forced into the command of this department against my will."[3] His apprehensive mind caused him to exaggerate the dangers around him and he labored desperately to bolster the state's defenses against what seemed to him, in his highly nervous condition, an imminent attack by far superior Confederate forces—better armed and under more efficient discipline. He was further depressed to witness on every side inefficiences and procrastination, which served only to intensify his irritability and impatience, an attitude which he made no effort to conceal. What seemed to strike even more deeply into him was the apparent lack of appreciation, or lack of interest, on the part of the War Department concerning the peril in which the Union's cause then stood in Kentucky. General Sherman also had reason to be deeply concerned over the state of affairs from a strictly personal point of view, as he feared that he was to be placed in a position in which he must fail in his assignment. Such a position to one of Sherman's temperament was almost unbearable. With admirable self-restraint, he had directed Secretary of War Cameron's attention to the fact that Kentucky was receiving only a trickle of troops, and those largely green volunteers. Further, he had no effective arms, in spite of the promise to send him modern Springfield muskets. The very fact that outmoded Belgian weapons, refused at other points, had been sent to him in Kentucky was further proof to him that those in power either were neglecting Kentucky or else refused to recognize the immediate danger in that state. Sherman's bitterness welled up as he complained to his brother of the official attitude which brought from him the conviction that "I am to be sacrificed."[4] He began now to press his views on Washington with increasing urgency and intensity, even going so far as to write directly to President Lincoln.[5]

Under the strain of responsibility and beset by the fear of failure, Sherman's reaction was to throw the blame on Washington, and in letters and telegrams he reiterated his need for men, for arms and for recognition of the importance of Kentucky to the Union. His insistence that Washington must take action became a mania with him. He wrote to Adjutant General Lorenzo Thomas on October 22 from Louisville: "You know my views, that this great centre of our field was too weak, far too weak, and I have begged and implored until I dare not say more." Concluding the same letter, after outlining the seriousness of the difficulties he faced in not being able to clothe and arm such volunteers as presented themselves, he again warned: "I repeat again that our force here is out of all proportion to the importance of the position. Our defeat would be disastrous to the nation; and to expect of new men, who never bore arms, to do miracles, is not right."[6]

"I have begged and implored until I dare not say more"— but more he did say to anyone who would listen and with such growing intensity of feeling that little doubt has been left as to his state of nervous excitement. Washington was ignoring him, apparently absorbed in the larger preparations of General Fremont in Missouri and General McClellan near Washington—siphoning off the troops and supplies which should have been dispatched to Kentucky.

Sherman wrote to his brother on October 5, 1861, from Muldraugh's Hill, about 40 miles from Louisville, where he had rushed with such troops as he had to prevent the Confederates from cutting the railroad. His letter reflected his fears:

> But this road can be cut at a hundred different points which would starve us out, or force me to strike out and live on a country which produces only beef and corn. . . . It will require near one hundred thousand men in Kentucky, and where they are to come from I don't know. . . . If the Confederates take St. Louis and get Kentucky this winter you

will be far more embarrassed than if Washington had fallen into their possession, as whatever nation gets the control of the Ohio, Mississippi and Missouri Rivers will control the continent. . . . You of the North never fully appreciated the energy of the South.[7]

In the atmosphere of confusion and disorganization which attended the Union efforts in Kentucky, Sherman lived under a pall of suspense and dread. His feverish mind pictured all too vividly an irresistible movement by Confederate forces against the inadequate, poorly disciplined Union troops. He lived in dread that General Albert Sidney Johnston would, at any moment, unite his Confederate forces with those of General Zollicoffer and attack the Union troops under General Thomas at Fort Dick Robinson or at any one of the many weak points in the Union line. Sherman recounted later that it always remained a mystery to him why General Johnston failed to do the very thing that Sherman anticipated, and he said:

> Had he [General Johnston] done so in October 1861, he could have walked into Louisville, and the vital part of the population would have hailed him as a deliverer. Why he did not, was to me a mystery then, and is now; for I know that he saw the move, and had his wagons loaded up at one time for a start toward Frankfort, passing between our two camps.[8]

Had Sherman been in complete control of his powers of reason, Albert Sidney Johnston's actions, or failure to act, would not have mystified him. Or had the Union commander's sources of information been more dependable,[9] he would have been greatly encouraged to learn that the Confederates were faced with obstacles fully as great as his own and with far smaller forces at hand.[10] The Confederate forces were never more than half the size of their Union opponents at any point, and the resources available to the Federals were much greater than those available to General Johnston. The reason for Johnston's failure to attack is best stated in his own memorandum, written at the time he took command at Bowling Green, October 28, 1861. He noted: "My force was too weak and too illy appointed to advance against greatly superior numbers, perfectly equipped and provided, and being much more rapidly reenforced than my own."[11]

Sherman had urgently written President Lincoln that Confederate General Simon B. Buckner had 20,000 men and sufficient transport to move them. Actually it is doubtful that Buckner ever commanded more than 6,000 men at any one time. In October, from Muldraugh's Hill, even as Sherman stared with gloomy eyes southward toward Bowling Green, his mind magnifying the poorly equipped Confederates into legions of gray before whom he felt powerless, his own command was almost twice as large as that of the enemy he feared.[12]

Nothing seems to demonstrate General Sherman's hysterical state of mind while in Kentucky more than his confused estimation of the military force opposed to him. He was convinced that the Confederates had between 25,000 and 30,000 men on the line from Bowling Green to Clarksville, when the total Confederate force "from the Big Sandy to the Mississippi, was only about 19,000 men."[13] Sherman had available, according to his own estimate, approximately 30,000 men, not including Home Guards.[14] In addition to his serious exaggeration of Confederate strength, Sherman had constantly harped on the inescapable fact that the Kentuckians would hail the Confederates as saviors and deliverers. His suspicious eye saw the shadows of traitors at every turn. He informed Washington early in November: "Our enemies have a terrible advantage, in the fact that in our midst, in our camps, and along our avenues of travel they have active partisans, farmers and business men, who seemingly pursue their usual calling but are in fact spies."[15]

It could not be denied that there were numbers of Southern partisans throughout Kentucky, and doubtless many of them passed information along to the Confederates; but Sherman exaggerated the eagerness of the Kentuckians to throw themselves into the arms of the Southern armies. General Johnston noted his disappointment over the attitude of the Kentuckians in the latter days of October: "Our advance into Kentucky had not been met by the enthusiastic uprising of friends, which we, and many in and out of the State, had believed would take place. Arms were scarce and we had none to give them."[16]

To the pessimistic Sherman, besieged in his headquarters at Louisville, the picture took on a darker and darker hue. His mind became weighted down with anxiety, and his demeanor gloomy and morose. He felt, in common with most neurotics suffering the pangs of anxiety, utterly helpless and defenseless in the face of impending danger. He who ordinarily liked to express himself became strangely silent and uncommunicative. He was in a deep state of melancholy and he later admitted, "I doubtless exhibited it too much to those around me."[17] His subordinates had become increasingly alarmed over their commanding officer's condition, and when his personal servant reported that he was eating and sleeping very little, they felt something should be done. It was one of these officers, interested in the General's welfare, who finally summoned Mrs. Sherman to Louisville.[18]

Upon Mrs. Sherman's arrival at Louisville, she immediately wrote Senator Sherman of her grave concern for her husband's sanity, and continued:

> Several of the army officers are staying at this house, and all seem deeply interested in him. He however pays no attention to them or to anyone and scarcely answers a question unless it be on the all engrossing subject. He thinks the whole country is gone irrevocably and ruin and desolation are at hand. For God's sake do what you can to cheer him and keep him in the position most advantageous to his mind and reputation.[19]

How well Mrs. Sherman sensed the great conflict in her husband's mind—that it was the fear of failure that colored his thinking, failure which he had convinced himself he was powerless to avert. She urged John Sherman to "at least write to me what is best to advice [sic] Cump to do. You know he is sometimes very peculiar and stands very much in his own light."[20]

During his time in Kentucky Sherman had failed to make friends of the newspapermen stationed there. The war correspondents were not long in noting the change in General Sherman's attitude, and his lack of consideration for them caused them to seek occasions to irritate him. They began to highlight his actions and to place their own interpretations upon them in their reports to their newspapers. They severely criticized Sherman's soft treatment of "political enemies" of the Union and intimated that he was encouraging disloyalty and treason. Weighed down as he was by the strain of unwanted responsibility and under the peculiar nervous excitement of the time, Sherman was goaded into ill-considered threats against the newspapermen—threats which served to alienate them and deprive him of their influence and support, which would have stood him in good stead when adversity struck him.[21]

Sherman's attitude toward the war correspondents offers a striking illustration of his inconsistencies, as it would be assumed that such a seeker after fame and fortune would have realized the value of such friends. Likewise, with his sense of caution and fear of premature criticism, it would appear that he would have been alert to the potential damage that men who exert such influence over public opinion could do him if opportunity presented itself. Sherman, however, continued to complain about reporters meddling and prying into military affairs, and he did not conceal his feeling that they were not only officious, but criminally careless in the type of information which they sent to their papers.[22] His open threat to bar all correspondents from his military department, thus earning their open enmity, is another indication of the extreme nervous tension under which Sherman labored.

The General was a familiar figure to the newsmen in the Associated Press rooms in Louisville in the fall of 1861, where he remained from early morning until late at night, pacing up and down in his nervous manner, smoking one cigar after another. A reporter for *The New York Tribune* stated that Sherman was very erratic, and noted that "his eye had a half-wild expression, probably the result of excessive smoking."[23] So immersed was Sherman in his concern over the impending attack of the Confederates and his inability to hear from Washington that he would not reply to direct questions put to him.[24]

The General's bluntness and gruffness of speech often amounted to rudeness, and it was due to his inconsiderate treatment of a reporter of a New York paper that the charge of insanity brought against him at this time received such notoriety and wide circulation. A newsman who knew Sherman recounted that the reporter approached the General in the Associated Press rooms and requested a pass through the lines to the South as a correspondent. Upon Sherman's refusal of the request, the reporter impertinently informed the General that Secretary of War Cameron was in the city, and he would secure the pass from him.

> Sherman at once ordered him out of his department telling him he would give him two hours to make his escape; if found in his lines after that hour he "would hang him as a spy." The fellow left the city immediately, and on reaching Cincinnati very freely expressed his opinion that the General was crazy. A paper published in that city, on learning the story of the interview between Cameron and Sherman, which soon became public, employed the fellow to write up the report which was thus first circulated of Sherman's lunacy.[25]

The interview referred to took place between Sherman and Secretary of War Cameron at the Galt House in Louisville on October 16, 1861. Secretary Cameron decided to stop over in Louisville on his way back to Washington from St. Louis to confer with the distraught Sherman. Cameron was apparently convinced that Kentucky had sufficient troops and needed only money and arms. When Sherman was asked by the Secretary what, in his opinion, was the number of troops required to defend Kentucky, he replied promptly that he considered 200,000 men necessary to rid Kentucky of rebels. Cameron was said to have thrown his hands up and exclaimed: "Great God! Where are they to come from?"[26] Nevertheless, Cameron asked Adjutant General Thomas, who accompanied him, to make a note of Sherman's recommendation so that something might be done upon his return to Washington. Sherman in recounting the matter said:

> On reaching Washington, Mr. Cameron called on General Thomas, as he himself, afterward, told me, to submit his memorandum of events during his absence, and in that memorandum was mentioned my *insane* request for two hundred thousand men. By some newspaper men this was seen and published, and before I had the least conception of it, I was

universally published throughout the country as "insane," "crazy," etc.[27]

The risks involved in wielding full authority at this time were a matter of deep concern to Sherman. In April he had written his brother from St. Louis that he wanted to avoid responsibility in the first days of the war, as failure or misfortune so early in the game would be sure to doom a commander to oblivion.[28] In Kentucky after he took over command from General Anderson, he was so anxious to escape the dangers inherent in high position that he reminded the War Department in his earliest communications that his elevation to full authority was in violation of President Lincoln's promise to him that he was to be left in subordinate position.[29] Sherman's insistence to the President that he be left in subordinate position cannot be ascribed to a sense of modesty or to a sincere desire to efface himself. A complete picture of the man and his personality, as reflected in his letters, his *Memoirs* and the estimates of those who knew him personally, would not credit him with genuine modesty. There can be little doubt that the General was insuring himself against the misfortunes which he had previously stated might likely befall those first in full authority. In this instance, at least, his conclusions appeared to be based on sound reasoning drawn from a knowledge of history, which shows the instability of high command in the early phases of war—a period during which the public is most critical and during which the shaking-down process is at work.

Sherman's egotism, in itself, greatly intensified his fears of failure. He must not fail—he could not afford to fail—and it was under this compulsion apparently that he decided to give up his command rather than face what seemed to him inevitable—Union defeat in Kentucky and oblivion for the responsible officer. By early November he could endure the situation no longer, and his actions are best described by Mrs. Sherman, who had come to Louisville to be with her distraught husband. She informed Senator Sherman that General Sherman himself "had telegraphed to General McClellan to have him relieved." And she continued: "Cump's mind has been wrought up to a morbid state of anxiety which caused him to request McClellan to make the change."[30]

About the middle of November Brigadier General Don Carlos Buell was ordered to Louisville to relieve General Sherman, who was transferred to Major General Henry W. Halleck's Department of Missouri. Sherman was ordered to report to his new commanding officer at St. Louis.

Buell's assumption of the responsibilities of command at Louisville was a great relief to General Sherman, as he had confessed his inability to cope with the situation. He had written his brother on November 21:

> I know that others than yourself know that I take a gloomy view of affairs without cause. I hope to God 'tis so. . . . Now that Buell is in command I might divest myself of all care on this score. We have been out to camp inspecting the troops and he has entered upon his duties, and I have delayed here simply to give him information.[31]

With his assignment to Halleck at St. Louis, Sherman was presented with an opportunity to continue his service without the strain of direct responsibility; and he proceeded to his new post apparently more determined than ever to prove his detractors wrong and to rebuild quietly and reestablish his reputation. He had assured his brother: "For myself I will blindly obey my orders and report to General Halleck in Missouri, but until I can see daylight ahead I will never allow myself to be in command."[32]

In Missouri, however, General Sherman was able neither to quiet his fears nor to "blindly obey" his orders. Almost immediately after reporting in Missouri he permitted his agitated mind and the exaggerated pictures it conjured up to give General Halleck cause to question his competence in command. At Sedalia, Missouri, where Sherman was ordered to inspect the Union troops, he became so convinced that Confederate General Price was poised to destroy the Union forces there that he issued orders for a concentration of all Union military units in the area. In taking this step General Sherman went over the head of the Union commander, General Pope—an unforgivable violation of military courtesy. Pope complained at once of such unauthorized action on General Sherman's part, and General Halleck, having more accurate information on the Confederate movements, at once countermanded Sherman's orders and ordered him back to St. Louis.[33] General Halleck was not unaware of Sherman's melancholy view of affairs, and he had heard of the General's ill-considered statements in St. Louis, forecasting the doom of the Union cause and predicting that no power could now save the North.[34] This thoughtless action on Sherman's part, together with his panicky conduct at Sedalia, convinced Halleck that Sherman needed rest.

Upon Sherman's return to St. Louis he found Mrs. Sherman, apparently summoned by General Halleck, waiting to accompany him to Lancaster. The General noted later that Mrs. Sherman was "naturally and properly distressed at the continued and reiterated reports of the newspapers of my insanity."[35]

Halleck had urged a 20-day furlough on Sherman, and he returned with Mrs. Sherman to his home at Lancaster, Ohio, for a period of rest and relaxation. It was while he was at home, however, that the full fury of the charges of insanity beat about his ears, and Sherman noted in his *Memoirs* that "this recall from Sedalia simply swelled the cry."[36] The charges questioning the General's mental competence appeared on the same date, December 11, 1861, in *The Cincinnati Commercial, The Cincinnati Gazette,* and *The St. Louis Democrat.* The Sherman family was considerably upset over the reports, and Philamon Ewing called personally on the editor of *The Cincinnati Commercial* to see the proof behind the article appearing in that paper. Ellen Sherman wrote at once to Senator Sherman, urging him to come to his brother's defense. "I think as you have political power you ought to use it and I know you will protect him and confuse his enemies."[37] Senator Thomas Ewing used his influence to discover the sources of the malicious campaign against his son-in-law. He wrote General Halleck to clear up Halleck's position on the Sedalia matter, and as late as February 1862 received a detailed reply from Halleck. General Halleck obviously attempted to clear himself of any culpability in contributing to rumors regarding Sherman.[38] The appearance of similar charges against General Sherman on the same day in different newspapers indicated to

Ellen Sherman that it was the work of one person, and she wrote John Sherman that she was convinced it was the work of Brigadier General O. M. Mitchel. General Mitchel had been Sherman's subordinate in the ill-fated Cumberland Gap fiasco,[39] and she felt he had influenced both Halleck and Pope against Sherman. It is obvious that, had Sherman had friends among the war correspondents, the reports would never have received the widespread notoriety which they attained. Mrs. Sherman in her letter to Senator Sherman quoted part of the story from *The Cincinnati Gazette,* which for insinuation and back-handed viciousness would be hard to beat. The writer, appearing reluctant to discuss so delicate a matter, said: "The family and friends of General Sherman had desired to keep his insanity a secret but the matter having been dragged into the papers it is proper to say he was not *stark mad* whilst commanding in Kentucky, etc."[40]

Here, indeed, was a setback for one who so ardently longed to go his way, quietly and unobtrusively at first, building reputation and gaining public acclaim in order to secure his future. Certain it was that the charge of insanity brought Sherman deep anguish of mind, and the unfavorable publicity which he received greatly depressed him in spirit. The extent of the suffering to which his naturally nervous disposition subjected him can never be fully known. That his mind was dark and filled with doubt is clearly shown as it turned in upon itself, and he began to question the motives behind the orders transferring him from Louisville to St. Louis. He began to doubt that it was done at his request. He later described his attitude:

> At the time I was so relieved I thought, of course, it was done in fulfillment of Mr. Lincoln's promise to me, and as a necessary result of my repeated demand for the fulfillment of that promise; but I saw and felt, and was, of course, deeply moved to observe, the manifest belief that more or less of truth in the rumor that the cares, perplexities and anxiety of the situation had unbalanced my judgment and mind.[41]

Ellen Sherman observed the effect of those trying days upon her husband and, knowing him as she did, she appeared to realize that in addition to his fears for his career, he suffered an agonizing sense of shame and humiliation. Sherman had returned to Lancaster more than once to lick his wounds and more than once Thomas Ewing had offered help after something had gone wrong. Now, doubtlessly exaggerating the series of failures which seemed to follow him, he recalled his brother's words to him in April, in which the Senator had urged him to "avail yourself of these favorable circumstances," offered by the national emergency, "to secure your position for life."[42] Ellen Sherman hoped to rebuild his self-respect when she urged the miserable General to go and see his brother and Mr. Ewing and talk the matter out with them. She wrote John Sherman from Lancaster on December 16, 1861, that she felt an expression of confidence in him would reassure General Sherman. She pointed out that "now he fears that Father and you are overwhelmed with mortification on his account."[43]

General Sherman would not be persuaded to go to Washington to see Mr. Ewing and John, and "he is feeling terribly about the matter," Mrs. Sherman noted.[44] Once again, after all his careful planning, it appeared that he was to drink deep of the wormwood of defeat—again the haunting fear of failure reared itself before his eyes. All individuals do not react to failure or frustration in the same manner, and often those suffering from humiliation and a sense of inferiority, instead of withdrawing from the field, react with dogged determination or even exaggerated aggressiveness. It is possible that Sherman, as distracted and disheartened as he was, acted under a compulsion to succeed, when in obedience to orders from General Halleck, dated December 23, 1861, he reported to his new command at Benton Barracks, a camp of instruction for recruits near St. Louis.

The first days of Sherman's return to duty were far from happy for him. He had written Mr. Ewing while on furlough at Lancaster that the charges that he was mentally unstable "will be widely circulated and will impair my personal influence for much time to come, if not always."[45] Ellen Sherman likewise was concerned over the attitude his subordinates might take toward the General. She pointed out to Senator Sherman that, "if his feelings were not already in a morbid state," she would feel less worried, and she continued, "as it is I cannot bear to have him go back to St. Louis haunted by the spectre, dreading the effects of it in any apparent insubordination of officers or men."[46]

Although there is no record that Sherman was subjected to insubordination from his officers, for months he could not hide from himself the fact that many of the officers and men coming under his command regarded him with mingled curiosity and suspicion.[47] This experience seemed to reopen the wounds resulting from his troubles in Kentucky, and he appeared consciously to castigate himself for his actions. Early in January he again confessed to his brother his failure to handle his assignment there: "By giving up command in Kentucky I acknowledged my inability to manage the case, and do think Buell can manage better than I could, and if he succeeds he will deserve all honor."[48] His self-esteem wounded by a realization of how poorly he had conducted himself, he wrote his brother again on January 4, 1862, from Benton Barracks:

> I am so sensible now of my disgrace from having exaggerated the force of our enemy in Kentucky that I do think I should have committed suicide were it not for my children. I do not think that I can again be entrusted with a command . . . though I do believe myself better qualified for a Disbursing Department—suppose you see McClellan and ask him if I would not serve the Government better in such a capacity than the one I now hold. . . . Telegraph me what you think and would do.[49]

Sherman had entered into his duties at Benton Barracks with great industry, and he gave his personal attention to drilling the recruits sent to him, forming regiments of them and rebuilding the physical equipment of the camp. But even this activity could not dispel the ghost of disgrace. His letter to his brother of January 8, 1862, expressed his distress at the suffering he had caused him, Ellen and his children. He could not resist another reference to the unfortunate incident in Kentucky and the ignoble role he had played, nor could he forgive himself for surrendering in the face of difficulties:

I ought to have endured and then would have been responsible only for my part, whereas by giving up the command I not only confessed my inability to manage affairs entrusted to me but placed the burden on other shoulders. Still Buell can and will do far better than I could, and the country gains by the change.[50]

Buell did manage better than Sherman, who, incapacitated by mental disorganization and confused by his fears, had been unable to coordinate his command. Buell on assuming command found the Kentucky forces a mob, without head or front. Noted for his abilities in the organization and disciplining of troops, Buell soon made a fine army out of the soldiers. Later his timely arrival at Shiloh, with the thoroughly disciplined ranks formerly commanded by General Sherman, was one of the deciding factors in saving the day for the Union. It was said that Sherman's position itself was doubtless saved from annihilation by these men, who after less than a year of strict discipline and training appeared as veterans, though they had never fought a battle.[51]

Even though Sherman was troubled at Benton Barracks and concerned for his future, he was not too occupied to keep his eyes open to the military situation. Early in January he wrote to his brother mentioning a very important characteristic of the war which he had observed—a type of warfare employed by the South and thus far apparently overlooked by the military authorities:

Now Halleck has in Missouri about 80,000 men on paper, and there are not in organized shape more than 10,000 or 20,000 opposed to him, yet the country is full of Secessionist, and it takes all of his command to watch them. This is an element that politicians have never given full credit to. The local Secessionist are really more dangerous than if assembled in one or more bodies, for then they could be traced out and found, whereas now they are scattered about on farms and are very peaceable, but when a bridge is to be burned they are about. . . .

I wish I could take another view of this war, but I can-

39

not. It thrusts itself up at me from every side and yet I hope that I am mistaken. . . .

Halleck has been successful thus far, and I hope may continue, but he cannot by mere written papers cope with Price, who is in the field bothered by no papers or accounts, taking what he lays his hands on. I think he [Halleck] has orders to move down the river, but the moment he moves a man from the interior to go to Cairo, Price will return. That is his game. And in that way with a comparatively small force he holds in check five times his number.[52]

This was not the first time that Sherman had referred to this problem. He had observed it in Missouri, noting at that time that, although the Union army held the city of St. Louis and the railroads, the secessionists actually held the surrounding country. This all-important point was beginning to develop a serious doubt in his mind as to the wisdom of occupying cities and expending the great energy required to retain a tenuous hold on vital lines of communication. The cost of the effort was not worth the advantages gained, if the people, though not openly unfriendly, quietly but effectively destroy those communications—only to disperse, blending themselves back into the surrounding scene. Sherman's thinking along this line again shows that he was determined to connect all the people of the South with the actual fighting of the war. His observations in early 1862 made their contribution to the evolution of his concept of war. He would not forget what he saw in Missouri. Instead, he would carefully file it away in his mind. The time was not ripe to work out a carefully rationalized plan to punish those who held the Union armies impotent and afraid to move too far away from their bases of supply. His mind would seize on these early impressions as a jumping-off place, from which he could proceed to work out his concept for a new kind of warfare.

Under the circumstances, General Sherman determined upon a policy of keeping his own council until such time as he could stand forth before his accusers, and those who had listened to them, as a man of ability and power—a soldier to be reckoned with, to be admired by men and officers alike. In later years he was to boast, with his singular lack of modesty, that his men idolized and revered him and that they would go anywhere and risk any danger simply at his order.[53] In the meantime Sherman, remaining in subordinate command, appeared content to carry out orders and to permit the nation to forget that his sanity had been questioned.

III

⁀⁀⁀⁀⁀⁀⁀⁀

Shiloh—Renewed Confidence
and a New Friend

Fort Henry on the Tennessee River had fallen on February 6, and Grant was attacking General Buckner at Fort Donelson on the Cumberland River. General Sherman was ordered to command at Paducah on February 13, 1862, to expedite the movement of troops and transports up the Tennessee River. John Sherman, ever ready to offer encouragement, wrote his brother on February 15 congratulating him on his new command. In his letter, written apparently in the flush of the victory at Fort Henry, John made an observation with which General Sherman might have agreed immediately after Bull Run, but which he now regarded in a new light:

> Do not the cheers with which our gun-boats were received in Tennessee and Alabama show you what I have always contended, that this rebellion is a political one, managed by Southern gentlemen and not grounded in the Universal Assent of the people?[1]

Certainly to General Sherman this was the viewpoint of one who, at a distance, saw only the outline of things. True it might have been that at the outset the rebellion was encouraged, its sparks fanned into flames by the courtly but fiery political leaders of the South. But that its principles were "not grounded in the Universal Assent of the people" Sherman could not agree. His mind reverted with quick irritation, characteristic of his nervous temperament, to Confederate General Price's small force, holding in check five times his number. Even worse, his vivid imagination pictured for him the elusive, innocent-appearing country people who struck paralyzing blows at transportation, only to appear blandly incredulous when they looked up from their plowing to answer the questions of a searching Union patrol. These in his opinion were neither politicians nor soldiers—these were the people!

Thus it was at Paducah, in the early months of 1862, that General Sherman first became fully aware of a new factor in warfare—one which he had not appreciated before. According to those who knew him, General Sherman had a peculiar mental characteristic which led him to immediate conclusions—conclusions which he arrived at by leaping over wide gaps of fact and reason. Boyd, his friend of Louisiana days, had noted this peculiarity and said of it:

> He could not reason—that is, his mind leaped so quick from idea to idea that he seemed to take no account of the time over which it passed, and if he was asked to explain how he came by his conclusions it confused him. This weakness, if weakness it can be called was due to his genius. His mind went like lightening to its conclusions, and he had the utmost faith in his inspirations and conviction. . . . Sherman reached his conclusions at a bound, and with him that was the end of it.[2]

Another who had opportunity to know Sherman attempted to describe this trait by saying:

> Sherman jumps at conclusions with tremendous logical springs; and though his decisions are not always final, they are in effect so, for, if he is forced to retire an inch, his next jump will probably carry him forward an ell.[3]

If he arrived at a definite conclusion at this time, it was the conviction that the people of the South would have to be reckoned with somewhere in the months of war ahead. He recognized them as an obstacle, but it was months later, at Memphis, that they became such a problem that he could develop a personal hatred for them—a hatred first directed toward what he called "guerillas," and then through generalization extended to all of the inhabitants who lived in the vicinity where resistance was offered.

There were busy days at Paducah, as Sherman went about the job of securing transports and forwarding men and supplies to Grant, who was besieging Fort Donelson. Grant was impressed by the enthusiastic support given him by Sherman, particularly in the face of the highly critical attitude which Major General Halleck began to adopt toward Grant. Although Sherman was Grant's senior in rank, he was willing to waive rank if Grant required his services.[4] Sherman was apparently anxious to be on the scene of action, as fame could not be expected as long as he remained a glorified steamboat dispatcher.[5]

It must have been with keen pleasure that General Sherman received orders on March 10 to take the field with a division which he had been organizing while dispatching transports to Grant and Buell. He was to take part in the great southward movement of General Halleck's forces, which had as its objective the capture of Corinth. The Confederate armies in the Mississippi Valley used Corinth as a central supply depot and base of operations. General Sherman, after steaming up the river beyond Fort Henry with his division, met General C. F. Smith, who ordered him to push on and destroy the Memphis and Charleston Railroad between Tuscumbia, Alabama, and Corinth. High waters and downpours of rain prevented the execution of the orders, and Sherman returned to Pittsburgh Landing, where he remained until the battle of Shiloh.

The attack of the Confederate army under General Albert Sidney Johnston upon the Union forces commanded by General Grant at Shiloh came as a surprise; and one of the bloodiest encounters of the war followed, with the two armies locked in heavy engagements all of Sunday and Monday, April 6 and 7.

This battle, which took a heavy toll in casualties on both sides, shocked the North particularly. The conduct of the Union army became a source of considerable controversy, as early reports, widely circulated in the North, told how its army had been caught by surprise. The Northern press expressed its grief and shock, and leveled harsh criticisms, both just and unjust, at the heads of those in command. General Grant was the focal point of the charges. He was accused of gross negligence in stories reaching the North and East—negligence contributing to the needless loss of life. Reports were circulated that whole regiments had been killed in their tents. Grant, who had gone up the Tennessee River to meet Buell at Savannah, was severely criticized for not being closer to his command.

Sherman apparently conducted himself well under fire, and he was obviously well pleased with himself, as he wrote Ellen Sherman from Shiloh on April 11:

> I won't attempt to give an account of the battle, but they say that I accomplished some important results, and General Grant makes special mention of me in his report, which he showed me. I have worked hard to keep down, but somehow I am forced into prominence and might as well submit.[6]

Little more than a month later, as a result of General Halleck's recommendation,[7] he was elevated to the rank of Major General of volunteers. He informed Mrs. Sherman of his promotion:

> I received today the commission of Major General, but, I know not why, it gives me far less emotion than my old commission as 1st Lieutenant of Artillery. The latter I know I merited; this I doubt, but its possession completes the chain from cadet up, and will remain among the family archives, when you and I repose in eternity.[8]

Later, in writing of that day at Shiloh, Grant said that Sherman's division actually held the key point of the Federal positions and "his division was at that time wholly raw, no part of it ever having been in an engagement, but I thought this deficiency was more than made up by the superiority of the commander."[9]

With the charges of negligence hurled at his head, Grant apparently made no reply, refusing to be goaded into an exchange of correspondence which could accomplish nothing.[10] Not so with his friend Sherman, who, with the bitter taste of his treatment at the hands of newspapers still fresh, dipped his pen in vitriol and wrote scathing indictments of reporters, editors and the press in general.

Senator Sherman had tried to persuade his brother back in February to let up in the harshness of his criticism of newspapermen. This was shortly after the insanity charges had dropped into the background and Halleck had placed Sherman in command at Paducah. Senator Sherman apparently feared that his brother's bent for making blunt, uncompromising statements might once again endanger his career. It was the politician who had written on February 15, 1862:

> You will have a noble opportunity to answer those who have belied you. Take my advice, be hopeful, cheerful, polite to everybody, even a newspaper reporter. They are in the main, clever, intelligent men, a little too pressing in their vocation. Above all things, be hopeful and push ahead. Active, bold, vigorous action is now demanded.[11]

General Sherman apparently had not forgotten the assurance that bold, vigorous action was demanded, and his conduct in the bloody line at Shiloh showed his determination to push ahead. The reassuring knowledge that he had received official recognition for his part in that battle had helped him to regain some measure of his poise and self-confidence. A reporter for a New York paper who interviewed Sherman after the battle remarked on the difference in him since last he had seen the General in Missouri. "Since I first saw him, his eye had grown much calmer, and his nervous system healthier," he reported.[12] Newspaper criticism, striking hard at Grant, threatened now to bring on a relapse. Sherman was convinced that the charges against Grant were unjust and were reported to the press either by misinformed officers or by those who, after their courage returned, hoped to justify their own actions in leaving the field. He could not forget that he had suffered at the hands of "irresponsible" newsgatherers, and he would not heed John Sherman's appeal for politeness, "even to a newspaper reporter." He expressed his contempt for those who hurled charges from a safe distance in a letter to Mrs. Sherman:

> I hope the war won't end until those who caused the war, the politicians and editors are made to feel it. The scoundrels take good care of their hides, run up after a fight and back again before there is a chance for another.[13]

In a letter three days later to his father-in-law, Sherman's resentment flared anew as he complained of the injustice of the charges:

> We all knew we were assembling an army for an aggressive purpose. The President knew it, Halleck knew it, and the whole country knew it, and the attempt to throw blame on Grant is villainous. The fact is, if newspapers are to be our government, I confess, I would prefer Bragg, Beauregard, or anybody as my ruler, and I will persist in my determination never to be a leader responsible to such a power.

Near the end of his letter he struck a new note—one which reflected his returning confidence in himself—as he said: "I am not in search of glory or fame, for I know I can take what position I choose among my peers."[14]

As late as June he was still agitated over the press's attacks on Grant, and writing to Mrs. Sherman from near Corinth, he unburdened himself: "I will get even with the miserable class of corrupt editors yet. They are the chief cause of this unhappy war. They fan the flames of local hatred, and keep alive those prejudices which have forced friends into opposing hostile ranks."[15]

It is not unlikely, even in the face of his attachment for Grant, that Sherman was expressing his own concern over the effects unfavorable notoriety could have on his own future hopes for a brilliant career. He knew from personal experience how much influence the press had over public opinion. Certainly he took to heart Grant's situation—one day the hero of Donelson, and the next, the scapegoat of Shiloh. In the same letter he indignantly observed:

> Worse than this at the North, no sooner does an officer rise from the common level, but some rival uses the press to malign him, destroy his usefulness, and pull him back to obscurity or infamy. Thus it was with me, and now they have nearly succeeded with Grant. . . . If this be pushed much further officers of modesty and merit will keep away, will draw back into obscurity and leave our armies to be led by fools or rash men.[16]

Many officers in the army were openly ambitious—particularly those who, as local politicians, had secured commissions with state troops—and they were not above writing favorable reports of their own deeds to their local newspapers, to build up their popularity in their home districts. Sherman commented on this practice and referred to officers who kept reporters close at their sides. He observed that often press reports intended for county circulation reached national attention, "making their little heroes big fools."[17] Sherman objected to such practices on the grounds that they placed the emphasis in the wrong place and directed the spotlight of acclaim on those less worthy of such mention, and he pointed out an example of such inaccuracies:

> Thus at Shiloh for a month, all through Illinois and Missouri, a newspaper reader would have supposed McClernand and Lew Wallace were away ahead of my division, whereas the former was directly behind me, and the other at Crump's Landing.[18]

Then he sounded a note of resignation, indicating that even should he be the one to be sacrificed, he would rise above the sordidness of self-seeking. He expressed his sentiments to Mrs. Sherman:

> Let them scramble for the dead lion's paw. It is a barren honor not worth contending for. If these examples and a few more will convince the real substantial men of our country

that the press is not even an honest exponent of the claims
of men pretending to serve their country, but the base means
of building up spurious fame, and pulling down honest merit,
I feel that I have my full reward in being one of the first to
see it and suffer the consequences.[19]

The war in the West moved on and General Sherman, with
renewed confidence, moved with his division, under Halleck's orders, to lay siege to Beauregard's Confederates, who were entrenched and well supplied in Corinth. On May 29 the Union
troops dug in, not taking any chances on a repetition of Shiloh.
The same night there were peculiar noises emanating from inside Corinth, and the whistling of locomotives puzzled the besieg-
ers lying behind their earthworks outside the city. Toward dawn
there were a series of explosions, followed by billowing smoke
over the town. When the Union forces advanced to feel out the
defenses of Corinth they found that Beauregard had evacuated
the town, removing all of his troops except his wounded. He had
carried with him all his supplies and destroyed such stores of
ammunition as he could not transport.

Major General Halleck was a cautious, methodical and thorough officer, and he had moved ponderously, consuming nearly
the whole of the month of May to cover the distance between
Shiloh and Corinth, approximately 30 miles. With Beauregard's
evacuation, Halleck moved into Corinth and, making it his headquarters, undertook to fortify it from every angle. This action on
Halleck's part was observed with misgivings by Sherman and
Grant, and although there is nothing to show that they discussed
it openly, it is certain that they were both critical. They felt
that Halleck was committing a grave error. They were in agreement that their commander erred, not only in the size of the
works of Corinth, but, what was of greater importance, in his
consequent breaking up and dispersing of his force of nearly
100,000 men. Sherman, who held General Halleck in high esteem at this stage of the war, admired the manner in which the
General had placed such a powerful, well-equipped army, effi-
ciently supplied, into a strategic base such as Corinth, from which
it could strike out in any direction. But, said Sherman:

Had he held his force as a unit he could have gone to Mobile or Vicksburg, or anywhere in that region, which would by one move have solved the whole Mississippi problem; and from what he then told me, I believe he intended such a campaign, but was overruled from Washington.[20]

The empty victory at Corinth was described to Senator Sherman in a letter written on May 31, 1862. General Sherman enclosed a copy of his orders, issued to boost his men's morale, which had been adversely affected by their failure to strike the enemy.[21] Although he confessed that he could not foresee the next move, he was willing to hazard a guess, and he wrote:

I cannot imagine what turn things will now take, but I do not think Halleck will attempt to pursue far. I think that Beauregard cannot now subsist his army or hold it together long.

It must divide to live, and the greatest danger is that they will scatter and constitute guerilla bands. The people are as bitter against us as ever, but the leaders must admit that they have been defeated. I hope this army with some exceptions will be marched forthwith to Memphis. . . . We want the Mississippi now in its whole length and a moment should not be lost.[22]

The fear that Beauregard's army would be broken up into small units "constituting guerilla bands" was to recur to Sherman frequently in the months ahead. He would categorically attribute to "guerillas" the knifing attacks of small units of cavalry detached from main Confederate armies for the express purpose of harrying Union troop movements and interrupting communication and supply lines. As such attacks became increasingly effective, Sherman's hatred for the "guerilla" would become a part of his thinking, almost to the point of an obsession.

At Corinth Grant looked on, thinking thoughts strangely similar to those expressed by Sherman in his letter to his brother. Grant was in an uncomfortable position—that of only nominal command. Halleck had, for reasons never expressed, placed Grant in embarrassing positions more than once since Donelson, and he had repeatedly requested Halleck to relieve him of his command. Grant had been in direct command at the battle of Shiloh, and he could not easily forget that General Halleck had ignored him. Halleck had neither called for Grant's official report of the battle nor shown him the full reports submitted to Washington. In consequence, Grant never submitted a full official report of that engagement. Now at Corinth he again asked General Halleck for permission to resign, and he was prepared to leave. Again his friend Sherman came to his support and urged him to stay with such warmth that Grant reconsidered.[23]

As he sat in enforced idleness, Grant's mind, too, played with the possibilities of the next move, and it appeared that he deplored the tying down of an army to a stationary base and the occupation and holding of places, rather than rapid movement in pursuit of the opposing armies. Said he:

> General Halleck at once commenced erecting fortifications around Corinth on a scale to indicate that this one point must be held if it took the whole national army to do it. . . . They were laid out on a scale that would have required 100,000 men to fully man them. It was probably thought that a final battle of the war would be fought at this point.[24]

The construction of such extensive works and the proper manning of them made necessary the constant guarding of vital lines of supply. That this was not an easy task was well demonstrated after Corinth was occupied. Buell was ordered east with the Army of the Ohio to repair the Memphis and Charleston Railroad as he advanced. His troops repaired the road only to have it destroyed by small bands as soon as the Union forces moved on. Observing this, Grant was impressed with the advantages of a mobile army as a more effective weapon.

Both Sherman and Grant realized that Corinth was of strategic value as a base of operations, but they were disappointed that the army was to stop there. Both would have preferred leaving a small garrison and pursuing the Confederate army with the main force. Grant later expressed it:

> On our side I know officers and men of the Army of the Tennessee—and I presume the same is true of those of the other commands—were disappointed at the result. They could not see how the mere occupation of places was to close the war while large and effective rebel armies existed.[25]

Thus, Major General Halleck's course of action, both before and after Corinth, was to make a deep and lasting impression on the minds of the two Union generals. Their thinking and later actions were to reflect the influence of the lesson unconsciously taught them by their commanding officer. There is nothing to indicate that the two men, destined to play the most prominent roles in the war in the months ahead, arrived at any common agreement at the time as to the most effective military moves. Their conclusions at Corinth in the spring of 1862 were strikingly similar and certainly laid the groundwork for future cooperation, based on mutual understanding.

Shortly after the occupation of Corinth, General Halleck began the dispersal of the large Union forces at his command. The Army of the Ohio, under Buell's command, was ordered to Chattanooga, via Huntsville and Stevenson, Alabama, to seize the mountain openings there. General Pope's forces were sent back to Missouri, and Grant was left in command of the District of West Tennessee and Northern Mississippi. General Sherman was ordered to proceed with his division to Chewalla, a point ten miles northwest of Corinth, to attempt repairs on the railroad and to salvage as much as he could of the abandoned rolling stock and locomotives which had been left in Beauregard's wake.

On the 9th of June, Sherman advised that neither salvage efforts nor repairs of the railroad were worthwhile, and General Halleck ordered him to Grand Junction to repair the Charleston and Memphis Railroad west of that point and to guard it against interruption by Southern forces in the vicinity. Sherman directed a part of the force under his command against Holly Springs, from which point he was being worried by roving Confederate cavalry units. He was not to be permitted, however, to undertake the ambitious program he had in mind of occupying and holding that place. General Halleck, informed of the action, ordered

Sherman not to attempt to hold Holly Springs, but to fall back and protect the railroad.[26]

Later in the month General Price occupied Holly Springs in force with his Confederate Army of the Trans-Mississippi and held Grand Junction as an outpost. General Grant requested permission of Halleck, now in Washington as general-in-chief of the armies, to drive Price out, and to his astonishment Halleck replied that the best use that Grant could make of his troops was not to scatter them out.[27]

On July 16, 1862, Sherman was informed by telegraph that General Halleck was called to Washington to assume command of the Armies of the United States. Grant was to assume Halleck's place and take up his headquarters at Corinth, while Sherman was to proceed immediately to Memphis as commanding officer of the District of West Tennessee, just vacated by Grant. Thus, with the departure of Halleck for Washington, Grant became Sherman's commanding officer, a relationship which was to continue unbroken to the end of the war. The two men had much in common, and the closing chapters of the war would show how firmly founded was the understanding which existed between them. Later, as they mapped the Vicksburg campaign, they worked well together—the superior officer asking the advice of his subordinate, and the subordinate offering suggestions with complete ease and freedom of expression. That they did not always see eye to eye would be shown in Sherman's objections to Grant's decision to run transports past the deadly guns of Vicksburg. His viewpoint was the product of the quick, imaginative mind, which seized at once upon the many hazards involved and feared the responsibility for the heavy loss of life which would surely attend such a venture. Grant, on the other hand, deliberate and practical-minded, faced problems as he saw them, apparently willing to face any criticism which might follow his efforts to solve them. He seemed to feel that when it was necessary to place troops in the most strategic positions for effective action, they should be put there in the most direct manner, and in consequence Grant was later to expend many lives in massed, frontal attacks on General Lee's defenses in Virginia. In contrast to Grant, Sherman was by nature inclined to avoid tight positions insofar as possible, preferring mobility and strategy to direct assaults on the enemy. In those cases where Sherman's recommendations were overruled by his chief, Sherman carried out Grant's orders without argument or complaint. The history of this period bears witness to what a fortunate working team was here established for the Union cause by the promotion of Halleck to general-in-chief in July of 1862.

IV

⟨⟨⟨⟨⟨⟨⟨⟨

Memphis Commander—
The Theory of Collective
Responsibility

General Sherman entered upon his duties as military commander
of Memphis on July 21, 1862, and his time was well occupied in
the administration of civil affairs and in drilling and organizing the
two divisions under his command. Memphis had been one of the
Confederacy's strong points on the Mississippi, and when the
Southern forces were forced to evacuate the town they left behind them countless Southern sympathizers and even members of
their families. Sherman's letters written during the summer and fall
of 1862 from Memphis leave no doubt that he was fully conscious
of the hostility and enmity on the part of certain elements of
Memphis's inhabitants. He was likewise acutely aware of the
hostile attitude of the surrounding countryside, and he was not
alone in his certainty that the Union forces in the Mississippi
Valley were surrounded by a populace who looked upon them
with unfriendly eyes. Grant, too, was uncomfortable in his headquarters at Corinth, and he expressed the uneasiness he felt after
Halleck departed and left him with insufficient strength, when he
wrote: "The remainder of the magnificent army of 120,000 men
which entered Corinth on May 30 had now become so scattered
that I was put entirely on the defensive in a territory whose popu-

lation was hostile to the Union."[1] Further, Grant recognized the danger of his position and just how insecure his hold on the country was, and he said:

> The most anxious period of the war to me was during the time the Army of the Tennessee was guarding territory acquired by the fall of Corinth and Memphis and before I was sufficiently reinforced to take the offensive. The enemy also had cavalry operating in our rear, making it necessary to guard every point of the railroad back to Columbus (Kentucky), on the security of which we were dependent for all our supplies.[2]

It was an anxious time for Sherman, too, and he rushed work on Fort Pickering in front of Memphis, putting all Negroes coming into the town to work on the fortifications. The problem of these slaves, hundreds of whom were being sent into Memphis every day from territory occupied by Union forces, was one of the many vexations which faced Sherman at Memphis. He wrote his brother that he could not see how his army was to clothe, feed and provide employment for these Negroes and their families, whom the government at Washington had, by command, declared free without providing any machinery for preventing their deterioration into idlers and thieves and worse. He pointed out that "you cannot solve this Negro question in a day."[3]

In his post as supreme military commander of the city Sherman apparently handled civil affairs smoothly. Insofar as was consistent with existing war conditions, he left the civil government in the hands of the mayor and other civil officials, even encouraging the use of the civilian police force for the maintenance of law and order. He further assured the mayor that the military would not interfere, unless necessary, with the functions of the civil courts. The assistance of the Union troops was offered, if needed, to collect taxes imposed by the municipal council, provided the tax plan was first approved by Sherman as one for the purpose of community improvement.[4]

The policy followed by the United States in buying cotton was a matter of irritation to Sherman. The United States needed the South's cotton, worth approximately 300 dollars a bale, and it served as coin in the balance of trade. That aspect of the matter was not so important to Sherman as was the vital question of "aid and comfort to the enemy." He was convinced that the policy contributed directly to the supplying of "guerilla bands" with guns and ammunition. Nor could he fail to see the horde of speculators and traders who flocked to Memphis to profiteer on the government's offer to buy cotton. Their purpose was to obtain cotton for resale to the government, and they were not overly scrupulous as to the means employed. It was regarding this phase of the matter that Sherman wrote to Secretary of the Treasury Chase on August 11, 1862. He pointed out to the Secretary that the policy of buying cotton from any and all who offered it, without too much inquiry as to where the money went or how it was employed, was fundamentally wrong. The avaricious cotton buyer, he said, soon discovered that salt, bacon, powder, firearms and percussion caps would entice far more cotton into his hands than would gold. With a concrete example in mind, he wrote:

> And I have no doubt that Bragg's army at Tupelo, and Van Dorn's at Vicksburg, received enough salt to make bacon, without which they could not have moved their armies in mass; and that from ten to twenty thousand fresh arms, and a due supply of cartridges have also been got, I am equally satisfied.[5]

Sherman used his letter to Chase, not only to attempt to set the government straight as to where its cotton policy was leading, but also to clear up his own thinking toward the war. The letter provided an opportunity for him to set down in black and white some important conclusions which he had been turning over in his mind for some weeks and which he summed up to the Secretary: "This is no trifle when one nation is at war with another, all the people of the one are enemies of the other; then the rules are plain and easy of understanding." He assured Chase that at the outset of the war there was apparently no understanding of such a simple matter, and he continued:

> The Government of the United States may now safely proceed on the proper rule that all in the South *are* enemies

of all in the North; and not only are they unfriendly, but all who can procure arms now bear them as organized regiments, or as guerillas. There is not a garrison in Tennessee where a man can go beyond the sight of the flagstaff without being shot or captured.[6]

Thus did Sherman strip war of all the rules of conduct voluntarily subscribed to by the civilized nations of the nineteenth century and set up a single very simple one—that all of the people of the South were enemies of those of the North, and the Union armies might therefore proceed on the "proper" rule that no line was to be drawn between the military forces of the South and the noncombatant civilian population. Sherman here stated, in simple language, the basic premise upon which the waging of total war rests and upon which efforts to justify it are founded.

Sherman now focused his attention on the countryside around his headquarters at Memphis, and he became more and more impressed with the disadvantages faced by an army invading enemy territory. He observed the ease with which his enemy, Bragg, moved about the Mississippi Valley, entraining his troops and sending his wagon convoys across country without fear. On all sides he received wholehearted cooperation and assistance from a friendly, sympathetic people.[7] In contrast, Sherman sat in Memphis, his force rendered ineffective by forces far inferior in numbers, but dangerous by reason of their flexibility of action and the rapidity of their movements. The serious effects of "guerilla" action on communications and supply lines occupied a large place in Sherman's thinking, as indicated by the frequency of his mention of it in his letters and reports in the early weeks at Memphis. There were good reasons for his concern as frequent scattered attacks were made on Union foraging parties, railroads and wagon trains—attacks sudden and vicious, with the attackers moving out of reach before effective resistance could be offered. Sherman had described his helplessness in a report to General Grant as early as August 1862. He pointed out the difficulty of coming to grips with the enemy and said that, although he sent his cavalry out in all directions, they usually returned empty-handed. The elusiveness of Southern units brought from Sherman a characteristic recourse to generalization, as he assured Grant: "All the people are now guerillas, and they have a perfect understanding."[8]

With his mind absorbed in his problem, it is highly probable that Sherman was inclined to overemphasize the "guerilla" threat and to build it up out of all proportion to its importance. General Nathan B. Forrest's Confederate cavalry, as well as that of General Van Dorn, was operating in the vicinity of Memphis,[9] and doubtless most of the damaging attacks reported to Sherman were made by units from these forces. Many of Forrest's cavalrymen were irregulars,[10] and uniforms were not available for a large number of them. These troops were listed on Confederate muster rolls as soldiers, and their officers held commissions from the Confederate government. It was a practice of both Van Dorn and Forrest to detach units from their main forces to strike at several different points simultaneously, and it is therefore not unlikely that Sherman heard of more "guerillas" than actually there were. The tendency to generalize his problem was not surprising in one of Sherman's temperament—quick, nervous energy made him irritable and impatient at the countless stings he suffered from an enemy with whom he could not come to grips.

The estimate made by Sherman of the numbers resisting the Union troops based at Memphis was a tribute to the strategy of the Confederate officers directing that phase of the war, and their consistent attacks wherever the enemy was weakest and most exposed was a source of very real trouble to the Union commander at Memphis.[11] His letters and reports are filled with threats and anger at their activities. With a rising note of conviction he wrote John Sherman on August 26, 1862: "All their people are armed and at war—you hear of vast armies at Richmond, Chattanooga, and threatening New Orleans, whilst the whole country is full of guerilla bands, numbering hundreds."[12]

Almost a month passed before he again expressed himself on the matter uppermost in his mind, but it was evident that his peculiar restlessness of mind had driven him on and that he was beginning to clear up his thinking. In the vain, opinionated manner so noticeable throughout his correspondence, he expressed his impatience with those in the North who were unable to see a truth so long known to him. In this vein he wrote his brother in

September: "It's about time the North understood the truth. That the entire South, man, woman and child, is against us, armed and determined." He assured his brother that not only was the South more confident than ever, but that he felt certain that it had hopes of conquering the Northwest; and he continued with stubborn insistence: "I guess you now see how, from the very first I argued, that you all underestimated the task."[13]

It was evident at this time that Sherman was determined to consider the resistance encountered in the surrounding territory as the treacherous acts of the civilian populace. He was to shut out any thought that his troubles were caused by Confederate cavalry. What he brought himself to believe, through a process of generalization and rationalization, was what governed his attitudes and actions. It mattered not that he had not investigated or weighed the evidence to establish the truth of the proposition—he had convinced himself that it was true, and that was what he would act upon.

It was apparent that Sherman had done an excellent job of convincing himself that the larger part of his troubles as well as those facing the other Union armies in the Mississippi Valley were directly attributable to the lawless and underhanded methods employed by civilian sympathizers with the Southern cause. Gradually his ideas had taken form, and he saw the "guerilla" as one who, when confronted with danger, disposed of his rifle and assumed the appearance of a citizen—or, when captured, demanded treatment as a prisoner of war, basing his claim on a commission or on protestations that he was duly enrolled as a soldier.[14] A few guerillas could endanger the lives of thousands of noncombatants who had already submitted to the Union arms, and some force must be applied to combat them. Sherman had been searching around for some means of crippling those he was coming to hate, and as early as July 31, a few days after he took command at Memphis, he wrote to his wife giving her an insight as to the direction things would take. He had sized up the situation, as he wrote:

> We are in our enemy's country, and I act accordingly. The North may fall into bankruptcy and anarchy first, but if they

can hold on, the war will soon assume a turn to extermination, not of soldiers alone, that is the least part of the trouble, but the people.[15]

John Sherman had written the General shortly before the Union army occupied Corinth, outlining the optimistic hopes of those in official circles for an early end to the war, and he had pointed out how sound the country's financial condition was. It would be advantageous for the North if the war could be ended while they were so prosperous. But John Sherman had warned his brother:

> However delay, defeat or a much longer continuation in the barbarity of rebel warfare will prepare the public mind in the North for a warfare that will not scruple to avail itself of every means of subjection.[16]

Sherman could have interpreted this statement from his brother, a senator who sat in the high councils of the government, as an indication that the practical application of a new type of warfare which he would put into effect as soon as it crystallized in his own mind would not receive too much adverse reaction in the public mind.

Rapidly now, General Sherman's mind was preparing itself to abandon such scruples as he might have had at the outset of the war. He had come a long way since the battle of Bull Run, where he had observed the actions of his volunteer troops with shock and disgust. Could their destructive tendencies be the answer he sought as to an effective means to reach the people of the South? But he was not quite ready yet to change the shadow of his thought into the substance of direct action. Even as he wrote exaggerated accounts of his situation and concentrated his faculties on the discovery of some effective means to strike back at those who attacked and ran away, he made public, in a letter to a newspaper, his stand on laws promulgated by Congress with reference to looting and pillage by the armies of the United States. Sherman's attitude, publicly expressed, was that of the orthodox army officer and West Point graduate:

> Straggling and pillaging have ever been great military crimes; and every officer and soldier in my command knows

what stress I have laid upon them, and that so far as in my power lies, I will punish them to the full extent of the law and orders.

But, he informed the editor of the paper, it is one thing to know what the law is, and quite a different matter to enforce it; and the letter continued:

> I admit the law to be that "no officer or soldier of the United States shall commit waste or destruction of cornfields, orchards, potato-patches, or any kind of pillage on the property of friend or foe near Memphis," and that I stand prepared to execute the law as far as possible.[17]

In the light of what happened within three or four days after Sherman's public statement outlining his attitude toward pillage and the destruction of property, there is every reason to question his sincerity and to suspect that he made it for the record and to justify his future course.

General Sherman grew more and more fretful as he watched the hostile countryside, and his anger mounted as he observed how effectively he was checkmated by what he insisted, time and again, were small "guerilla" forces. The personal angle began to enter his consideration—were the people of the South, lending their aid and support to unscrupulous "guerillas," to be permitted to interfere with his career, which had begun so auspiciously at Shiloh? He was particularly irritated by the Southerners' efforts to interrupt the passage of steamboats bringing supplies from the North down to Memphis. It was these snipers, lying along the banks and bluffs, firing on the boats, who brought to a head the strain of weeks of nervous tension, uncertainty and anger. They had assumed such formidable proportions in his mind that again he suffered from a deep-seated anxiety in which an overpowering sense of danger and a defenselessness against it were present. Because of his excessive sensitivity to the possibility of new humiliation he now stood at the point where desperate steps were required to save his self-esteem. His was the type of egoism which it is not safe to dam up, tempting the explosion of primal forces.

Thwarted to the danger point, he exploded into action with an order to Colonel C. C. Walcutt, which read in part:

> The object of the expedition you have been detailed for is to visit the town of Randolph where yesterday the packet Eugene was fired on by a party of guerillas. Acts of this kind must be promptly punished, and it is almost impossible to reach the actors, for they come from the interior and depart as soon as the mischief is done. But the interests and well-being of the country demands that all such attacks should be followed by a punishment that will tend to prevent a repetition.[18]

Now he was to exact payment and fulfill the long pent-up craving to get back at his enemy. There was no doubt now, as the instructions to the commander of the expedition were explicit:

> I think the attack on the Eugene was by a small force of guerillas from Loosahatchie, who by this time have gone back, and therefore you will find no one at Randolph, in which case you will destroy the place, leaving one house to mark the place.

All restraints were now cast aside. A steamboat near Randolph had been fired on by "guerillas." They had done so before; apply the torch and destroy the town utterly. What did it matter that Sherman "thought" that the guilty persons came from a place far from the scene of the attack? This was retaliation pure and simple —the visitation of punishment on a community for the acts of those coming from outside the vicinity, the wreaking of vengeance upon a town because it happened to be near the scene of trouble. Here Sherman put into effect the theory that his generalizations had inevitably led him to the theory of collective responsibility. "All the people are armed against us"—"man, woman, and child" —this had been his refrain for months.[19] His correspondence indicated how systematically he had built his case in his own mind, and how thoroughly he had convinced himself that he was surrounded by an ever-watchful, unseen enemy, one who could rob him of his opportunity to demonstrate his abilities as a soldier.

He had counted "guerilla" bands in numbers far greater than actually existed.[20] All of this was a part of mental processes of rationalization through which he reduced his problem to its lowest common denominator. Collective responsibility placed in his hands a weapon, simple in its application, to strike back at his enemy with telling blows. The wording of his orders to Colonel Walcutt clearly indicates that Sherman was not only uncertain that the attack was made by guerillas, but that he could only hazard a guess as to the direction from which it came. It is noteworthy that no investigation was made to ascertain the facts or to establish the complicity of the inhabitants of the town of Randolph in the attack. The theory of collective responsibility rested on the assumption that proximity to the scene of the act constitutes guilt and no further proof is required. Thus Sherman felt relieved of following the accepted rule of civilized warfare, which required that thorough investigations be conducted to establish the participation of the residents of a community before inflicting punishment. Justification for his irregular act was a part of the orders: "The interests and well-being of the country demands . . . a punishment that will tend to prevent a repetition." Thus was the plea of necessity offered to condone the transgression of the laws of war. But the inherent danger in placing the emphasis on necessity permits its advocate to proceed to any extreme. The days following the destruction of Randolph would demonstrate the extremes to which Sherman was now willing to go as he broadened the scope of his changed point of view toward war.

Having now brought the enemy into focus and satisfied himself that war could be carried to the people, it required no great jump in reasoning to cross the narrow line between the destruction of property to punish a community and the application of punishment directly to the individual. Sherman had wanted to retaliate more than a month before his anger had spurred him into ordering the destruction of the little river town, but he was still cautious. His report to Grant at the time showed that he was not deterred by any moral or ethical considerations as he had written: ". . . and I would favor the condign punishment of anyone committing such outrage, but we must be careful not to render ourselves too harsh, or they will naturally seek revenge."[21]

Having struck the first blow, he wrote to his brother telling of his action and preparing him for the realization that this war would require a new set of rules—rules which were not in accord with the accepted viewpoint. He had been forced to take positive action, he assured John; and he continued:

> I rather think you now agree with me that this is no common war, that it was not going to end in a few months or a few years. For after eighteen months of war the enemy is actually united, armed and determined, with powerful forces well handled, disciplined and commanded on the Potomac, the Ohio, the Missouri. You must now see that I was right in not seeking prominence at the outstart. I knew, and know yet that the Northern people have to unlearn all their experience of the past thirty years and be born again before they will see the truth.[22]

The obvious truth, as Sherman saw it, was that the tactics of the South, if permitted to continue, would stretch the Union armies out into one grand guard detail, keeping them ever on the alert to protect their lines of supply and communication. He was convinced that the Northern armies could defeat the South by sheer weight of numbers, provided they could use their full combat strength in actual fighting. It followed, in his reasoning, that the people of the South would first have to be rendered ineffective before the Northern armies dared to move with direct strides against the armed forces of the South. This he had expressed to his brother: ". . . and though our armies pass across and through the land, the war closes in behind and leaves the same enemy behind."[23]

Property destruction was not the complete answer. Sherman was convinced of this, since the "guerilla" attacks continued even after the example offered in the fate meted out to Randolph. There was something lacking—an element to complete the new concept of war—if the part played by the people of the South was to be eliminated. With acceptance of the fact that destruction of property was not the final answer, Sherman's mind leaped the gap and seized on the solution—terrorism. He would so thoroughly inject the shock of fear into the South that it would lead to its complete demoralization. Such demoralization would work like a slow poison, resulting in paralysis of the Confederate armies through wholesale desertions as men returned home to assure the safety of their families. More important, dread would so sicken the people of the South that they would clamor for cessation, and to obtain relief they would exert every pressure on their government to end the war. Here, then, in Memphis, was the mold made. The months ahead would see it filled in: it would harden into the completed philosophy of total war, employing a program of devastation and waste, the turning loose on the countryside of a horde of pillagers and looters who would do their work systematically and well.[24]

V

Experiments in Terror

It could properly be said that at Memphis Sherman was at the experimental stage in the development of his philosophy, and the series of acts which followed his ordering the burning of Randolph bear witness to the energy with which he set about applying his ideas to the people around Memphis. His correspondence with Grant and the orders issued from his headquarters speak for themselves. On September 27, three days after the destruction of Randolph, Sherman issued his Special Order No. 254, which read:

> Whereas many families of known rebels and of Confederates in arms against us having been permitted to reside in peace and comfort in Memphis, and whereas the Confederate authorities either sanction or permit the firing on unarmed boats carrying passengers and goods, for the use and benefit of the inhabitants of Memphis, it is ordered that for every boat so fired on ten families must be expelled from Memphis.
>
> The Provost Marshall will extend the list already prepared so as to have on it at least thirty names, and on every occasion when a boat is fired on will draw by lot ten names, who will be forthwith notified and allowed three days to remove to a distance of 25 miles from Memphis.[1]

With this order Sherman apparently abandoned whatever scruples he had. The former West Pointer was now willing to resort to the most extreme application of vindictive retaliation: the holding of hostages and the threat of punishment held over the heads of those suspected of being the friends or kin of those charged with crime.[2] What did it matter that those referred to in the order made their homes in Memphis, perhaps owned property there; and that, although avowedly sympathetic with the Southern cause, they were submissive to the authority of the Union army in possession of their city? The arbitrary visitation upon them of the miseries attendant upon breaking up their homes, giving up their vocations and removing themselves into the harshnesses of the countryside was a new departure, in complete violation of accepted conduct of an invading army. This willingness on Sherman's part to ignore the rights of noncombatants in occupied territory indicated that he was prepared to use any means to neutralize the enemy. It can be safely assumed that he knew the attitude of military men toward the conduct of armies in the field. The question was discussed among them; and the civilized nations of the world in the nineteenth century had voluntarily subscribed to certain special rules governing the waging of war. Major General Halleck, Sherman's own commander-in-chief, was an accepted authority of his day on the rules governing the intercourse of nations and the laws of war. Sherman had attended West Point with Halleck, and certainly curiosity if not actual interest in the subject would have prompted him to look into Halleck's *International Law*. Had he consulted that work at Memphis in the fall of 1862 to refresh his mind on the rules governing the treatment of the enemy's civil population, he could have read:

> So long as they refrain from all hostilities, pay the military contributions which may be imposed on them, and quietly submit to the authority of the belligerent who may happen to be in military possession of their country, they are allowed to continue in the enjoyment of their property, and in the pursuit of the ordinary avocations.[3]

It was said of General Sherman that he was in the habit of "starting new notions constantly in his own brain, and following

68

them up, no matter how far or whither they led."[4] On October 4
he reported to General Grant that two more steamboats had been
fired on—the attacks being described by Sherman as wanton and
cruel—and he informed Grant of the new notion that had occurred to him:

> I caused Randolph to be destroyed, and have given public
> notice that a repetition will justify any measures of retalia-
> tion, such as loading boats with their captive guerillas as
> targets (I always have a lot on hand), and expelling families
> from the comforts of Memphis, whose husbands and brothers
> go to make up those guerillas. I will watch Randolph closely,
> and if anything occurs there again I will send a brigade by
> land back of Randolph and clean out the country.[5]

From this modest beginning—the experiments to discover the
effectiveness of the practical application of his concepts of total
war—the destruction of property, the holding of hostages and now
the improper exposure of prisoners to the fire of their own forces,
would be enlarged on in the weeks ahead and their effects carefully noted.

Whether Sherman himself ever entertained any doubts or hesi-
tations as to the course to which he had committed himself cannot
be stated accurately, but it is noteworthy that during this period
no mention is made in his correspondence of the rules of war, nor
does he suggest that his actions were not in accord with them.
There are threads of justification woven into his letters and his
orders for his extreme severity and barbarism; and a definite impression is left that many of these were included with one eye on
posterity and the hope for ultimate vindication.[6]

Sherman had no fears or worries insofar as the opinion of his
brothers-in-arms was concerned. On the contrary, it might be said
that he was left alone in Memphis to work out and perfect his
unorthodox philosophy, secure in the assurance that he had
Grant's sympathy and understanding, and that the latter was
watching his experiments with keen interest.[7] He had, as well, the
silent assent, if not the outright approval, of his general-in-chief,
Halleck.[8]

Grant, fully aware of the course on which Sherman had now embarked and familiar with Sherman's personal characteristics and temperament, must have sensed that under the impetus of Sherman's driving nervous energy these experimental moves would have far-reaching effects. Recognition of the fact that Sherman's headstrong, impetuous nature could lead him to extremes might have caused Grant some twinge of misgivings at this time. He doubtless observed that his subordinate would require delicate handling if he was to be effectively employed. Grant had noted at Shiloh, and he would become more and more impressed in the months ahead, that Sherman had peculiar abilities which if directed into the proper channel and carefully controlled would indeed make an effective weapon.[9]

It must have been with deep interest that General Grant sat in his headquarters, now at Jackson, and read Sherman's full report of October 4, 1862—a detailed report characteristic of the Memphis commander—outlining the problems which faced him, their solutions, comments on the war, personal opinions of other generals, as well as numerous suggestions, freely offered, as to how the war should be conducted.[10] Here Grant read Sherman's summation of his final remedy—the employment of terror. If Grant did not immediately grasp the full implications of the concept, he at least could have had no doubt that its sponsor was convinced, ready and willing to carry out the program to its ultimate conclusions. These lines, so filled with the shadow of events to come, passed before Grant's eyes:

> Detachments inland can always be overcome or are at great hazard, and they do not convert the people. They cannot be made to love us, but may be made to fear us, and dread the passage of troops through their country. With the Mississippi safe we could land troops at any point, and by a quick march break the railroad, where we could make ourselves so busy that our descent would be dreaded the whole length of the river, and by the loss of negroes and other property they would in time discover that war is not the remedy for the political evils of which they complained. I hold myself ready to carry out promptly and cheerfully any plan you may make.[11]

Having thus assured Grant of his willingness to apply the program of which he was actually the author, he let it appear that it was Grant's idea—an admirable application of practical psychology.

Sherman had steadily grown in poise and self-confidence in the months since Shiloh, and he was almost cheerful in the fall of 1862 as he was left to operate largely on his own initiative in Memphis.[12] Here, as military commander, all power and authority lay in his hands—his word was law. Now, for the moment at least, he was free and unhampered by politicians—free to follow out his own course of action and to notify headquarters of what he had done only after it was an accomplished fact. There is a noticeable absence of requests of the commanding officer for approval before certain orders were issued. His reports and letters to General Grant simply notified Grant as to the orders already promulgated, and in many cases already executed, before headquarters was notified of them. In one case, at least, Sherman wrote Grant of his intentions to visit summary punishment on a locality near Memphis, and his orders for the execution of the sentence were issued the same date.[13] Sherman apparently felt the full thrust of his arbitrary authority, and he would make certain that nothing was permitted to interfere with him in the free exercise of it.

Further in this same report of October 4 Sherman expressed his confidence in the future, assuring Grant that now for the first time since the war started, the number of men involved was commensurate with the game. His conviction that his philosophy of war was workable was strengthened in this flush of confidence. He appeared to be so completely absorbed with the idea of having found a solution that his fascination with his concept of war seemed to give rise to an irresistible urge to restate it, play with it and emphasize it, as much for his own sake as to impress it on Grant. For the second time in the same letter he pressed the matter on Grant's attention:

> We cannot change the hearts of those people of the South, but we can make war so terrible that they will realize the fact that, however brave and gallant and devoted to their

country, still they are mortal and should exhaust all peaceful remedies before they fly to war. This is all I hope for, and even this will take time and vast numbers.[14]

And he added a statement which in the light of later events appeared significant:

The scramble for money, for office, of our Northern people makes me sometimes sick, but still we must take them as they are, and I begin to feel that the Northern people will soon realize that words and deeds are different things.

Too long had the North fought with words and it was therefore Sherman's sacred duty, self-conceived, to translate their oratory and threats into the cold realities of war, directed against the hostile South, her armies and civilian population alike.

The next two weeks witnessed a rapid series of events. Sherman had reported to Grant on October 9[15] that his retaliatory actions had been effective in stopping the attacks on the riverboats, but a few days later he was again stung into an angry mood by even more intensified attacks, both above and below Memphis. He had previously described the attacks as "wanton and cruel" and "fiendish in the extreme"[16] and he referred to the latest ones as "cowardly acts." This is an excellent illustration of Sherman's inconsistences in reasoning: the denial of the right of resistance to the people of an invaded country. It further demonstrates how effectively he could rationalize a problem. He justified on these grounds, together with his personal anger and irritation and his conviction that those who fought "hit and run" warfare could prolong the war indefinitely, the harsh measures he enforced. Such acts, he felt, cast reflections on the abilities of Northern generals. He had pointed out more than once, and there can be no reason to doubt, that he was fully aware of the risks which an invading army ran the farther it penetrated enemy territory. Such hazards were acknowledged among military men, who recognized that in the occupation of hostile territory "forcible possession extends so far only as there is an absence of resistance."[17]

Union forces, under General Sherman's command, actually occupied and held the city of Memphis, and under such circumstances the citizens of that place, regardless of their sympathies, were required to submit to the rules and regulations of the occupying forces. But for Sherman to require the country surrounding Memphis to recognize his authority and submit to his control was in complete disagreement with the rights of the inhabitants of an invaded country. As long as resistance was offered, the rights which ordinarily accompanied military occupation did not exist. An accepted military authority of the day stated it:

> . . . and he [the invading army] therefore cannot pretend to govern it [the invaded territory] or to claim the temporary allegiance of its inhabitants, or in any way to direct or restrict its intercourse with neutrals. It remains as the territory of its former sovereign,—hostile to him [the invading force], as a belligerent, and friendly to others, as neutrals.[18]

Had Sherman's judgment been based on reason rather than being distorted, as it appeared to have been, with an obsession to eliminate all resistance through the employment of any and all means at his disposal, he could have understood the natural efforts of the South to resist invasion. He would have observed his inaccuracy in branding their resistance as "cowardly" and "wanton and cruel." Instead, Sherman steadfastly refused to understand or, if he understood, to acknowledge that his steamboats, wagon trains and railroads operated in an unconquered enemy territory and that they were the means which enabled him to penetrate farther the land which the South defended with her blood. The steamboats, the immediate irritant arousing Sherman's hatred and vindictiveness, brought to Memphis not only "many women and children passengers,"[19] with regard to whose safety Sherman seemed so intent, but they brought also great stores of supplies and munitions.[20] It was not strange that attacks were made to prevent the arrival of the materials of war, which strengthened and sustained the enemy's hold on the South. In calling such attacks "cowardly" Sherman appeared to proceed along the lines that he was betrayed—stabbed in the back—as though he, commander at Memphis, had issued a blanket parole to the countryside, requiring, if not the people's allegiance, at least their docility and inactivity, only to have them strike at him from every point and wherever he was most vulnerable.

However, it was results that Sherman wanted, and he was not to allow ethical considerations to enter the question. If the people of the South persisted in their resistance, they would be punished, and he would not be restricted in the methods he used to inflict that punishment—whether through destruction of their property or through the fear and uncertainty which is the lot of the hostage who is held responsible for acts beyond his knowledge or control.

No longer did the rules of war serve Sherman's purposes: nowhere did they provide for the employment of terror as an instrument of war, and it was just such a program that he was now beginning to round out in his mind. He wrote Grant again on October 18 concerning attacks along the river, attacks which typified for Sherman the resistance to be expected from the South, and he stated:

> We will have to do something more than merely repel these attacks. We must make the people feel that every attack on a road here will be resented by the destruction of some one of their towns or plantations elsewhere. All adherents of their cause must suffer for these cowardly acts.[21]

No discrimination was to be made; all were to pay a tribute in suffering. Thus, generalization, an easier process than that of investigating individual cases in the search for truth, again served Sherman well.

Nowhere can Sherman's hardness of heart be better shown than at this stage of his plans. That he had hardened his heart and shut out the voice of conscience was shown as he acknowledged that there was an element of injustice in what he proposed. He was fully aware that the innocent must suffer with the guilty. Since it was the South's innocent, it was regrettable, but they must suffer, if as a result of their pain and grief Union cavalry and infantry could range at will throughout the land, freed from the fear of surprise attacks. He expressed himself to Grant:

> I propose to expel ten secession families for every boat fired on, thereby lessening the necessity for fighting boats for

their benefit, and will visit on the neighborhood summary punishment. It may sometimes fall on the wrong head, but it would be folly to send parties of infantry to chase these wanton guerillas.[22]

On this same day Sherman issued Special Orders to the Forty-sixth Ohio, the troops who had proved their willingness to execute their general's orders by the thoroughness with which they had erased the little town of Randolph from the riverbank. The orders to the officer in command were explicit:

> The Forty-sixth Ohio, Colonel Walcutt, will embark to-night on board of steamboat _____, and before day-break drop down to a point on the Arkansas shore about 15 miles below this, near Elm Grove Postoffice, and there disembark. He will then proceed to destroy all the houses, farms and cornfields from that point up to Hopefield.[23]

There was no doubt that the troops executed their orders, as Sherman's report to General Grant on October 21 assured him:

> I ordered parties to Island 21, also to the point where the Catahoula was fired into. At the latter place the officer in command, Colonel Walcutt, Forty-sixth Ohio, found much evidence of complicity with the guerillas, and he burned their places.[24]

General Sherman's procedure was clear—a report of a steamboat fired on reached Memphis, or a cavalry unit demonstrating against the Confederate Generals Price and Van Dorn was attacked—the matter could be dealt with easily. A glance at the map, the place of the attack marked and the nearest localities indicated—orders were issued, and to the soldiers was assigned the task of executioners. It was not their business to listen to supplications or fervent protestations of innocence—their duty was to punish without pity. Let terror answer the people of the South.

It is noteworthy that no efforts were made now by Sherman simply to balance accounts. It had been the practice of the Union army to levy against a community for damages sustained through attacks on wagon trains or other supply transportation when such attacks occurred in or near settled communities. This had been ordered by Grant as early as July 1862, when he was commanding at Memphis, in the belief that payment for damage done would encourage the residents of such communities to refuse to entertain or harbor their own troops. Grant's orders, however, specifically stated:

> It is ordered that whenever loss is sustained by the Government collections shall be made by seizure of sufficient amount of personal property from persons in the immediate neighborhood sympathizing with the rebellion to remunerate the Government for all loss and expense of collection.[25]

Under the rules of war Grant could have justified, to some extent, the issuance of his orders. It was held, where satisfaction was demanded and milder methods failed to secure it, that the military might levy on the inhabitants. In each case, however, the levy was not to exceed the amount of the actual damage.[26] As early as eight days after the order Sherman had availed himself of it, obtaining General Halleck's permission on July 11 to send an expedition to the settlement of Rising Sun. Permission was asked to seize 35 mules, the exact number stampeded and lost from a wagon train which had been the victim of attack in the neighborhood. The mules were to be taken from planters who, Sherman said, "were knowing to the attack." Here, as he was to do later, no proof was offered to show that the planters in question were "knowing to the attack." He was apparently content to act on the assumption that proximity was sufficient to establish guilt.[27] In this instance Sherman made his collection in orderly manner. His force was accompanied by a quartermaster who was instructed to issue receipts for the property seized.[28] Several days before the request to visit Rising Sun, the same Sherman had felt such concern over the theft of a few head of livestock that he warned his subordinate, General Stephen A. Hurlbut: "Try and prevent petty thieving and pillaging; it does us infinite harm. I hear of some horses taken by your men near Holly Springs, and a pair of mules taken by your train from near La Fayette."[29]

As an entirely different Sherman commanded at Memphis in October 1862, gone was the nice observance of the rules of war. This was not the same Sherman who in July was careful to exact 35 mules, and no more, to replace 35 mules lost. No longer was it a question of indemnity, the amount of which was determined by the extent of the harm done. A code no longer existed—there was no legal procedure or judicial process. Sherman was the commanding officer; his word was law and he decided in his own manner, according to his whim, mood, needs, or the degree of terror which he wished to inspire.

Although Sherman consistently denied that he supported or condoned pillaging and needless waste, he could not contend, in the face of the massive evidence to the contrary, that his corps did not resort to looting and the theft of personal property. He always maintained that he could not help it,[30] or he attributed such depredations to camp followers and stragglers. He was always careful to observe outward appearances, and the dreaded march of his army was clothed in the precise, clipped orders approved by the military handbook for the conduct of a civilized army in enemy territory. Even after the expert training of his troops in destruction of property in and around Memphis, a practice tending to release them from the legal and moral restraints and to lower their respect for the sanctity of private property, he could still issue orthodox orders such as those which covered the line of march from Memphis toward Holly Springs. These orders stated in part:

> The chief quartermaster may seize any wagon or carriage or other vehicle suitable for the transportation of stores, for the sick, to be added to the train, and forage will be obtained in the same manner as during the march last summer, viz., brigade quartermasters or commissaries will take from the farmers and planters, giving a memoranda receipt, which receipt will be taken up by the chief quartermaster or commissary by loyalty vouchers. Pillage or robbery by the soldiers or subordinate officers must be promptly checked and punished.[31]

A month earlier a force composed of several units had been organized to strike separately but simultaneously at different points on the river. Sherman's orders outlining this maneuver were interesting, in that they not only stated concisely the nature of the operation to be carried out, but also included a statement of purpose, inspiring in both men and officers a sense of the righteousness of their cause and a justification of the harshness of the measures they applied. The orders read:

> The people at large should be made to feel that in the existence of a strong Government, capable of protecting as well as destroying, they have a real interest; that they must at once make up their minds or else be involved in the destruction that awaits armed rebellion against the national will.
>
> Subordinates and privates must not pillage, but commanders may do anything necessary to impress upon the people that guerillas must be driven from their midst, else they must necessarily share the consequences.[32]

Under such orders, the troops operating out of Memphis doubtless witnessed shameful actions on the parts of their officers in the deliberate pillaging of the country homes around Memphis, acts of lawlessness not only officially sanctioned in their orders but limited only by the officers' discretion.

Discipline and the conduct of soldiery have ever reflected the characters of the officers commanding them. Smart, well-disciplined troops, instantly obedient to orders, are not the result of laxity and vacillation on the part of those in authority; for soldiers conduct themselves no better and no worse than the officers who command them. Thus in the fall of 1862, Sherman's soldiers observed the actions of their officers and through them felt the current of the General's thinking. There can be little doubt that they were infected with his terrorist philosophy and that they began to be convinced that it was a duty laid upon them to punish the South for its obstinate refusal to submit to the North.

Sherman's orders, when read to troops, must have caused the rank and file to wink knowingly to each other in their understanding of the real meaning underlying the formal wording of the orders—orders which, in the light of actual practice, lacked the ring of sincerity. The men were quick to sense that Sherman

78

was paying lip service only to the rules of war, and the enthusiasm and thoroughness with which they later wrecked and destroyed, looted and pillaged showed how fully they understood. They were not long in recognizing that they could operate unhampered by the fear of disciplinary action from their higher officers.

Sherman was notorious as a poor disciplinarian, and it appeared that his laxity in discipline was either an inability to cope with the unruly spirit of his men,[33] which he had encouraged either deliberately or indirectly through failure to assert his authority; or, more likely, through studied indifference he permitted his men to develop a spirit of recklessness. He doubtless recognized in their growing disregard for law and order an effective weapon in the accomplishment of his purpose. Whatever his motives, there seemed to be no doubt that the armies falling to his command were soon aware of a loosening of the reins of discipline, and it was said of Sherman by one who knew him personally:

> His faults as a commander are as glaring as his faults of character. As an organizer of armies for the field, as a tactician in battle, he was an utter failure. He never commanded an organized army whose discipline did not become relaxed under his administration, and he was never commander-in-chief in any battle which was not a failure. Instead of being an organizer, Sherman was a disorganizer; he was chief among the "Bummers" which he made his soldiers, and by which name they were eventually designated.[34]

When confronted with Sherman's inability to organize the army in Kentucky and with the breakdown of discipline in the Army of the Tennessee after Sherman took over its command from Grant, Sherman's admirers point out that he had no bent for discipline, but sacrificed it for greater mobility. If the morale of his army was bad, its marching was good. It is obvious that such reasoning is faulty and that it is presented by way of justification, as it is an accepted military maxim that well-disciplined troops in well-ordered, compact units move more rapidly from one objective to another. Sherman's army was well suited to Sherman's purpose. Loose, flexible, flung out over a wide area, they could do their work well, without the fear of any formidable enemy force in the vicinity to offer resistance.

Later, the most convincing indictment of General Sherman's attitude toward the lawlessness of his corps would be found in the diary of Major Henry Hitchcock, an officer of his staff. Major Hitchcock was in intimate daily contact with the General throughout the Georgia and South Carolina campaigns, and he would note in his daily record that he could not see any satisfactory explanation or excuse for Sherman's indifference toward his men's conduct. Hitchcock observed Sherman's attitude toward the wanton destruction of the town of Millen, Georgia; he described the manner in which General Sherman sat on his horse, unmoved, as the place was burned and then looted. The effect on Major Hitchcock was reflected in his diary:

> There is but one comment on these things; no need to repeat it. I cannot think there is any sufficient excuse. Admit (as we must) the difficulty of preventing all lawlessness in a large army, especially that of negroes and camp followers, who *cannot* always be reached,—yet I am sure that a Headquarters Provost Marshall, if necessary with a rigid system of roll calls in every company required at any halt—severe punishment inflicted not only on men who straggle but also on officers who *fail to prevent it,*—and the absolute prohibition and summary punishment even of legitimate foraging except by regular details,—would go far to prevent these outrages,—the general orders contemplate and call for this,—but they are *not* enforced, at least not as I think they should and might be.[35]

Hitchcock's diary would indicate the change which he observed in Sherman's attitude toward pillage and needless waste, becoming more pronounced after the march from Atlanta started; and Sherman would inform Hitchcock that he had done as much as any officer, in the first two years of the war, to control the vandalism of his men, and without too much concern he would remind Hitchcock that he had issued orders forbidding unlawful acts on the Georgia march. Sherman would point out to his subordinate that, after all, it was the duty of regimental and company officers to enforce the orders.[36] Major Hitchcock's reaction to his general's attempts to justify his attitude is interesting, as the entry for December 1, 1864, would say:

> At the same time I don't think General would take same trouble now—indeed he admits as much—to hunt out and punish it. Evidently it is a material element in this campaign to produce among the *people of Georgia* a thorough conviction of the personal misery which attends war, and of the utter helplessness and inability of their "rulers," State or Confederate, to protect them.[37]

Sherman's staff officer would permit himself to wonder whether the General had not sacrificed discipline to obtain and improve his personal popularity with his men.[38] Sherman would later admit that he capitalized on the unruly spirit of the men whom he had so carefully instructed and encouraged in 1862. He would say of the junior officers particularly that they had learned their lesson along the banks of the great river, and he would comment upon their initiative, as he wrote of the march through Georgia:

> In a well-ordered and well-disciplined army, these things might be deemed irregular, but I am convinced that the ingenuity of these younger officers accomplished many things far better than I could have ordered, and the marches were thus made in the most admirable way.[39]

At Savannah in December 1864, Sherman would have an opportunity to look back over the preceding two years and sum up what his philosophy of total war had accomplished since Memphis days. He would recognize that the terror inspired by his corps in the Mississippi Valley had crippled the people as much as had their actual loss of property. The dread in which the passage of his forces was held had been built up by the stories of viciousness and cruelty which preceded him. He later wrote:

> It was to me manifest that the soldiers and people of the South entertained undue fear of our Western men, and, like children, they had invented such ghostlike stories of their

own inventions. Still this was a power, and I intended to utilize it.[40]

Thus would he sum up the power of terror and its effect on a people at war, a power which revealed itself to him at Memphis in 1862 as he put his troops through their paces on practice grounds extending up and down the Mississippi River. Here, from a concept which became clearer and clearer, he observed the results of his experiments in terrorism. Here he schooled his corps in the savage art of destruction. Here under his orders they learned to strip the country of livestock and the fruits of field and orchard. It was then that the rank and file, under the skillful tutelage of Sherman, first recognized their hated enemy in the people around Memphis. On the side, through their own initiative, encouraged by the negligence or indifference of their officers, the troops acquired proficiency in pillaging and looting defenseless communities.

To sum up: the logic of Sherman's doctrine was worked out at Memphis. He started with the principle that necessity permitted and justified the violation of all rights.[41] By deduction supplemented by his ability to generalize the matter, he arrived at the most extreme consequences, to which having abandoned himself it was easy to confound the utility of the moment with real necessity. The final outcome was the theory of collective responsibility, on which the philosophy of total war was founded, a mode of warfare which transgressed all ethical rules and showed an utter disregard for human rights and dignity.

It was in Mississippi, Georgia and South Carolina that Sherman's philosophy would be applied on a grand scale. Whereas at Memphis ten square miles were devastated to punish a community, in Georgia a swath 60 miles wide, diagonally across the state, would be laid waste. These states particularly would be marked by a trail of burned houses, needless destruction of the necessities of life, and the wholesale theft of private property. Where the little river town of Randolph paid for its sins in flames, the capital cities of Mississippi and South Carolina would be reduced to ashes to punish those states. Ten secession families were forced to move out of their homes at Memphis, but the whole city of Atlanta was to be arbitrarily depopulated, without regard to the harshnesses involved. On the Mississippi River prisoners were placed on the boats exposed to the fire of their own forces, but in Georgia Sherman would force them to uncover Confederate mines by marching them over suspected areas —or, in South Carolina, threaten to hang them if his foragers were molested. The hostage idea would be improved upon through the seizure of prominent citizens as a guarantee for the safe return of prisoners captured from his line of march by Confederate forces.

The Mississippi, Georgia and South Carolina campaigns were the finished product, the polished performance of the corps, who under the direction of General Sherman spent the fall of 1862 in a rehearsal for total war.

Part II

TOTAL WAR
Practical Application

VI

Devastation of Mississippi

The fall of Vicksburg after a long seige of 47 days was the cause of great jubilation in the North. The capitulation of the last great Southern stronghold on the Mississippi, together with the surrender of Port Hudson less than a week later, literally cut the Confederacy in twain. The whole length of the great river was now in Union hands, and almost within a matter of hours the river was lined with steamers along the levee.

General Sherman was highly pleased over the victory at Vicksburg. Although he was 20 miles east of that besieged city on the day it surrendered, he had had a vital part in bringing about its capitulation. The day following the surrender he wrote his wife that the fall of the river fortress "is the event of the war thus far." And he expressed the feeling that "the capture of Vicksburg is to me the first gleam of daylight in this war."[1]

The capture of Vicksburg had not been an easy feat, and Sherman could recall the efforts and disappointments, the planning and discussions with Grant before the final day of triumph had dawned. Just a few short months before, in December 1862, General Sherman had embarked a force of some 32,000 troops to go down the river from Memphis. He was to assault Vicksburg from the rear while General Grant engaged Confederate General Pemberton to prevent him from reinforcing the Vicksburg garrison. Sherman had had no way of knowing that General Van Dorn's Confederate cavalry had dashed into Holly Springs on December 20, 1862, and left Grant's advance supply depot in flames. Grant, stripped of stores, was forced to abandon the advance and had failed to hold Pemberton. Sherman had proceeded according to plan and debarked his force into the cold waters of Chickasaw Bayou and assaulted the Confederate works. The Confederates were prepared for the attack, and the Union losses in dead and wounded had been shocking. The newspapers had turned on Sherman again, harrying him to the point where he threatened to resign his commission. President Lincoln had sent General McClernand, a political appointee, to assume command as Sherman's superior, and this act, hard on the heels of the humiliation of his failure at Vicksburg, had brought General Sherman to the point of actual resignation. He endured only because John Sherman had insisted he owed it to his wife and children to do so.[2]

General Van Dorn had dealt Grant a serious blow at Holly Springs, as Union losses of vital stores could not be replaced without great hardships. The Federal line of communications stretched from Columbus, Kentucky, to Holly Springs, Mississippi, and it was constantly disrupted by the depredations of the Confederate cavalry under General Nathan B. Forrest.[3] This setback had cost the Federal armies five long months before General Grant could put into motion the plan which led to the day of victory over the Confederacy's great fortress on the Mississippi.[4]

A few days after the surrender of Vicksburg, Grant had sent General Sherman some 20 miles east of that city to a camp on Big Black River where he was preparing a movement in force against the Confederate army under General Joseph E. Johnston. General Grant had written Sherman what was expected:

> The object of the expedition you are commanding being to break up Johnston's Army and divert it to our rear, and, if possible, to destroy the rolling stock and everything valuable

for carrying on war, or placing it beyond reach of the rebel army, you may return to Vicksburg as soon as this object is accomplished.[5]

This would be General Sherman's second visit to Jackson, and he informed Mrs. Sherman that, "if not held back by Johnston," he intended to "enter Jackson and there finish what was so well begun last month."[6] In the previous May, Sherman had taken part in General Grant's movement against Confederate reinforcements assembled at Jackson.[7] On May 14 the Confederates had abandoned Jackson, and Sherman had been entrusted by Grant with the job of destroying everything of value to the enemy.[8] Sherman had immediately dispatched his First and Third Divisions to the task of railroad wrecking, instructing them to destroy the roads "out as far as possible"[9] and as completely as possible. On May 15 Sherman had urged General Joseph A. Mower to "push the work of destruction, especially of types, presses, sugar, and everything public not needed by us."[10] Again, apparently writing for the record, he had warned General Mower against permitting his soldiers to pillage houses or remove goods from stores, which he had heard the provost marshal himself was authorizing. This must be corrected, Sherman had assured the General, or "the feeling of pillage and booty will injure the morals of the troops and bring disgrace on our cause."[11]

The Federal forces under Sherman's command had remained in Jackson on the first occasion in May just long enough to destroy the railroads, military factories, the arsenal and public stores, and then he had rejoined the main army in the siege before Vicksburg. Now, in July, General Grant ordered him to push General Johnston out of the Mississippi capital again. This time Sherman was determined to employ his theory of total war to wreck Jackson and cripple that section of Mississippi permanently.

The state of Mississippi had already been badly hurt. Federal armies had roamed and ranged it since the summer of 1862, destroying railroads, bridges and culverts and everything that might have been useful to the Southern armies. After the loss of his supply depot at Holly Springs in December 1862 and his inability to maintain communication to the north, Grant had learned, to his surprise, that his army could subsist off the enemy's country, and he had written General Halleck that there would be little left within a few weeks in northern Mississippi to support guerillas.[12] Sherman realized that this new mode of operation without fixed base and the necessity for extended lines of communication placed a new and powerful weapon in his hands. Now his cavalry and infantry corps could move rapidly across the country, accomplishing a dual purpose: they could strike with full ranks, using troops formerly required to guard railroads and cumbersome wagon trains; and they could eat well off the countryside, destroying the enemy's substance, placing the heavy cost of war where Sherman felt it properly belonged, on the noncombatants of the South.

The General's experiments in devastation and destruction around Memphis had given his men and officers the needed training, and when he moved down the river in December 1862 to attack Vicksburg he had ordered that wherever the boats were fired into from the shore, troops were to be landed and all neighboring houses and barns were to be burned.[13] This order was fully enforced, and all during the winter and the spring of 1863 this policy was continued.

A private of the Sixth Wisconsin Battery wrote in his diary concerning incidents that occurred in April 1863 which graphically illustrate Sherman's methods of retaliation:

> 12M. a miscreant fired into the boat and wounded a member of the 93rd severely, the ball entering his left breast. The boat rounded to and tied up, and in an instant the whole regiment was in confusion, running for their arms, etc., etc. Skirmishers were sent out, while Colonel Putnam went with a force in a yawl in search, but returned in an hour; failed to find him, but brought along a man of the house that harbored him as prisoner, after reducing his house to ashes.

Later the same afternoon the boat had tied up near a large river plantation. While the artillery horses were being exercised, Private Jenkins Lloyd Jones noted in his diary:

> Foraging parties out in all directions, and chickens, hogs,
> beef, onions, etc., poured in. Several negro villages were set
> on fire, also the cotton gins, corn-cribs, within reach. The
> whole air was bright at night with fire.[14]

This followed the practice Sherman had instituted while at Memphis. The Confederate government had ordered all families living along the Mississippi to move 12 miles inland, and they had been ordered to burn all their cordwood within easy reach of the river.[15] This had been done to hinder as far as possible the movement of Federal boats. Sherman had moved his troops by river transport in the winter and spring of 1862–1863, and he had solved this difficulty by equipping his men with axes which they used to supply the boats with wood from the houses along the shore.[16] His troops had wantonly destroyed many houses and barns, burning and robbing many of them.

A prominent Mississippi planter's letter to his wife had testified to the attitude of the Union soldiers in the winter of 1862 toward private property. He had written his wife, who had sought safety in Alabama, of occurrences in the neighborhood:

> . . . the cavalry went as far as Oakland and then all returned,
> they made sad havoc on their march; burnt old man Shelby's
> gin-houses also Hulls—and Hatchez—burnt all Hull's fences,
> killed most of his stock, took all that they had left, clothes,
> bedding, burnt all his doors, broke out his window sash, and
> burnt two of his cabins; at Hulls they broke all that fine
> furniture and threw it into the yard, searched the house and
> robbed it of ten thousand dollars in money. . . . Friars Point
> is *status quo* but every house at Delta is burned, *every one*.[17]

Sherman had personally encountered an example of his soldiers' handiwork in the havoc wrought at the Bowie plantation in Louisiana in the spring of 1863, just before he had crossed the Mississippi below Vicksburg. He noted:

> The house was tenantless, and had been completely ransacked; articles of dress and books were strewed about, and
> a handsome boudoir with mirror front had been cast down,

shivering the glass. The library was extensive, with a fine collection of books.[18]

The General had found a Union soldier sitting on the spacious porch of the fine plantation house when he rode up. The soldier was sitting in a satin-covered armchair with his booted heels on the keys of "a magnificent grand-piano." The General had taken no disciplinary steps, but had simply "started him in a hurry to overtake his command." Concerning this instance of the destructiveness of his soldiery, he had written Mrs. Sherman, whom he did not fully inform as to the harsh war he was waging against the civilians of Mississippi:

> It is done of course by the cursed stragglers who don't fight, but hang behind and disgrace our cause and country. Of course devastation marked the whole path of the army, and I knew all the principal officers detest the infamous practice as much as I do.[19]

The same night the Bowie plantation house had been burned to the ground, library, furnishings, family portraits and all.

General Sherman had admitted to his wife that he had no objection to taking anything he could find to feed his army, and he urged his officers to feed off the country. He could see no great wrong, he said, in using fences for firewood, but "this universal burning and wanton destruction of private property is not justified in war."[20] Yet he had acted quite differently at Memphis in the early fall of 1862.

He recalled what a thorough job General Frank P. Blair had done in May in executing Sherman's orders to strip the Yazoo Valley and render it useless to the Confederates. Blair had reported the Yazoo section to be one of the most fertile that his troops had yet seen in Mississippi. After informing Sherman that his troops had used everything they could, his report continued:

> We must have burned five hundred thousand bushels of corn and immense quantities of bacon, most of which was concealed by its owners, but discovered and either appropriated or destroyed by my order.

I destroyed every grist mill in the valley, and have driven in to this place about 1000 head of cattle. I brought with me an army of negroes nearly equal to the number of men in my command; and the cavalry and infantry have seized and brought in 200 or 300 head of mules and horses. I have also ordered the empty wagons to load with cotton, and I think they have brought 30 or 40 bales. I burned all the balance of the cotton I found.

Joe Johnston will find very little for his army in the country between the Black River and Yazoo, for 45 miles north of Vicksburg.[21]

Several days later Confederate General William H. Jackson, who had been detached by Johnston to observe the movements of Federal troops, reported: "Enemy destroyed property of every description; burned sixteen houses in Mechanicsburg and several on the road; also gin houses; destroyed all bridges behind them."[22] Other reports had come in from the Confederates, reflecting only too well how thoroughly Sherman's troops had laid waste the country. Confederate General John Adams informed headquarters on June 5, 1863:

The enemy is still burning mills, gins, corn, etc., taking all provisions from the citizens indiscriminately, killing cattle, hogs, chickens, and so on, with the evident intention of destroying the subsistence and forage which could be of service to our army.[23]

This same Confederate officer reported again the next day concerning the activities of the Union troops:

They destroy everything like forage and provisions, as well as all mills, gins, etc., expressing their object to be to prevent General Johnston's army from advancing, at the same time expressing a determination to lay waste the State of Mississippi.[24]

This was only a part of the story of the waste and destruction that Sherman had visited on Mississippi and her citizens. On July 4, the day that Vicksburg surrendered, he issued his orders for the movement against Jackson, Mississippi, and the Confederates under Joe Johnston.[25] He realized full well how effectively his destruction at Jackson in May had prevented that Southern army from rendering any assistance to the besieged city of Vicksburg. General Johnston had confessed in a letter to Secretary of War Seddon his inability to move to Vicksburg's relief. He could not move without supplies and the exhausted countryside could not provide them.[26]

Sherman moved three corps against the city of Jackson: General Edward O. C. Ord's Thirteenth Corps, the Fifteenth, which Sherman commanded, and General Parkes's Ninth Corps. They marched by different routes to converge at Bolton. By July 10, Johnston entrenched himself at Jackson, the fortification of which Sherman found much stronger than when he had been there in May.[27] General Ord was ordered to send all available cavalry to the south to destroy the railroad and as many bridges as possible for at least 15 miles from Jackson. Colonel Bussey, with all the force he could raise, was to proceed north of Jackson with the cavalry and destroy the railroad at Canton, the trestle across the Black River and as many other bridges as he could reach.[28] Sherman now settled down to bombard the town of Jackson, and he ordered a systematic fire to be poured into the town:

> From General Parkes; front; a rifle shot, aimed in the general direction of the State-house, infilading the town of Jackson, to be fired every five minutes, day and night, and oftener, when the chief of artillery observes good effect.[29]

The same procedure was to be followed on the fronts held by Generals Steele and Ord, except that they were to add the fire from ten- and 20-pound Parrott guns. Thus a pattern of fire was formed which began to make the Confederate position untenable. The impending fate of Jackson was felt throughout the countryside and was noted by General Grenville M. Dodge, Union commander at Corinth, who reported to General S. A. Hurlbut that "there is a big stampede. Every ferry on the Tombigbee is crowded with people, running their horses and negroes east. Many of the negroes are coming into our lines."[30] General Hurlbut reported a little later on the same day that "great consternation prevails all through Mississippi. It is believed that Joe Johnston was defeated at Jackson on 9th and 10th."[31]

General Johnston had not been defeated on the dates referred to, but he realized full well that the Union forces were too formidable for him. In addition, he was kept informed as to the extent of the damage to the country and towns around Jackson and knew that he must retreat eastward as promptly as possible before his last avenue of escape was closed. The Union forces which had fanned out around Jackson were ordered among other places to Hazlehurst Station near Gallman to burn a section of railroad, "any bridge near, with cars, depots, turnouts etc." They were to push on to Brookhaven to burn locomotives and cars. The officers of detached groups were always to remain within supporting distance of each other. Their orders read:

> Having completed the work of destruction, you will return to your division by such route as you may choose, loading on your return the wagons with corn or property useful to this army, and will gather and bring in beef, cattle, sheep, and hogs.[32]

With the countryside being stripped of subsistence and his lines of communication destroyed,[33] Johnston ordered his wagon trains and droves of cattle east to the remaining connections with the Mobile and Ohio road. On the night of July 16, 1863, General Johnston evacuated his Confederate forces from the town of Jackson and withdrew to the east. Sherman made no attempt to pursue, but instead immediately ordered General Steele to occupy the town.

The capital of Mississippi was in the hands of soldiers well versed in the art of destruction. These men, who, since the fall of 1862, had been permitted to live off a countryside largely without effective defense, were no longer amateurs in the use of torch and wrecking bar. Sherman's troops, who now held the town of Jackson, were imbued with a sense of irresponsibility and recklessness—a natural consequence of months of burning gins and mills. There was a sense of exhilaration in the freedom of action brought about by indiscriminate destruction. The soldier, anonymous in the uniformity of his fellows, was swept on by mob psychology to commit acts in violation of all rights, both moral and civil. These men into whose hands had been placed the torch, with orders to burn the little river town of Randolph and later the gins, mills and barns of the people along the Mississippi, did not find the transition from barns and mills to private residences a difficult one. Men who had for months ruthlessly shot down hogs, cattle and sheep, after appropriating all that they could use, did not find that the taking of personal possessions from helpless citizens particularly hurt their consciences.

Sherman reported to General Grant that the Confederates had fired a building containing commissary stores, which spread and consumed one of the most valuable blocks of the town. Many fine residences had been reduced by flames, he said, set by the Confederates. "Indeed," he informed Grant, "the city, with destruction committed by ourself in May last, and by the enemy during the siege, is one mass of charred ruins."[34] Writing to Admiral Porter, Sherman referred to the fires set by General Joe Johnston's troops and added, "Our men, in spite of guards, have widened the circle of fire, so that Jackson, once the pride and boast of Mississippi, is now a ruined town."[35]

Amid the flames which ruined the business section and left many fine homes in ashes, the soldiery proceeded to sack the town completely. Pianos and articles of furniture were dragged into the streets and demolished. The aroused soldiers entered residences, appropriating whatever appeared to be of value or happened to strike their fancy. Those articles which they could not carry they broke or trampled underfoot or otherwise damaged. They thrust their bayonets into pictures and knocked out windows and even removed doors from their hinges.[36] An eyewitness described how household furnishings, including beds and costly coverings, were thrown into the streets and burned. Among the private residences wrecked by the soldiers was that of Bishop Green of the Protestant Episcopal Church. His home was noted for its taste and refinement and even more for its fine library of 3,000 volumes. Sherman's soldiers, no respecters of persons, committed it to the flames. "It was a sad sight," stated one who viewed the ruins; "nothing remained of it but broken walls."[37]

On the night of July 18, General Sherman called his generals together for a banquet in the Governor's mansion,[38] while the work of destruction continued unabated throughout the town. The Confederate Hotel was burned, the penitentiary, Greene's cotton factory and the Catholic church. *The Mississippian* office, together with a block of private buildings, was destroyed. In the case of the newspaper, the soldiers broke the presses and scattered the type in the street.[39] Books were stolen from the Mississippi State Library. Some of these were later returned by General Ewing in 1867.[40] The final scene in Jackson was described by a newspaper correspondent:

> Finally after every other excess had been committed in the destruction of property, the torch was applied. The entire business portion of the city was in ruins except a few old frame buildings. One residence after another has been burned until none of the really fine ones remain, save those occupied by some of our general officers. Such complete ruin and devastation never followed the footsteps of an army before.[41]

A captain in an Illinois regiment was just as impressed by the shocking scenes in Jackson. On July 17, 1863, he entered the following in his diary:

> During the day some of our men—the roughs—after pillaging the place set fire to a great many buildings some of which were very fine. . . . I never saw or heard of a city being so thoroughly sacked and burned as this place.[42]

Sherman carried out General Grant's orders to destroy the railroads in and around Jackson and all property which might be of value to the enemy. The thoroughness with which he accomplished the assignment can be judged from his report:

> Besides the breaks at the North and South, before recounted, 12 miles north and south of the town were absolutely destroyed; every tie burned and every rail of iron

warped so as to be utterly useless. About 20 platform cars and about 50 box and passenger cars were burned in the city, and all the wheels broken. About 4000 bales of cotton, used as parapets, were burned. Two heavily rifled six-inch guns, with an immense pile of shot, shell, and fix ammunition, were destroyed and cast into Pearl River.[43]

General Ord had previously been ordered south to Gallatin and Brookhaven, some 60 miles, breaking up the railroad, destroying rolling stock and damaging the railroad in its whole extent. General Steele with three brigades was sent to Brandon, where he destroyed a three-mile section of road.[44]

Even while Jackson was being sacked Colonel Charles R. Woods was at Canton, where he reported to Sherman:

> The whole infantry force was occupied during the day in destroying railroad tracks, iron, buildings, etc. There were destroyed 5 locomotives, 30 cars of all kinds, 2 turn-tables, 13 railroad buildings, including engine-house for 7 engines, with repair shops filled with fine machinery, attached; 1 machine-shop, depots, offices, etc.; 300 feet of trestle and bridge work, and miles of rails burned and bent. Much more of the track was torn up.[45]

Even while detached forces from Sherman's army moved rapidly and effectively to disrupt all lines of communication and render the state of Mississippi north of Jackson useless to Confederate armies, his foragers were damaging the countryside just as effectively in their destruction of foodstuffs. Sherman informed General Grant while Jackson was besieged that his foraging parties, protected by infantry, were ranging the whole area, and the thoroughness of their work impressed him enough for him to write:

> We are absolutely stripping the country of corn, cattle, hogs, sheep, poultry, everything, and the new-growing corn is being thrown open as pasture fields or hauled for the use of our animals. The wholesale destructions to which this country is now being subjected is terrible to contemplate, but it is the scourage of war, to which ambitious men have ap-

pealed. . . . Therefore, so much of my instruction as contemplated destroying and weakening the resources of our
enemy are being executed with rigor.[46]

The area in the vicinity of Jackson, Brandon, Clinton and other
towns was not the only one to suffer such complete ruin. Sherman was now thoroughly devastating an area which other Union
forces had hit only crippling blows in the spring of 1863. Grierson's raid in April 1863 had carried him in a slashing dash from
LaGrange, Tennessee, across the whole state of Mississippi and
was estimated to have left destruction amounting to four million
dollars in terms of money[47] and incalculable damage in human
suffering and misery.

> From La Grange, his starting point, to Holly Springs, a
> newspaper correspondent in September, 1863, found only
> five plantations out of fifty occupied. In the majority of in-
> stances the buildings had been burned.[48]

Colonel R. V. Richardson, a Confederate cavalry officer sent to
drive Grierson off, had admitted the success of his raid and reported to General Pemberton that Grierson "captured mules and
horses, negroes, forage, subsistence, and stole money and jewelry
from the people in his course." Grierson commanded the Sixth
and Seventh Illinois Regiments of cavalry, which were, according
to Colonel Richardson, "the pride and boast of the United States
Army."[49] The Second Iowa Cavalry had burned Okolona, destroyed barracks and roads, then moved on Tupelo, where they
destroyed large amounts of provisions.[50] Colonel George E. Bryant of the Twelfth Wisconsin Infantry was later Third Brigade
commander under Sherman on the Jackson campaign. He reported that on a raid through Hernando in April 1863 his expedition had "captured 80 prisoners, 200 horses and mules (100
of them good cavalry horses), 70 stands of arms, 12,000 pounds
of bacon, 10,000 pounds of which were destroyed, also a quantity of dry goods, medicine, etc."[51] The same vicinity had been
visited again in June by the Second Iowa Cavalry, whose colonel
reported:

This morning Company M, of the Second Iowa Cavalry, was sent to the right flank, where they found in the woods a long house filled with stores (flour, salt, sugar, candles, boots, shoes, bacon, etc.) which they destroyed. On the route from Panola to Hernando immense quantities of grain—in buildings, in the stack, and in the field—were destroyed. . . . Many grist mills, tanneries, and stores were destroyed during the march from Panola to Hernando.[52]

Brigadier General J. Z. George of the Mississippi Guard, who was ordered to break up the raid in the Hernando-Panola vicinity, reported that the conduct of the Federals had gone far beyond the requirements of military necessity. He wrote:

The track of the enemy in this last raid is marked by robbery and arson. They stole every mule and horse, buggy, carriage, and wagon which they could seize. They carried off every valuable slave which they could entice or force to accompany them. They burned corn-cribs, mills, gin-houses, fences, blacksmith-shops, and wheat which had been cut and was then in the shock. In many instances they robbed the citizens of clothing and furniture.[53]

On the evening of July 18 a Federal cavalry unit, under Major Hugh Fullerton of Sherman's command, entered the little town of Brookhaven and proceeded to sack and pillage it completely. The Confederate report to General Johnston informed him that they "burned 113 hogsheads of sugar, destroyed the post-office, and burned two engines and all the rolling stock" before withdrawing.[54] Fullerton's cavalry together with Colonel John G. Fonda's mounted infantry swept southward in their destructive course and destroyed four locomotives, 52 cars, a number of bridges, the depots at Byram, Bahala, Crystal Springs, Gallatin and Hazlehurst. One mill and a large quantity of lumber were burned at Hazlehurst. In addition, they destroyed 70 hogsheads of sugar and tore up a half mile of railroad track.[55] Several days before this, the Federal cavalry and a regiment of Steele's division of Sherman's army had visited Brandon, burning the courthouse and jail.[56]

Sherman had so far exceeded the earlier devastations that he reported to Grant regarding the net results in and around Jackson: "We have so exhausted the land that no army can exist during this season without hauling in wagons all his supplies."[57] If this was true for the military forces of the Confederacy, it applied even more cruelly to the noncombatants in the blasted sections of the state.

Such widespread devastation and waste left untold suffering in its wake. The civilian populace in those areas visited by Sherman's army were in an almost hopeless situation. Their transportation system, by means of which relief supplies of food might have reached them, was thoroughly broken and rendered useless. Their horses and mules, together with wagons, both essential to planting, were either confiscated or wrecked, effectively closing that avenue of relief. Even the making of a subsistence crop appeared hopeless. The civilian populace found their whole economic structure undermined—their slaves had either gone along with the Union armies or had been herded together and driven to concentration points along the river.[58] There was little or no livestock left to pull the plows and perform the many other duties essential to farming. It was a stricken and destitute people about whom General Sherman wrote Grant. "The inhabitants are subjugated," he said, "they cry aloud for mercy. The land is devastated for 30 miles around."[59]

Sherman himself was deeply impressed with the extent of the ruin he had brought about, and he remarked to Senator Sherman that "I even am amazed at the effect."[60] Hopelessness and sheer hunger were working on the Mississippians. The people of the desolated and ravaged areas were faced with outright starvation. They had not been beaten, but as noncombatants they were, as Sherman phrased it, "subdued."[61] Many of the inhabitants had removed themselves to the eastward, farther into the inner citadels of the Confederacy, but others had remained to face the fortunes of war. Those who remained now had the choice of perishing for want of the essentials of life or bowing to the victor and begging for sufficient food to sustain them. From Jackson, Sherman informed Grant that "there are 800 women and children who will perish unless they receive some relief."[62] He had moved to supply the immediate needs of the state asylum and hospital at Jackson, and he now asked General Grant's approval to give 200 barrels of flour and 100 barrels of salt pork to relieve the pangs of hunger.[63] Of course, such supplies were to be made available only if the needy citizens "give me pledges that it shall be devoted to pure charity."[64] On July 23 the citizen's committee at Clinton, Mississippi, gave its written pledge that supplies furnished by the United States would be used only for relief of the destitute, and they received 15,000 rations.[65]

The town of Raymond had suffered almost complete destruction at the hands of the Union cavalry and the citizens of that community were in dire circumstances. Their plight caused General Grant to write Sherman:

> The Confederates at Raymond have sent in for medicines and provisions for their sick left there, about a hundred and fifty in number. Having stripped the country thereabouts we can do no less than supply them, but they have brought no teams. The country having been stripped of them also, I will have to call on you to forward these things from Big Black as soon as I can get them there, and if you have captured teams and carriages, you may send them there in place of our own and they need not be returned.[66]

Grant followed up this dispatch with another the next day reminding General Sherman that the passage of Federal troops "have left the country destitute both of transportation and subsistence,"[67] and urged him not to delay in sending the necessary supplies.

Colonel John M. Corse, commanding a brigade at Oak Ridge, was so affected by the sufferings of the citizens in that area that he was moved to apply to General Sherman for permission to relieve them. He was informed on August 9, 1863, that the commanding general granted him approval to "supply such of the destitute families in your neighborhood as may be by you deemed worthy with necessary provisions, and the amount will be made up to you."[68]

Warren County, Mississippi, had been so devastated and stripped that General Grant found it necessary to give it special consideration in general orders issued from his headquarters on August 1. Paragraph IV ordered:

> Within the county of Warren, laid waste by the long presence of contending armies, the following rules to prevent suffering will be observed:
> Major-General Sherman, commanding the Fifteenth Army Corps, and Major-General McPherson, commanding the Seventeenth Army Corps, will each designate a commissary of subsistence, who will issue articles of prime necessity to all destitute families calling for them, under such restrictions for the protection of the Government as they may deem necessary. Families who are able to pay for the provisions drawn will in all cases be required to do so.[69]

Sherman's harsh theory of war, carried without pity to noncombatants, was now levying its full tribute in sorrow and suffering. The people of the South were feeling the bitter hatred of an invading army which spared nothing in its path. Haggard, hopeless women and children stood in shattered doorways throughout Mississippi, left to face the days ahead without sufficient food to sustain them, and more and more often with insufficient clothing and shelter. Although forced to beg sufficient rations from those who had violated their homes and carried away even their intimate personal possessions, they were not broken, and the flames of their spiritual strength, on the whole, seemed harder to extinguish than that of their men. General Sherman was not insensitive to the attitude of the women. He had described them to Mrs. Sherman in June:

> I doubt if history affords a parallel to the deep and bitter enmity of the women in the South. No one who sees them and hears them but must feel the intensity of their hate. Not a man is seen; nothing but women with houses plundered, fields open to the cattle and horses, pickets lounging on every porch, and desolations sown broadcast, servants all gone and women and children bred in luxury, beautiful and accomplished, begging in one breath for the soldiers' rations, and in another praying that the Almighty or Joe Johnston

will come and kill us, the despoilers of their homes and all that is sacred.[70]

Although Sherman, more than once, expressed pity for these unfortunates, it always appeared to be in a detached manner. First and foremost he justified the violation of the rights of noncombatants on the ground that they had brought their fate down upon their own heads. There runs through all of Sherman's correspondence a thread of fanatical belief that he held a special commission to punish the rebellious South and all its people. He continued his letter to Mrs. Sherman:

> Why cannot they look back to the day and the hour when I, a stranger in Louisiana, begged and implored them to pause in their career, that secession was death, was everything fatal? . . . They have sowed the wind and must reap the whirlwind. Until they lay down their arms and submit to the rightful authority of the government they must not appeal to me for mercy or favors. [71]

The treatment meted out to the civilian populace in Mississippi by the Federal armies did not pass unnoticed in other sections of the Confederacy. A cry of indignation and anger came from *The Augusta Chronicle,* which printed an editorial captioned: "Outrages by the Federals in Mississippi." This editorial recounted some of the more sensational actions of the Federal soldiery, declaring that "the outrages lately committed by the Federal soldiers in Mississippi exceed in barbarity, if possible, those perpetrated by the vandals in other sections."[72] *The Richmond Daily Dispatch* had demanded that the Confederate armies invading Pennsylvania under Lee should use their golden opportunity to retaliate for the needless and shameful waste by the Federals in the South. In an editorial headed "The Sword of the Lord and of Gideon" it was demanded that the South exact "an eye for an eye and a toothe for a toothe." The editor pointed out that fear and dismay were evident in the rich Pennsylvania farming areas, as "fat farmers drive off their fat cattle to the mountains" and "public records are moved out of the way of danger."[73] Immediate and unbounded retaliation was urged as the only manner in which such outrages in the South could be prevented, and the editor demanded "a half a dozen eyes for each eye, and half a dozen teeth for each tooth." He further expressed his dissatisfaction over reading in the Northern press that "the Confederate armies in Pennsylvania conducted themselves in a highly exemplary manner, and he pointed out that the rebels respected private property."[74]

Concern and indignation were reflected in the Confederate army, which was far more vital to the Confederacy than the outbursts of its press and public spokesmen. The rank and file of the army began to feel the strain. The first flush of wrath was replaced with a deep-seated concern for the welfare of families left in vicinities at the mercy of Union forces. The men in Confederate military service faced the difficulties of poor rations, insufficient and inferior clothing, and poor and infrequent pay without too much grumbling. Their morale continued high even in the face of reversals in the field. Much more depressing, however, than these personal hardships "was the knowledge that wives, children and parents were deprived of sufficient food and clothing."[75] As stories came to the Confederate armies of the mistreatment of the folks at home, anxiety caused many of the soldiers to set out for home without observing the formality of securing a furlough or discharge.

The effect on the Southern armies resulting from Sherman's unrestricted warfare on women and children went beyond anything that even he could have calculated. There had been desertions from the ranks of both armies, but the loss of manpower through this avenue had really begun to be felt in Confederate ranks even before General Joseph E. Johnston evacuated Jackson, Mississippi. While that city was besieged by Sherman, General Johnston had reported to President Davis that "our men are deserting in large numbers by the fords on Pearl River."[76] On July 23, from Morton, Mississippi, where he had set up temporary headquarters, the Confederate general had informed Davis again that "desertions continue, especially of Mississippians."[77] Later, in his complete report of his operations in Mississippi, he stated: "Desertions during the siege and on the march were, I regret to say, frequent."[78] So alarming had become the number of those leaving without official sanction that Major Carter of the Seventh Mississippi Infantry at Monticello asked for cavalry reinforcements in order that he might "capture 2000 or 3000 deserters and return them to their commands." He informed the commanding general that "the country is full, and they are still coming in by squads of 10, 15, and 20, who will resist any small force, or even double that of their own."[79] General James R. Chalmers, the Confederate commander at Grenada, complained to General Johnston several days later that "the country is filled with stragglers and deserters, whom it is difficult to arrest, because they are hidden and protected by the citizens."[80] A minor Confederate official at Meridian was so deeply concerned over this situation that he felt constrained to offer his counsel to General Johnston and informed him that "the number of absentees, stragglers, and deserters from the army scattered over the State is also alarmingly great." He offered the gratuitous suggestion that "could all these men be restored to the ranks, a great change would at once be effected in our prospects."[81]

Mississippi was in a turmoil in the late summer and fall of 1863. Not only were deserters and stragglers from the army moving about, hunting their families or trying to evade the authorities, but countless numbers of refugees streamed eastward and northward in their efforts to escape a relentless enemy. The movement of these refugees hindered the Southern armies, according to General Chalmers, particularly with regard to available supplies. In his report of July 22, 1863, from Grenada, he advised that the areas from which the Confederacy could hope to draw supplies had been greatly reduced by the movements of armies, and "this difficulty is greatly increased by the emigration of large numbers of our citizens with their families and selves from this and other States to localities where they will be protected by our arms."[82] A Union surgeon wrote his wife of the "filthy crowd" he encountered on the steamboat to Vicksburg from upriver, and how wives of men who were in the rebel army reported to the commissary in Vicksburg to draw enough food to sustain life.[83] As late as October an artilleryman in Sherman's army noted in his diary while en route to Chattanooga that he passed the camp of the First Alabama Cavalry, U.S.A., some

1,300 strong, "consisting mostly of refugees from the rebel army, many of whom have their wives and children along."[84] He observed further that every train was loaded with refugees from the interior.

Leaving chaos and confusion in his wake, General Sherman in the latter part of July issued orders for the withdrawal of his army to the Big Black River, where the troops were to go into summer quarters to rest and furbish up their arms and equipment. A part of the special orders issued by the General were interesting in that they required both officers and men to relinquish all loot and booty which had been wrested from the helpless citizens of Mississippi. They were not to be permitted to keep the horses and mules which had carried infantrymen in the style of staff officers. On this subject the orders required that the quartermaster set up corrals on the bank of Big Black "in which to collect horses, mules, etc., now in possession of soldiers and officers belonging to this army, which have been plundered and taken from the inhabitants of the country." Nor were the men to be allowed to keep the more personal possessions of the people whose homes they had forced, and whose trunks and chests they had broken open with the ever-handy bayonet. The order further instructed the quartermaster:

> He will appoint suitable officers or agents of the quartermaster's department to take, by force if necessary, all horses ridden by any officer or soldier of this army not entitled by law to be mounted, and collect out of the wagons all articles of furniture, chairs, tables, books, papers, etc.,—anything not belonging to the usual equipment of the officer or soldier.[85]

Such property referred to in the order as "useless" would either be burned or "sent to Vicksburg for sale for the benefit of the United States."[86]

So widespread was the unrestrained looting and robbery of private homes that General Grant officially recognized the shameful practices in his orders of August 1, 1863. A section of the orders was directed particularly at the actions of Federal cavalry. These mounted groups, ranging far and wide on the flanks of the infantry columns, had much better opportunities to rob and burn country houses and those in the smaller villages. They dashed in, wrecked or appropriated everything of value, and as rapidly withdrew after covering their depredation by reducing the houses to ashes. Paragraph V of General Grant's Orders No. 50, stated:

> Conduct disgraceful to the American name has been frequently reported to the Major-General commanding, particularly on the part of portions of the cavalry. Hereafter, if the guilty parties cannot be reached, the commanders of regiments and detachments will be held responsible, and those who prove themselves unequal to the task of preserving discipline in their commands will be promptly reported to the War Department for muster-out. Summary punishment must be inflicted upon all officers and soldiers apprehended in acts of violence and lawlessness.[87]

This order appeared to impress Sherman only to the extent that on August 4 he transmitted to General Grant court-martial proceedings against a private, a sergeant and a captain of the Thirty-fifth Iowa. They were charged with burning a cotton gin during the return march from Jackson. He had caught these men in the act, he stated, and he regarded their act as sheer vandalism, inasmuch as "the burning of this building in no way aided our military plans."[88] No enemy was within 50 miles at the time, Sherman pointed out. It was obvious that he chose to make examples of these men to show that he was carrying out Grant's orders to punish men "apprehended in acts of violence and lawlessness." Had the General sincerely wished to punish the lawless men in his army, he had sufficient evidence to do so since only a few days earlier he had acknowledged the possession of loot by his men in his order to the quartermaster to use force if necessary to relieve the soldiers of "chairs, tables, books, papers, etc.," which they had stolen from defenseless citizens. Sherman had entertained his staff at a banquet in Jackson in the red glare of burning buildings and homes while these same men were sacking the town. No action was taken to punish either men or officers even though they stood self-indicted of the misconduct referred to by General Grant the moment the quartermaster removed from their baggage the many personal possessions which they had appropriated out of private homes and which were obviously not a part of a soldier's field equipment.

It was obvious that Sherman had no intention of executing his order of July 24 and Grant's of August 1 against vandalism, and thereby dulling the most terrifying instrument of war which he had employed so mercilessly. He would continue his devastations,

> till all traces of war are effaced; till those who appealed to it are sick and tired of it, and come to the emblem of our nation, and sue for peace. I would not coax them, or even meet them half-way, but make them so sick of war that generations would pass away before they would again appeal to it.

Nothing would be permitted to interfere with his program of terror in which he was determined to,

> remove and destroy every obstacle, if need be, take every life, every acre of land, every particle of property, everything that to us seems proper; that we will not cease till the end is attained; that all who do not aid us are enemies, and that we do not account to them for our acts. If the people of the South oppose, they do so at their peril; and if they stand by, mere lookers-on in this domestic tragedy, they have no right to immunity, protection, or share in the final results.[89]

Despite Sherman's orders, evidently issued for the record, officers and men under his command did not seriously feel the heavy hand of discipline for their lawless conduct. The General himself apparently succumbed to temptation in September 1863, if one witness can be believed. Miss Anne Martin, writing a friend in that month about the depredations committed by the Union army, said:

> Sometimes property was merely confiscated and not destroyed, as was the case with a Warren County woman, from whom Sherman confiscated fifty loads of fine furniture, leaving behind only a table, a chair, and a curt egalitarian ra-

tionalization to the effect that "a woman who has fifty loads of fine furniture deserves to lose it."[90]

The men were in complete agreement with the attitude of their commanding officer toward the practice of pillaging and plundering at which they had now become so adept. The spreading of terror had now become not only a pleasure, but a mission for which they had been well trained.

On October 27, 1863, Sherman received General Grant's order "to drop all work on the Memphis & Charleston Railroad"[91] and hasten eastward to the relief of Rosecrans at Chattanooga. This was a hurry call, and there was little time for the wholesale destruction and waste which usually accompanied the passage of Sherman's forces. However, the soldiers did manage to keep up their record for sacking and robbing the communities through which they passed. An artilleryman of the Sixth Wisconsin Battery recorded the actions of his Division in Iuka:

> The Division, as usual, pillaging down-town. Nearly $3000 worth of goods having been stolen, the outlaws being in the shape of a regiment led by a Major "straps and colors" etc. Luckily the artillery boys were all in camp.[92]

This Wisconsin soldier left no doubt that this was nothing unusual for his fellows when he noted in his diary for the day following the sacking of Iuka:

> I think that our Division is getting to be the worst in the Department. Everything is left unmolested by other troops, but when we come along, jayhawking and pillaging is the order of the day. It is done by unscrupulous young men or boys rather, having been removed from all restraint of society and parents.[93]

It was with a sense of disgust that the diarist watched the men of his division strip poor people in northern Alabama of their meager supplies. He wrote: "I could not think of laying hands on the small stock of the poor half-clad old women and children we saw."[94] The guards placed to protect the helpless were of no avail to prevent foraging at gun point, the soldier observed, as "the guards sat down and always looked the wrong way, and meat in plenty was brought."[95]

After participating in the battle of Chattanooga, Sherman was ordered by General Grant to proceed immediately into eastern Tennessee to relieve General Burnside. He was to drive off the Confederate Longstreet and break the railroads between him and General Bragg. Putting his columns into motion on November 29, Sherman rode into Knoxville on December 6, 1863, and finding that General Burnside's position in Knoxville was not so desperate as had been represented, he withdrew around the 16th of December. The presence of Sherman's army in eastern Tennessee was soon felt by that section. On December 8, General Oliver O. Howard with the Eleventh Corps of Sherman's command issued a circular to his troops. He had hoped to congratulate them for their conduct in the campaign, and he had no complaint as to their loyalty and cooperation in military duty, but the General continued:

> I will frankly say that acts are done and allowed to be done which are a burning shame and excite my hearty indignation. From Union men, women, and children articles of every description have been stolen, and the thieves not brought to punishment. Piteous cries come to me every day of this dreadful misconduct. I call upon you as men and as officers who have a care for our common reputation to use every exertion to put a stop to these crimes and irregularities, to punish the offenders with the utmost severity, to catch up stragglers from other corps and turn them over to the provost-marshal for punishment.[96]

Such conduct on the part of Union soldiers could not contribute much toward a deeper sympathy and understanding by the people of Tennessee for the Union cause. Sherman acknowledged to General Grant that Union people were being hurt. He pointed out: "We have eaten and are eating up much meat, meal, flour, etc., and though we try to forage on the enemy, I fear we take much of Union people."[97] On the same day this was written from his headquarters at Athens, Tennessee, Sherman instructed General Jeff C. Davis, a division commander, to "scout up the Ocoee and forward, grind all the meal you can, collect good hogs, sheep and beeves, and generally take care of yourselves."[98]

With Chattanooga and eastern Tennessee firmly in Union hands, Sherman, now in command of the Military Department of the Tennessee, was ordered to Huntsville, Alabama, to put his troops into winter quarters. It was not toward Alabama that the General directed his attention, however. Once more he looked toward Mississippi, where affairs had not gone as planned. The crippling blow which he had dealt that state in July, and which he had said should paralyze Mississippi for 20 years, had failed. The Confederates had moved back into Mississippi and in small detachments were tearing up railroads and launching knifing attacks on the scattered Federal garrisons. General Joseph E. Johnston had established his headquarters at Meridian, and the chief commissary was also there.[99] General W. W. Loring, with his command, was established at Canton.[100] Confederate General William H. Jackson had his headquarters at Livingston. These Confederate forces were causing the Union forces great anxiety and provoking even greater efforts to prevent the Southern army from taking over control in the state.[101] The Confederate cavalry commands under Generals Stephen D. Lee, Forrest and Ferguson were on the loose and threatening the hold of the Union army on the country.[102]

The forces left by Sherman in Mississippi had continued to spread terror through devastation, in their effort to hold on to that state. General Chalmers, a Confederate cavalry leader, reported their activities in October. In their efforts to concentrate against him he reported:

> In addition to other outrages upon the persons and property of unoffending citizens, they made it a point to visit the houses in which I had had my headquarters, and, when they did not entirely consume, to injure them as much as possible by destroying their furniture and clothing, and wantonly wasting their supplies and forage. . . . In addition to this they burned the villages of Wyatt and Chulahoma (the latter without any provocation whatever), and desolated the plantations along their route, burning corn-cribs, etc., and driving off horses and cattle.[103]

A resident of Washington, D.C., entered in his diary:

> Oct. 30th [1863]. More burning. General McPherson of the
> Fed. Army made a raid recently to Canton, Miss. with 2000
> cavalry. He burned farmhouses, barns, in fact everything that
> would burn in the line of his march. The women & children
> driven houseless & homeless out in the pelting rain. Can such
> brutes be called men?[104]

In November 1863, Sherman, from his camp near Chattanooga,
ordered the Federal commander at Eastport, Mississippi, to keep
communications open through Corinth. "There is a small nest of
the worst sort of guerillas back of Savannah that I want killed
and their property destroyed," he wrote.[105] This ruthless treatment of the people in that community, in Sherman's opinion,
would serve as an example to others.

In spite of their terrible losses in wagons, farm stock and
slaves, the people of Mississippi had managed to grow another
crop, to raise hogs and cattle. The specter of starvation as well
as their dependence upon their conquerors had somehow been
averted. Sherman was aware of this development, and he realized that the Confederate forces in Mississippi were gathering
these supplies as rapidly and thoroughly as possible[106] and stor-
ing them in protected areas.

To Sherman this lodgment of Confederate armies in Mississippi
meant that the Mississippi River was threatened. Full control and
the unimpeded use of the great river by the Union had always
amounted almost to an obsession with Sherman. The riverboats
were no longer free to travel the Mississippi except under the
constant threat of attack from the shores. *The Canton Tri-Weekly
Citizen* on January 17, 1864, in its column headed "Latest from
the Mississippi River," recounted the exploits of a Brigadier
General L. S. Ross, a Texas cavalry leader, who had crossed
into Mississippi and was playing havoc with the Federal boats.
The newspaper reported:

> Near Greenville, Washington County, Miss., he planted his
> batteries on the banks of the river, and soon had a chance to
> try their efficiency The splendid steamer Delta came puffing

proudly along— . . . When the batteries were opened upon her and she was sent to the bottom—another evidence of the impossibility of navigating the Mississippi, except by mutual agreement, and casting into ridicule the boastful order of General Banks, that the same was now open for navigation and trade.[107]

The report further assured the reader that the Confederates succeeded in crippling the Union gunboat which was sent to the rescue. *The Canton Citizen,* in its edition of January 20, carried a reprint of "Yankee" reports of General Ross's activities:

> Several boats have been fired into lately. On the 6th [January] thirty shots were fired at the steamer Delta, three taking effect. . . . Several shots fired at the ram Hornet, two taking effect. Steamer Emma fired into with musketry by guerillas 7th inst., at Greenville; also the Belle Creole.[108]

The seriousness with which Sherman regarded these developments and the extent to which he was willing to go to put a stop to Confederate activities in Mississippi is clearly shown in his letter from Nashville to General John A. Logan in December 1863. General Sherman had gone to Nashville to confer with General Grant, and the safety of the great river had occupied an important place in their deliberations. He assured General Logan, now in command of the Fifteenth Corps encamped at Bridgeport, Alabama, that he (Sherman) "must do something to check the boldness of our enemy in attacking boats on the Mississippi River." And he continued:

> To secure the safety of the navigation of the Mississippi, I would slay millions—on that point I am not only insane, but mad. Fortunately the Great West is with us on that point. I think I see one or two quick blows, that will astonish the natives of the South, and will convince them, that though to stand behind a big cottonwood tree and shoot at a passing Boat is good sport and safe, that it may still reach and kill their friends and families hundreds of miles off. For every bullet shot at a Steamboat, I would shoot a thousand 30 pdr. [pounder] Parrotts into even helpless Towns on Red River,

Washita, Yazoo, or wherever a boat can float or a Soldier can march. Well, I think in all January and part of February I can do something in this line.[109]

By February 3, 1864, General Sherman had perfected his plans to strike eastward from the river to Meridian, Mississippi, where General Leonidas Polk, the fighting bishop, now commanded the Confederate army in the state. Weather conditions were ideal for the movement of Sherman's columns, and this in itself was unusual. Mississippi weather in February was usually cold and rainy and the roads muddy morasses. *The Augusta Daily Chronicle and Sentinel,* in its news from Mississippi, noted on February 6, 1864: "The weather is mild and pleasant—the roads are getting in excellent condition, and military movements on a large scale can be made." And in the same item the reporter furnished news which must have heartened Sherman's army, marching with few wagons, hoping to live off the countryside. The news item continued: "Affairs in Mississippi are emphatically improving. The people have plenty to eat and the stock are all fat. Cows and hogs are abundant and the country is well supplied."[110]

Sherman drove eastward through Jackson to strike directly at Meridian and encountered little determined resistance from the Confederates. He had issued orders that there was to be no straggling or laxity on the march. His columns were compactly formed, with cavalry on the flanks, to minimize the effects of dashes of Confederate horsemen.[111] General Stephen D. Lee's Confederate cavalry met Sherman's army at the Big Black and fought him all the way, hoping only to keep his foragers in as much as possible. General Lee stated that it was not General Polk's intention to fight Sherman. Polk had hoped Sherman would overextend himself into the piney woods, where he could be effectively crushed with the cooperation of Confederate reinforcements expected from Georgia. According to General Lee, "the movement of troops for the purpose [Hardee's Corps] was at the time in progress."[112]

Apparently plenty of forage was found, even though the Union foraging parties lost men here and there, picked off by the vigilant cavalry of the Confederates. Robert J. Campbell, a soldier in Sherman's army, recording in his diary on February 7, 1864, said: "Plenty of forage; roads good; Rebs in full retreat; pass through Brandon and halt east; more forage than I ever saw; rich country; a general good time."[113] Again, on February 9, he remarked on the plentiful forage. The next day he passed through Hillsboro and reported tersely that the "town burnt up; plenty of forage."[114] Captain Hickenlooper of the Fifth Ohio Battery passed through Brandon on February 7, and his report stated that he found sufficient forage "for one trip; no surplus."[115] This officer also passed through Hillsboro and described it "nearly deserted, and now mostly destroyed by fire."[116]

On February 14 and 15 the Union army rolled into Meridian, having encountered little or no resistance. *The Mobile Daily Advertiser and Register* reported on February 16, 1864:

> A private dispatch from Enterprise dated last evening states that our forces evacuated Meridian yesterday (Sunday) morning. The government property was all saved, and nearly all, if not all the machinery of the Railroad Company. Our troops retired in good order in the direction of the Bigbee river. The last train above on the Mobile and Ohio Railroad passed Meridian at 1 P.M. yesterday, and reported the enemy in full view, just entering the town. The train was fired on and no effort was made to stop or delay it.[117]

Sherman lost no time in setting his men at their work of wrecking the railroads, burning public property and unofficially destroying the town of Meridian. His report to General Grant gives a graphic picture of the scope of the destruction:

> For five (5) days, ten thousand of our men worked hard and with a will, in that work of destruction, with axes, sledges, crowbars, clawbars, and with fire, and I have no hesitation in pronouncing the work well done. Meridian with its Depots, Storehouses, Arsenals, offices, Hospitals, Hotels, and Cantonments, no longer exists.

In addition he summarized the extent of the damage to railroad and other public property:

The former [General Hurlbut] reports to me officially the destruction of sixty (60) miles [of railroad] with ties and iron burned and bent—one locomotive destroyed and eight bridges burned. The latter [General McPherson] fifty-five (55) miles of road destroyed, fifty-three Bridges, six thousand seventy-five (6075) feet of trestle work below Quitman burned—nineteen (19) locomotives, twenty-eight (28) cars and three (3) steam sawmills burned and destroyed. The Railroad is destroyed all the way from Jackson to Meridian, a hundred (100) miles; from Meridian south to and below Quitman—north to, and including a bridge at Lauderdale Springs, and east about twenty (20) miles.[118]

On the whole General Sherman was well satisfied with the Meridian campaign. He felt that he had accomplished most of what he had set out to do. He had pushed the enemy out of Mississippi and destroyed the only remaining railroads in the state, and these, he pointed out to General Grant, were "the only roads by means of which he [the enemy] could maintain an army in Mississippi threatening to our forces on the main River." He continued his report:

We also subsisted our army and animals chiefly on his stores, brought away about four hundred (400) prisoners of war, and full a thousand white refugees and five thousand negroes, about 3000 animals (horses, mules & oxen) and any quantity of wagons and vehicles. Beyond Pearl River we destroyed all C.S.A. Cotton that we encountered, and all that was used in the enemy's forts at Meridian—also many cotton gins and loose piles of cotton were burned by our soldiers and by the negroes without orders and without detection.[119]

Sherman was much chagrined that General W. Sooy Smith, Chief of Cavalry, failed to meet him at Meridian. General Smith had been ordered to leave Memphis in time to make a junction at Meridian with Sherman's infantry columns. His cavalry was to have destroyed General Forrest, but instead General Smith had fallen victim to General Forrest's cavalry and had been headed off and completely routed near West Point, Mississippi. Had Sherman been able to employ General Sooy Smith's cavalry around Meridian, the scope of the ruin and destruction would have been greatly increased. An examination of General Smith's report of his operations shows, however, that he had done a thorough job. He informed Sherman:

> I . . . moved the other two brigades right down the Railroad destroying it as we went tearing up the ties burning them & bending the rails. From Okalona to West Point we found government corn in immense quantities all along the road and this we burned until there was a line of fire from place to place. I had no means of ascertaining definitely what was government corn and what the property of private citizens and could only burn that that was cribbed near the Railroad. . . .
> The results of my trip are as follows:
> 1st   Corn burned from one to two million bushels
> 2nd   Confed. cotton burned two thousand bales
> 3rd   Thirty miles of R.R. destroyed
> 4th   Three thousand horses and mules and fifteen hundred negroes brought out of the enemy's country.[120]

The report added that forage and provisions for 7,000 troops were taken away from the people in the path of the army.

These were the official reports of the punishing blows inflicted on the state of Mississippi in early 1864, and the destruction and confiscation of property which they described might be justified in war, but nowhere in General Sherman's reports does he mention damages other than those directed against military objectives. His *Memoirs* simply sum up the Meridian campaign by stating that he destroyed "an arsenal, immense storehouses, and the railroad in every direction."[121] There is a strange silence as to the conduct of his men toward the defenseless citizens of Mississippi. These people, largely women and children and old men, suffered every indignity and humiliation at the hands of a ruthless soldiery, who ransacked their homes, appropriated and destroyed their most intimate personal possessions, and finally wrecked or burned their homes to the ground.

It was on the return march to Vicksburg that the Federal columns were loosed on the towns, villages and farms between

Meridian and the river. The withdrawal began on February 20, and by February 26 the infantry columns had all reached Canton. What transpired at Canton, the county seat of Madison County, demonstrated General Sherman's attitude toward noncombatants. He had expressed his feelings on January 30, 1864, in a letter to the naval officer cooperating in a movement up the Yazoo River. With reference to private property he wrote:

> . . . but so long as they have cotton, corn, horses, or anything, we will appropriate it or destroy it so long as their confederates in war act in violence to us and our lawful commerce. They must be active friends or enemies. They cannot be silent or neutral. . . . They may protest against our holding them responsible for the acts of the Confederate authorities, but in war we have a perfect right to produce results in our own way, and should not scruple too much at the means, provided they are effectual.[122]

Here then was the keystone of Sherman's harsh theory of war: strike with vengeance; unleash a horde of destroyers to prowl broadside over the country; offer no restraints to their cruelty, thievery and practice of arson; encourage by silence or studied oversight their utter lack of regard for law and order and the rights of private property.

Before leaving Meridian the Union soldiers had, in addition to destroying public property, almost completely demolished the town itself. A letter to *The New York Times* from Meridian said very few unoccupied buildings escaped destruction, and most of the private residences were also destroyed.[123] Soldiers instructed to burn unoccupied houses were not overly interested as to whether the houses were vacant or not.[124] Northern newspapers pictured the scene in Meridian: "Houses were broken open and plundered, every horse, cow and chicken in the place was seized, not a fence was left, the commissary stores were destroyed, and the slaves carried away with the army."[125] A citizen residing near Meridian described the efficiency and thoroughness with which the soldiery stripped his place. Writing to *The Mobile Daily Tribune* from Selma, where apparently he had been forced to go, he said:

On the 16th of February [1864] the infernal Yanks paid us a visit at Meridian and cleared us out. They took all our meat, about 6,000 pounds, 29 as fine hogs as were ever killed, cleared out our storeroom, took all our poultry, fired the mill, blacksmith shop, office, oxstalls, smokehouse, storeroom, house kitchen and chicken house, burnt all our wagons, platform, lumber, etc., kicked up the devil generally.

This man was more fortunate than most as he was successful in hiding several horses and cattle, and by great exertion he rescued his corncrib and a little corn. Most of his furniture and bedding he saved from the flames by fast action. His letter referred to the sufferings of the community, as he wrote:

They have destroyed everything in our neighborhood, all communication by letter or otherwise has stopped. They took nearly all the negroes, horses, mules, hogs and chickens in our settlement. I do not think you can hear a chicken crow for ten miles around Meridian.[126]

A Cincinnati boy in Sherman's army wrote home, describing how the Mississippians tried desperately to save some of their supplies. He said:

The planters throughout the State would run off their provisions and stock under charge of a negro, and he would either bring it into our lines or our foragers would find it before it had gone far, and bring it in. I think if a mosquito would go over that road now, or in the country for miles each side, he would not find provisions enough for three days rations.[127]

Jackson, the battered capital of Mississippi, was again subjected to the tender mercies of the national troops. A correspondent writing to *The Canton American Citizen* in April 1864 stated:

One must visit Jackson to learn the extent of the destruction it has sustained. . . . There are not exceeding ten buildings standing upon both sides of State Street . . . and look in whatever direction you may from the front of the capitol, ruin meets the eye. . . . So near complete their nefarious work that they now call the former capitol of the proud State of Mississippi, "Chimneyville." . . . The numerous chimneys still standing upon the burnt districts, and the undisturbed debris of charred walls and the destroyed wares, will remain until the end of the war, silent but terrible monuments of the devastating inroad of the vandal hordes.[128]

Confederate General Stephen D. Lee was shocked at the robbery of poor people, an action which certainly was not dictated by the necessities of war. He stated that "the track of Sherman and Smith was marked by the wanton destruction of private property —burning houses, etc." He continued:

Sherman alone carried back to Vicksburg about 300 wagons more than he started with. These wagons and their teams he took from an impoverished and already desolated country, and the very poorest (pecuniarily) class of people living in the thin piney woods country through which he passed. Over 10,000 bales of cotton and 2,000,000 bushels of corn were burned. Over 8000 slaves, mounted on as many mules (stolen) belonging to citizens of the country, were carried off. A Federal writer estimates the damage as $50,000,000. As over *three fourths of this was private property,* the future historian may possibly ask, was this and the towns burned (Meridian, Canton, etc.) the warfare of the civilization of the nineteenth century waged against those who had a few years before been brothers, and among whom General Sherman had lived and derived his livelihood?[129]

Jackson and Meridian were not the only towns to feel the heavy hand of ruin. A resident of Brandon wrote her husband, who was in the Confederate army, describing to him the treatment accorded her family by General Hurlbut's troops. McPherson's forces had passed through the day before, but apparently they had not conducted themselves as reprehensibly as those of General

Hurlbut. Excerpts from this private letter were published in a Montgomery newspaper. The letter writer reported:

> They [Union troops] were very destructive throughout the whole country where they have passed. . . . Papa has been one of the heaviest sufferers so far as heard from in his part of the country. The thieving rascals reached our premises whilst we were at the dinner table on Sunday, and kept up their plundering and stealing until dark. . . .
>
> Every horse and mule Papa had was taken away, hogs killed, and all the poultry taken. In the smoke-house nothing was left, except some meal which they emptied on the floor. Not a single pound of meat or sugar were we able to save, and none had been sent off.[130]

But the soldiers did not stop with the stealing of everything edible on the place. They next turned their attention to the house itself. The picture of their conduct is a sordid one. In this case, typical of countless others, the vandalism of the Federal soldiers reached a new low. The letter writer continued:

> In the house there was not a trunk, drawer, wardrobe, desk or anything they did not plunder and plunder well; and the contents scattered over the house, and everything stolen they wished. Not a garment of yours did they leave, except a few pairs of socks and some collars. A great deal of B's [her infant daughter] and my clothing were stolen; silk dresses, embroidered handkerchiefs, silk stockings and B's beautiful little hat and cloak . . . ; it is impossible to mention all. My money and jewelry I managed to save, by having them buried. What was left [of clothing] here was torn into pieces or abused in some way. Papa has nothing left but what he was wearing. Every bed was stripped of clothing. We managed to beg a few pieces from some of the thieves, but only enough for one bed; this one bed was the only one used for three nights, some of us sleeping one portion of the night, and the others the balance. For three meals we hadn't a thing but roasted potatoes to eat, and since that time what we have eaten has been done with our fingers; not a knife or fork was left, and but little earthenware. Mama

has not even a coffee pot left. All this stealing was done before our eyes, and neither words or tears would prevent it.[131]

The utter helplessness of the victims of such brutality, forced to stand by while such humiliations and indignities were heaped upon them, left lasting scars upon the memories of those so mistreated. The closing extract of this woman's letter would be repeated over and over again as time passed and the South came into its heritage of hate. "I hate them more now than I did the evening I saw them sneaking off with all we cared for," she assured her husband, and she added, "and so it will be every day I live."

In Brandon itself the soldiers burned the Methodist Church, the post office and the government stables around the town. Many buildings were fired, but the citizens managed to put out the flames. It was reported that every house on the square was fired, and that "Martin's store was robbed of everything."[132]

The village of Decatur, some 70 miles east of Jackson, was reported to have had 30 buildings destroyed by fire.[133] Lake Station nearby was utterly demolished. The Union cavalry destroyed "two livery stables, the machine shops, three locomotives, a railroad water tank, a turntable, thirty-five cars, two saw-mills, and a quantity of lumber."[134] But they did more than this, as testified to by the chief acting signal officer of the Seventeenth Army Corps. He reported that while the cavalry was pushing the Confederate defenders out, "the Signal Corps went through the town like a dose of salts, and just as we were leaving I noticed a man hunting around to get someone to make an affidavit that there had been a town there."[135]

A businessman at Enterprise, in Clarke County, described to his partner the entrance into that town of the ravaging army of Federal cavalry and infantry. "The Yankee cavalry entered our village on Tuesday evening," he wrote, "then the infantry 4000 strong came pouring in at double quick, and in ten minutes after the ravaging and plundering commenced."[136] They burned the depot, two flour mills, 2,000 bales of cotton, 15,000 bushels of corn, as well as two hospitals and other buildings.[137] In their carnival of destruction the aroused soldiers then turned their attention to the pillaging and looting of private residences. The

Enterprise businessman, himself a heavy loser, after describing the rapidity with which the Union troops set about their ruinous work, continued:

> No place or house escaped them. Locks and bars availed nothing. Every room, trunk, wardrobe, and the beds and bedding, were plundered and torn up, nor did the poor negroes, whom they came to set free, as they said, escape those low-down pilfering rascals. Not one negro cabin or kitchen in the town, and for miles around escaped. Everything they could carry off was taken, and what they could not, was torn up and destroyed, even to servants' underclothes, and as for horses, none escaped but those sent off for at least eight miles from their encampment. . . . Every horse and mule (8 in number) was taken; my stock hogs killed, wagon, harness, saddles and bridles, fodder, hay and some corn; poultry, even to the geese. On the plantation my gin-house with 60 bales of cotton, besides my little crop of this year . . . together with 5 or 600 pannels of fencing, were all consumed; and last, but not least, 6 of my negroes went off. . . . My loss will not fall short of $28,000 to $30,000.[138]

This man's losses, as high as they were, were no different from those of his neighbors. His letter mentioned some of his neighbors, apparently well known to the person to whom he wrote:

> John Cockran lost 151 bales of cotton, besides his two storehouses; . . . W. B. Smith about $35,000 in all; Doby some $8,000, perhaps $10,000. . . . Every store, warehouse and workshop in the place was laid in ashes.[139]

Another who witnessed the descent of Sherman's soldiers on Enterprise said, "The enemy came into this place on Tuesday evening last, about 5 o'clock, yelling like Indians and firing at everything and everyone they met, but fortunately without killing or wounding anyone." This force, the writer estimated, was made up of 11 regiments of infantry, one of cavalry and six pieces of artillery. They remained at Enterprise two days and three nights. The writer reported that a portion of this force proceeded to

Quitman, where they "burned the bridge and Sander's mill, Stalling's Hotel and the Courthouse."[140] Brigadier General W. Q. Gresham, commanding the Union brigade dispatched to Quitman, reported an additional destruction: "We also destroyed the railroad depot at Quitman, the large and elegant hospital buildings, recently erected, one large steam flouring-mill and one large steam sawmill."[141] The units of Federal troops which remained in Enterprise proceeded to indulge in the needless, wanton waste which now came so easily to them. The witness who wrote to *The Mobile Register* describes events in Enterprise very much as the one quoted above. He wrote:

> They burned all the gin-houses as they went, and took all the negroes that would go with them. I do not think they forced any to go. They took nearly all the bacon in this town and in the country around and all the horses and mules they could get hold of.
> The town is in ashes—that is, the business part of it. Otto Stein's tinshop and a blacksmith shop are the only buildings left standing on what was known as Commercial Row. The hotel, both livery stables, the row where the printing office was, in fact all that part of town except Kremer's house, was also burned.
> As I told you they took most of the bacon, and killed nearly the entire stock of hogs and cattle in the place. . . . Mr. G. Tolson lost $8000 in money, besides his wife's silverware.[142]

Among other towns suffering the same fate were Hillsboro, Bolton, Lauderdale and Canton. At the last place the Union colonel in command of cavalry stated that large numbers of Negroes and mules were captured, and several mills, two bridges over the Pearl River and other property were burned by order. His report showed restraint when he reported: "I regret to say that some other buildings were wantonly destroyed." He also stated that an officer caught in the act of firing a building was being reported through proper channels.[143]

Sherman had sent one wing of his army into the Yazoo country to punish the people of that section, and when the Union army abandoned Yazoo City on March 6, 1864, they attempted to destroy it. *The Canton American Citizen* reported:

> Before leaving [Yazoo City], besides depredations of a minor character, the enemy signalized their departure by setting fire to and consuming the west side of Main Street, from O'Donnell's to Barksdale's—six or eight of the finest brick stores in the place. On the east side they burned four framed and five brick stores, the courthouse, one dwelling occupied by a Mrs. Parsons, and three other, unoccupied.[144]

The flaming pathway of Sherman's army through Mississippi was marked by wanton waste, arson and the sacking and pillaging of towns, villages and homes. His troops robbed the finest plantations and the lowly cabins of the Negroes with equal greed and heartlessness. They applied the torch to private property, often to cover their depredations, with as little compunction as they burned public property. They spread terror through the sheer joy of the sense of power it gave them and to force their will, in most cases, upon a people who stood defenseless. With most of her able-bodied men in the Confederate armies, Mississippi discovered in suffering and sorrow that Sherman's theory of total war was no longer a theory or an experiment, but a stark, practical program of terror directed against the old men, women and children of the South. The tears, heartaches and deprivations of the civilian populace of Mississippi demonstrated vindictive retaliation carried almost to its ultimate application.

As Sherman looked toward the coming campaign in Georgia he declared that the great result of the Meridian campaign "is the hardihood and confidence imparted to the command, which is now better fitted for war."[145] The people of Georgia and South Carolina could draw no comfort from the warning General Leonidas Polk gave his troops when he assumed the command of Confederate forces in Mississippi. He solemnly declared of Sherman's armies: "The hate of these men has not been abated by the plunder and desolation and bloodshed upon which it has fed, but rather has been deepened and intensified."[146]

VII

/\WV/\WV/\WV/\WV

Atlanta and Northern Georgia

"General Sherman has taken Atlanta." This terse message reached
President Lincoln on Friday morning, September 2, 1864. The
telegram had been dispatched by General Henry W. Slocum, commander of the Twentieth Corps, the first to push into Atlanta over
the abandoned Confederate works. This message was followed by
one from Sherman, which reached General Halleck at Washington
on September 4. The opening sentence of Sherman's telegram, so
widely quoted in later years, said: "So Atlanta is ours and fairly
won."

The news of the capture and occupation of Atlanta threw the
North into a delirium of joy. People shouted and men threw their
hats into the air—an air of victory and exhilaration, mixed with a
sense of relief, permeated the speeches and newspaper editorials
praising this climax to a long and bloody campaign.[1] Sherman
became a great hero overnight, and he received letters of praise
from people in all walks of life. His name was mentioned favor-
ably by both the Democrats and the Republicans as a possible
candidate for the presidency or the vice-presidency. Sherman,
apparently unmoved by the political hullabaloo, did recognize that
his occupation of Atlanta had great political significance for Presi-

dent Lincoln, and he later said that his success at Atlanta "made the election of Mr. Lincoln certain."[2]

The Atlanta which the Union armies now occupied was a shattered and broken city. Sherman had subjected it to bombardment without notice. Heavy field guns had fired thousands of rounds of both solid and explosive shells into its houses, buildings and streets. Day and night Federal artillery had deliberately poured death and destruction into the town in such a systematic pattern that it seemed that no part of it remained untouched. A correspondent of *The New York Herald,* who was also one of Sherman's volunteer aides-de-camp, observed the artillery fire directed on Atlanta:

> The artillery had opened with shot and shell upon the city. . . . Major General [David S.] Stanley brought his artillery into position and kept up a warm fire. . . . From several points along the line we could plainly see the doomed city, with the smoke of burning houses and bursting shells enveloping it in one black canopy, hanging over it like a funeral pyre.[3]

Although the bombardment of a besieged city without notice was considered by most military men of the day as a violation of the accepted rules of war, no considerations on this score had deterred Sherman. For many months now he had dispensed with the orthodox concepts of war and set himself up to judge what constituted right and wrong. He was determined to reduce Atlanta to abject submission and therefore made no effort to confine his artillery fire to military objectives only. He had sent back to Chattanooga for a battery of four-and-a-half-inch rifles in order to test their effectiveness on the city. Confederate Captain Thomas J. Key, of an Arkansas artillery battery stationed in Atlanta, recorded in his diary for August 23:

> The wiley Yanks did not let the citizens or soldiers in Atlanta sleep much last night. They kept their 20 pound Parrotts throwing shells into the heart of the city the live-long night. Whether anyone was killed I have not heard. Not many days since, one shell killed a woman and her child

while another poor child, who was lying in the bed sick, was struck by a shell and torn to pieces.[4]

The night bombardments, part of a system to wear down the nerves and resistance of the defenders, were graphically described by Sherman's aide:

> From right, and left, and centre flew these dread missiles, all converging toward the city. From our commanding position we could see the flash from the guns, then the shells, with their burning fuses, hurtling through the air like flying meteors.[5]

This correspondent examined the city after the withdrawal of Hood's army and was able to judge at first hand the destruction wrought by Federal shells. He noted that the projectiles had played havoc with the city and said that "in some places the streets were blocked up with rubbish."[6] He was impressed with the extent of the damage in the suburbs, which, he said, "were in ruins, and few houses escaped without being perforated. Many of the citizens were killed, and many more had hair-breadth escapes."[7]

A soldier in the Commissary Office of the Fifth Connecticut Volunteers, occupying Atlanta, wrote his family describing what he had seen after he had walked around the city. Referring to the damage caused by the shelling as "astonishing," he continued:

> I knew our batteries threw over enormous quantity of shells but I couldn't think they were so effective. . . . The Macon Depot is in the center of the city and has been a good target for all our batteries I should judge by the way things are splintered up. . . . Shade trees a foot through are cut off, and fences broken down, in short every kind of mischief is done by these iron missiles. I don't see how anyone ever ventured to live there yet some did and escaped too.[8]

General Hood had censured Sherman for shelling Atlanta without proper notice of his intentions, and Sherman had attempted to excuse himself in a letter to Hood. He blamed Hood, he said, because "you [Hood] defended Atlanta on a line so close to town that every cannon-shot and many musket-shots from our line of investment that overshot their mark went into the habitations of women and children." This is a particularly interesting statement on Sherman's part in view of his telegram to General Halleck on August 7, 1864, in which he said that he had sent to Chattanooga "for two thirty-pound Parrotts, with which we can pick out almost any house in town." It was his intention, he said, to "make the inside of Atlanta too hot to be endured."[9] In their exchange of correspondence General Hood replied that he was pained by General Sherman's pretense that Union artillerymen had overshot their targets because of the proximity of Confederate defense lines to residences. Hood could understand an occasional shot going wild, and he wrote that he made no complaint over the firing into Atlanta, but he pointed out:

> There are a hundred thousand witnesses that you fired into the habitations of women and children for weeks, firing far above and miles beyond my line of defense. I have too good an opinion of the skill of your artillerist, to credit the insinuation that they for several weeks unintentionally fired too high for my modest field works, and slaughtered women and children by accident and want of skill.[10]

This violation of the accepted practices of war, however, was not the one which called forth the wrath and indignation of the whole South. Sherman called Mayor James M. Calhoun of Atlanta to his headquarters several days after the Union army occupied Atlanta and informed him that it was his intention to remove all the inhabitants of Atlanta from the city. His reasons for such an unprecedented measure were expressed in a letter to General Halleck. First, he declared, the Federal army needed "all the houses of Atlanta for military storage and occupation." In almost the next breath he stated that in order to contract the lines of defense of Atlanta it would be necessary "to destroy the very houses used by families as residences." He pointed out that the residence in Atlanta of a poor population "would compel us, sooner or later, to feed them or to see them starve under our eyes." And if these were not sufficient reasons for his action in depopulating the city, there remained the plain and simple fact that "as captors, we have a right to it."[11]

Sherman would permit the unfortunate residents the poor choice of going either to the north or farther south, but they could not remain in the city. Transportation by railroad would be furnished those citizens desiring to go north. Those wishing to go south would have wagons and ambulances placed at their disposal as far as Rough and Ready Station, where Confederate General Hood's army must take over. Sherman's ruthless depopulation of a surrendered city shocked the people of the South. He ordered into exile a people who had demonstrated their courage and their love for their homes by the manner in which they had endured the siege of their city. They had stuck it out through the days and nights of screaming shells; the nerve-wracking fears of imminent death had not daunted them. Many had remained in the face of impending battles because their homes were in Atlanta, and they preferred to risk all to preserve them. Others, having no place to go, could not flee the doomed city. Now at the point of the bayonet, men, women, and children were to be torn away from their homes, possessions and all that was familiar to them, and be bodily transported into the countryside. Most of the beloved personal possessions, accumulated by families over a period of years, must be abandoned—heirlooms, treasured paintings, little things, many of them closely intertwined with proud family histories—all must be left behind with little likelihood that they would ever be recovered. The enormity of Sherman's crime against the citizens of Atlanta cannot be fully appreciated unless the results of his order are considered in terms of the human suffering and unhappiness which it caused. These same homes from which their occupants were so ruthlessly removed would later either be consumed in the incendiary fires set by a reckless soldiery or be thoroughly sacked and robbed of their contents after the departure of the Union armies from Atlanta.

The people of the South could find no justification for Sherman's order for the depopulation of Atlanta. *The Montgomery Daily Advertiser* of September 16, 1864, in an editorial captioned "The Armistice of Atlanta," said in part: "The proceeding is justly regarded as very extraordinary—extraordinary for the inhumanity of the proceeding, and for the length of time employed for such a purpose. The proceeding, altogether, is perhaps without a parallel in history."[12] *The Macon Telegraph* in a similar editorial, headed "The Atlanta Exile," gave expression to the horror and indignation inspired by the depopulation:

> Modern warfare may be challenged in vain for an edict from a military satrap so utterly and inexcusably barbarous as this. To drive out a non-combatant population from their homes and effects, with nothing but the clothes upon their persons, is a military measure which we think is without example since the expulsion of the Moors from Grenada. . . . So horrible is this on helpless women and babies, that we might look for such an outrage as this to evoke a universal burst of indignation from Christendom; but the world does not like us, and no measure of outrage or tyranny against the South, excites any degree of repugnance to the perpetrators.[13]

The reaction of all the helpless noncombatants in the South seemed to have been summed up in the words of General Hood, who in his letter to Sherman accepting the armistice period concluded:

> And now, sir, permit me to say that the unprecedented measure you propose transcends, in studied and ingenious cruelty, all acts ever before brought to my attention in the dark history of war. In the name of God and humanity, I protest, believing that you will find that you are expelling from their homes and firesides the wives and children of a brave people.[14]

An appeal was made to General Sherman in the form of a petition signed by Mayor Calhoun and two city councilmen, E. E. Rawson and S. C. Wells. They pleaded that Sherman reconsider his order requiring the citizens to leave Atlanta. The removal was already in progress and the Mayor pointed out that it was resulting in untold inconveniences, losses and suffering. The consequences of the forcible exile of these people, the letter said, were "appalling and heart-rending." The petition further pointed out that there were no accommodations for the refugees farther south, where it was reported that many pople were even then "staying in churches and other out-buildings." Winter was not far off and these helpless people deprived of their homes would face the hardship of cold weather in the woods without shelter and subsistence. Such treatment would work a particular hardship upon the old and sick, as well as upon women far advanced in pregnancy,[15] the petition declared.

General Sherman was unimpressed by the picture of suffering and hardship which the Mayor's petition painted, and on September 12 he informed the Atlanta officials he would not countermand the order. He acknowledged in his letter, which from its tone was written for publication, the distress which his orders caused, but assured the Mayor and councilmen that the orders "were not designed to meet the humanities of the case." The people of the South, he declared, were suffering in consequence of their errors in reasoning which had lead them to disrupt the Union. Several highlights from this letter reflect how completely Sherman had dedicated himself to the practice of total war against the South: "You cannot qualify war in harsher terms than I will. War is cruelty and you cannot refine it; and those who brought war into our country deserve all the curses and maledictions a people can pour out." Nothing less than complete subjugation and a humble admission of their faults would be acceptable to General Sherman. He assured the Mayor, and through him the people of the South:

> You might as well appeal against the thunderstorm as against these terrible hardships of war. They are inevitable, and the only way the people of Atlanta can hope once more to live in peace and quiet at home, is to stop the war, which can only be done by admitting that it began in error and is perpetrated in pride.[16]

With this curt refusal from Sherman the removal of the Confederate families from their homes in Atlanta proceeded without interruption. Rufus Mead, Jr., of the Fifth Connecticut Volunteers, was one of the many Union soldiers to witness the exodus from Atlanta. He wrote his family:

The citizens are leaving in droves every day. The cars are loaded with those going north while about 100 six-mule teams go south as far as Rough & Ready & there meet the Rebel teams. The wagons carry the stuff only while the citizens walk or the women and children ride in ambulances. It makes an odd looking train when they all get together to start. The armistice lasts till 9 P.M. on the 21st Inst. September 1864. It raises quite a commotion in this community.[17]

Mrs. Mary A. H. Gay, a resident of Decatur, Georgia, on her way to Jonesboro passed the refugees from Atlanta where they were gathered to await Confederate wagons. The appearance of the miserable population of Atlanta was a gloomy one:

An autumnal mist or drizzle was slowly but surely saturating every article of clothing upon them. Aged grandmothers upon the verge of the grave, tender girls in the first bloom of young womanhood, and little babes not three days old in the arms of sick mothers, were driven from their homes and all thrown out upon the cold charity of the world.[18]

The truce agreed upon to accomplish the removal of the citizens of Atlanta expired on September 21, 1864. The next day Brigadier General Francis Shoup, Chief of Staff to General Hood, noted in his journal that the Confederate escorts had returned to the Southern lines, where they reported "a vast amount of suffering among the refugees, who have come South." Little had been done for them and a "large number of them are still at different stations on the railroad, without any shelter or anyone to provide for them."[19]

The suffering of the homeless citizens was increased by the absence of food in that section of Georgia around Jonesboro. Federal foraging parties operating out of Atlanta had so thoroughly stripped the surrounding country that the residents of Jonesboro themselves were in imminent danger of starvation. Now added to their misery, the Atlanta refugees had been set down in the same area. The situation was so serious that General Hood telegraphed

134

Georgia's Governor Joseph E. Brown on September 13, 1864: "The enemy having robbed the people in the vicinity of Jonesborough, I have about 1000 applications daily for rations for people in that quarter. I cannot subsist them. Can you not make arrangements and send food for them?"[20]

After the departure of the residents of Atlanta, the city was occupied almost wholly by the Twentieth Corps under command of General Slocum. Captain George W. Pepper, a war correspondent with the Federal army, was moved to the verge of poetry in describing the town bereft of its citizens. As he looked about him he wrote: "Here are the luxurious homes, now the scenes of no domestic joys; stately warehouses, where no wealthy merchants congregate; beautiful temples where resound no more the organ's swell or the notes of praise."[21]

In October 1864 Atlanta became a hive of activity as Sherman's base of operations against General Hood. The Confederates had circled around Atlanta and reappeared on the Federal line of communications to Chattanooga and the North.[22] General Wheeler's Confederate cavalry was cooperating with Hood to destroy the railroad and so threaten the Federal line of communication to the north that Sherman would be forced to withdraw from Georgia. While Sherman moved against Hood in northern Georgia in his efforts to repair and keep the railroads open, the army livestock at Atlanta began to suffer from the lack of sufficient feed. General Slocum was instructed to send strong foraging parties into the surrounding country to collect all the corn and fodder that could be found.[23] As these heavily armed parties pushed into the countryside Georgia began to feel the heavy hand of waste and destruction even before Sherman set out on his march through the state. On October 21, 1864, the First Brigade with one brigade from each of the divisions of the Twentieth Corps moved out of Atlanta east to Decatur and remained in that vicinity for four days. While loading the wagons with corn and fodder the troops subsisted entirely off the country. Colonel Selfridge of the Forty-sixth Pennsylvania Infantry reported that his brigade's part of this foray yielded "30,000 pounds of corn and 55,230 pounds of fodder, besides large quantities of provisions which were captured by the men and no record kept of the amount."[24] The size and strength of these foraging parties operating out of Atlanta furnish some indication of the extent of the damage done to the surrounding territory. Major Patrick Griffith of the Forty-sixth Pennsylvania Infantry reported that the foraging party which returned to Atlanta on October 26 brought in 800 wagons loaded with corn.[25] These parties were constantly threatened by Confederate cavalry, but were in such strength that little could be done to stop them. The 800-wagon train referred to by Major Griffith was guarded by three brigades of infantry and two batteries of artillery. On October 22, General Slocum, taking no chances, ordered this guard reinforced by the Second Brigade of the Thirteenth New Jersey Infantry.[26]

Although the stated objective of such expeditions was to gather corn and fodder for the thousands of horses and cattle in Atlanta, no troops so accustomed to plundering and pillaging a defenseless citizenry as were Sherman's men could have been expected to restrict themselves to the robbing of cornfields and barns. The fate of the civilians around Jonesboro testified to the fact that they did not confine themselves to fodder gathering alone. Colonel James S. Robinson of the Eighty-second Ohio Infantry moved out of Atlanta around the middle of October to accompany a foraging expedition of 733 wagons. His report said that his party brought back to the city 11,000 bushels of corn and "the troops obtained besides this a considerable quantity of fresh beef, fresh pork, poultry, sweet potatoes, and other species of provisions."[27] Later the same month Colonel Robinson foraged out toward Lawrenceville, Georgia, with only 300 wagons, and the expedition netted about 6,000 bushels of corn. Other items brought in by the party were judiciously clothed by the Colonel in a general statement that the troops secured "the usual amount of provisions and other promiscuous articles."[28] General Alpheus S. Williams, commanding the Twentieth Corps in General Slocum's absence from the army, reported the total results obtained by the expeditions from Atlanta up to the time it was abandoned by the Union army in November. He estimated:

> The four expeditions brought back on an average each of over 650 wagons-loads of corn and fodder, besides consid-

erable subsistence supplies of cattle, sheep, poultry, sweet
potatoes, honey, sirup and the like. The chief quartermaster
of the corps reports as turned over to him from these expeditions, corn, 1,932,468 pounds; fodder, 138,200 pounds.[29]

Thus it was that the citizens of Georgia who lived in the vicinity
of Atlanta began to experience the destructive practices of the
Union soldiers who, hardened to the supplications of many helpless communities in Mississippi, went about their work with energy
and enthusiasm. Had these troops required justification for their
illegal acts, they found it in General Sherman's letter written from
Alabama to General Slocum, their corps commander, on October 23:

> We find abundance of corn and potatoes out here [Ala-
> bama], and enjoy them much. They cost nothing a bushel. If
> Georgia can afford to break our railroads, she can afford to
> feed us. Please preach this doctrine to men who go forth,
> and are likely to spread it.[30]

Georgians north of Atlanta were likewise receiving a bitter
taste of the terrors of unrestricted warfare. Sherman was in command of all the forces in the field north of Atlanta, and he personally directed the Federal efforts to trap General Hood's
Confederates, who were attempting to cut his communications
with Chattanooga. He was no more inclined in Georgia to observe
the rules of war where civilians were concerned than he had been
in Mississippi. A new callousness marked his decisions and further
demonstrated that the only right he acknowledged was that backed
up by might. Previously Sherman had applied the theory of
collective responsibility against noncombatants by levying excessive
costs in destroyed property. In October 1864 he went far beyond
this point when he suggested with shocking callousness that, in addition to the destruction of property, civilians be killed in an area
where attacks had been made on Union communications. Sherman
made the suggestion in a letter to Brigadier General Louis D.
Watkins as casually as he might order a troop movement:

> "Cannot you send over about Fairmount and Adairsville,
> burn ten or twelve houses of known secessionists, kill a few

at random, and let them know that it will be repeated every time a train is fired on from Resaca to Kingston?"[31]

With this request, amounting actually to an order, Sherman now abandoned even the guise of legality. The noncombatants referred to were not charged with being "guerillas." No evidence was offered against them with the possible exception that they were secessionist, which was not strange since the Federal army had invaded the land of secession. Sherman deemed it sufficient, just as he had at Memphis, that the citizens were guilty simply because they lived in a community where unidentified parties had fired on a Federal train. Had he not caused the little river town of Randolph to be wiped out on no more valid evidence? A new element of terror was added to instill fear into a community in Georgia—some of that community's citizens, "chosen at random," were to pay with their lives.

As early as July 1864, while the Federal army was forcing its way toward Atlanta, the people of northern Georgia had realized that there was no assurance of personal safety for any of them. Although the persons of noncombatants were considered inviolate under the rules of war, Sherman had exploded this conception as he had others by ordering the summary arrest of every person employed at the cotton and woolen mills at Roswell Factory in Cobb County, Georgia. These employees, some 400 or 500 in number, mostly women, were to be charged with treason.[32] General Sherman, unhindered by any orthodox ideas, was now making his own rules with an even freer hand than ever. The Roswell factories manufactured both cotton and woolen cloth for the Confederate government, and Sherman reasoned that those who accepted employment which aided the Confederate government were guilty of a treasonable act. General Kenner Garrard's Union cavalry had burned the mills and broken up the equipment on July 6, 1864, and Garrard had been ordered to send the employees to Marietta. In order that there might be no misunderstanding on his subordinate's part, Sherman wrote: "I repeat my orders that you arrest all people, male and female, connected with those factories, no matter what the clamor, and let them foot it under guard, to Marietta, where I will send them by cars to the north."[33]

Sherman had written General Halleck on July 9, 1864, that the employees at Roswell Factory were "tainted with treason," and he intended to transport them bodily to Indiana "to get rid of them here."[34] This act of Sherman's had transcended any measures that he had yet taken against the noncombatants of the South. What was the crime of these citizens, and how had their guilt been established? The charges against them were that they had sought to earn their livelihoods in mills owned by the Confederate government. The sentence meted out by Sherman was that they should be torn away from their homes, friends and loved ones to be set adrift in new and foreign surroundings many hundreds of miles away. No justification could be offered for this action. The mill workers offered no threat to the Union army, as the equipment and machines which they might have used to continue their trade had been demolished. Sherman offered no justification other than his statement to General Halleck that sending these people away to try to earn a living in Indiana would "get rid of them" in Georgia. The war in Georgia was being conducted more and more according to the whim of the commanding officer of the invading army. *The Cincinnati Commercial* had remarked on this unorthodox measure by stating with some delicacy that "the capture was a novel one in the history of war."[35]

The prisoners had arrived in Marietta to await transportation to the North. General George H. Thomas, Union commandant at Marietta, observed their forlorn appearance, and apparently with some doubt as to the wisdom of Sherman's action, he had written to him on July 10, 1864: "The Roswell factory hands, 400 or 500 in number, have arrived at Marietta. The most of them are women. I can only order them transportation to Nashville where it seems hard to turn them adrift. What had best be done with them?"[36] The cruelty of the act had not impressed Sherman, who had relented only enough to inform General Garrard, the arresting officer, that he might "let them take along their children and clothing, provided they have the means of hauling or you can spare them."[37] He had ignored General Thomas's feeling that it was hard on these women and children, and had informed Thomas that he had arranged for them to be forwarded from Nashville to Indiana.[38]

While awaiting railroad cars the prisoners were confined in the old Seminary Building near Marietta. A soldier of the One Hundredth Indiana Infantry Regiment was a member of the detail which stood guard over the women, and he recalled what a difficult job it was to keep the Union soldiers away from them. "General Sherman says he would rather try to guard [sic] the whole Confederate Army, and I guess he is about right about it," he wrote.[39] Stories persist, however, in Cobb County until the present day concerning the brutal offenses committed against these women prisoners by Northern soldiers.[40]

Sherman's subordinate commanders followed his lead in their attitude toward the noncombatants in the areas in which their troops operated. On October 30, 1864, General John E. Smith, commanding the Fifteenth Corps, formerly Sherman's own, ordered Colonel Heath of the Fifth Ohio Volunteer Cavalry to proceed to Canton, Georgia, "where you will permit the citizens to remove what they desire, and burn the town, after which you will proceed to Cassville and make the same disposition as at Canton."[41] Usually in such cases this severe retaliation was visited upon towns or communities where Union foraging parties had been attacked or fired upon. This cold execution, differing from the firing of homes by impassioned soldiers, was given official sanction and demonstrated how harshly Sherman's officers applied their commander's theory of collective responsibility. It would be impossible to calculate the number of unfortunate people who were thus made homeless and who were forced to move out into the countryside to wander as refugees. There were countless numbers of these desperate people as shown by a brief but disclosing statement found in a divisional journal which indicated how they tried to force their way onto a Union train. Under date of November 12, 1864, the writer noted that the "last train passed up at 10:30; great excitement among the refugees; all assisted in keeping them off."[42] This was in the vicinity of Cartersville, where great damage had been done to the countryside. Where these people had to be beaten away from the train, others walked through the ruined areas carrying all that they could in packs and bundles.

In addition to towns and communities burned in retaliation,

Union commanders selected particular individuals who were to be punished through loss of their property. In many cases protesting citizens were charged with complicity in attacks on foragers and were arrested and jailed without trial.

General John E. Smith, who had ordered the burning of Canton and Cassville on October 30, on the same day issued the following order from his headquarters at Cartersville:

> Commanding Officer Forage Escort:
> Sir: You will burn the houses belonging to Joe Davis, Jolly, and Payne. The houses will be designated by your guide, who will report to you at Capt. H. Skinner's office.[43]

In November, Colonel Thomas Morgan was sent under Sherman's direct orders to search out and arrest "a list of men who were said to be more or less implicated with the guerillas."[44] With one William Lowry assigned as a guide, Colonel Morgan proceeded with his regiment to the neighborhood where the attack on the Union foragers had been made. He arrested the first men he met on the road and then others on the list. One of the arrested men was a Captain Hendricks, who claimed to be an officer of the First Georgia Cavalry. These men, civilians with the exception of Hendricks, were questioned, but no trial of any kind was conducted. His report shows that on the basis of his questioning he proceeded to mete out sentences on the spot: "Captain Denman's house was burned. Just as the goods were removed a 'charge' was blown, . . . Lindsay Hendricks' buildings were burned, and so was Wash. Henderson's house."[45] The citizens who were arrested were brought in and placed in custody of the provost marshal.

The next step in Sherman's campaign of terror against northern Georgians was the seizure of those living in communities where attacks were made on his ruthless foraging parties preying on a defenseless citizenry. Those so arrested were to be held as hostages for the return of captured Union troops. This violation of the rules of war was as cruel as any yet perpetrated by Sherman. The holding of hostages has ever been considered one of the most barbarous practices in war, as it holds individuals in jeopardy of life and limb and subject to loss of property for acts completely beyond their control. The fate of the hostage depends not on his own acts but upon those of others, and he is selected and held, not because of his own guilt, but upon the premise that fears for the hostage's safety may bring the guilty party to light. Halleck's *International Law,* in the section dealing with the rights of noncombatants in occupied territory, made it clear that no individual could be justly charged with the guilt of a personal crime for the acts of a community of which he is a member.[46] Although Sherman was fully acquainted with the "book," he did not hesitate to issue the following order to the commanding officer at Cartersville:

> Arrest some six or eight citizens known or supposed to be hostile. Let one or two go free to carry word to the guerilla band that you give them forty-eight hour's notice that unless all the men of ours picked up by them in the past two days are returned, Kingston, Cassville, and Cartersville will be burned, as also the houses of those arrested.[47]

Sherman here used the word "guerilla" as loosely as he had learned to do in his days at Memphis. It was a convenient word which he used to apply to any force or member of a military unit who dared attack Federal soldiers. It is interesting to note that Sherman used the designation "guerilla" far more frequently than did any of his subordinates. It seemed to offer at least a verbal justification for retaliation against those who did not receive his soldiers with open arms. Most of the references to attacks on foraging parties were attributed by the officers making the reports to "rebel cavalry." It is very doubtful that there were any organized guerilla bands in North Georgia in the fall of 1864, since no record of any such bands is found in Confederate correspondence of the period. Confederate cavalry units, in most cases operating under General Joe Wheeler's orders, were active against Sherman's foragers, the railroads and other units of the Federal army which were not too formidable for them to tackle. Sherman's charge of "guerilla" against these Confederate bands left the desired impression and permitted him to employ against the people the harshest measures he could devise.

On November 9, 1864, General Sherman's aide-de-camp, L. M. Dayton, requested that General Jeff C. Davis, Fourteenth Corps commander, secure hostages for men captured from his guard. He informed General Davis:

> Yesterday a small squad of my guard foraging were attacked, 1 mortally wounded, 1 slightly and the remainder, 7, were captured by some guerillas. The general commanding [Sherman] wishes you to send out a regiment in the vicinity where it occurred, seize some citizens, and send on to inform the enemy he must bring those men and all others captured in same manner back at once. They must be returned by tomorrow noon, else the regiment will burn a dozen houses in retaliation.[48]

The citizens seized by the regimental commander receiving these orders were duly brought in and General Jeff C. Davis received instructions as to their disposition. One was to be permitted to return to his home, while another, Hendricks, was "to be kept in confinement beyond a possibility of escape during the war."

> The other men arrested you will send under good guard to Chattanooga, to be imprisoned and held as hostages for the return of the wounded soldier at Houck's house, and 31 of our soldiers whom they admit having unlawfully captured and made prisoners.[49]

While foraging parties roamed and ranged northern Georgia, and every form of intimidation was employed by Federal commanders to subjugate the citizens, other towns and villages suffered destruction or serious damage at the hands of the invading armies. A Federal officer passing north to join General George H. Thomas at Chattanooga entered in his journal a glimpse of Dalton, Georgia:

> Dalton has been almost destroyed by the different armies that have been in it. Houses have been torn down, many being first stripped of the clapboarding to make bunks, etc., for the soldiers, and the remainder gradually destroyed for

firewood and the like. It was manifestly a pretty town once, and in a beautiful situation.[50]

Marietta, 20 miles north of Atlanta, had known the horrors of war for many months. Northern troops passing through there on November 14, 1864, saw its funeral pyre. A Federal colonel noted that "all the principal buildings around the public square in this town were burning as we passed. General Sherman was standing looking on."[51]

Major Hitchcock, Sherman's Assistant Adjutant General, sat his horse at the general's side as the courthouse burned and its flames spread to other buildings on the square at Marietta. Sherman assured Hitchcock that such occurrences could not be prevented, that the soldiers were the guilty ones and even the guards could not stop them. The same afternoon General Sherman with his staff rode out to a field near Marietta to review Kilpatrick's cavalry. Hitchcock pictures the scene as the cheering horsemen clattered by in review before the commanding general, while "a mile off on the right, lay Marietta, from which rose columns [of] black smoke and lurid flame—terrible commentary on this display and its real meaning."[52] Major James Connolly of General Absolom's staff, wrote in his diary for November 14, 1864: "When we reached Marietta we found that all the business part of town was burned by Kilpatrick's cavalry last night."[53]

Major Connolly had witnessed the burning of Acworth, Georgia, by the troops of the Fourteenth Corps the day before. Acworth had been a thriving railroad town, but that night Major Connolly noted in his diary, "it is a heap of ruins." He had tried to prevent the firing of the town but finally seeing it was hopeless, he had given up. He had succeeded "in saving a few houses occupied by 'war widows' and their families, but all the rest of the town went up in smoke."[54] This officer recognized the lack of discipline of the Union soldiers and their contempt for individual and property rights. He stated in his notes that "it is evident that our soldiers are determined to burn, plunder and destroy everything in their way on this march." The major showed an awareness of the intense hatreds engendered in Southern hearts by the humiliations and cruelties visited on them when he entered in his diary at Acworth, Georgia: "If we are to continue our devastations as we began today, I don't want to be captured on this trip, for I expect every man of us the rebels capture will get a 'stout rope and a short shrift.' "[55]

Rome, in Floyd County, was almost completely destroyed. The Union forces had occupied the town since early May 1864. In October, Sherman, following Hood's movements north of Atlanta, feared that Hood would attack the Federal garrison there and rushed heavy reinforcements to General John M. Corse, the Union commander at Rome. General Hood did pass within a few miles of the city, but crossed the Coosa River above and moved his columns on into northeast Alabama. On October 10, 1864, from Allatoona, Sherman had telegraphed explicit instructions to General Corse in the event Rome was attacked. Referring to General Hood, he wired: "In case he attacks, I wish you to burn down every house in Rome that interferes with your range of fire."[56]

General Corse, with his command, moved out of Rome to drive off three brigades of Wheeler's cavalry, reported in the vicinity of Dirt Town, Chattooga County,[57] 10 or 15 miles from Rome. It must have been these troops who visited Mrs. Naomi P. Bales at her father's plantation in Dirt Town Valley. She stated:

> On Oct. 14 and 15 the center of Sherman's army passed, following Hood. . . . Again our home was pillaged from foundation to attic. Large army wagons were loaded to the brim with corn, fodder and wheat; cows and hogs were driven off or shot, smokehouses stripped, pantries cleaned of every movable article, and such as could not be carried off was broken or damaged. The negroes huddled together in their houses, like sheep among wolves, scared out of their wits and frightened almost white.[58]

After the soldiers had thoroughly ransacked the house and broken or rendered useless everything they could not carry, the Federal wagoners descended on the wrecked home. Mrs. Bales said that a guard had been left with them for four hours, but was withdrawn, and then "we were at the mercy of 'wagon dogs.' " These men locked Mrs. Bales and her sister in a room, and while one of them guarded the door, the others thoroughly "ransacked bureau drawers, wardrobes, turned up mattresses, etc." Failing to discover anything of value, the prowlers threatened to strip the two women to search them, but apparently left them alone because of their tearful entreaties. It was just as well the women were not forced to submit to a search of their voluminous hoop skirts since Mrs. Bales confessed:

> I had several thousand dollars in Confederate money in a bustle around my waist, and my small amount of jewelry and a few keepsakes in huge pockets under my hoops. Em [her stepsister] had her jewelry and silver forks and spoons in pockets under her hoop.[59]

The passage of the Union troops through Dirt Town Valley left this woman with the very real problem of providing sufficient food to sustain not only her family, but a large number of slaves. They were reduced to eating whatever they could get. It was a depressing story she told:

> For three weeks a hundred in our family (including slaves) literally lived from hand to mouth. We picked up scraps of potatoes left in the fields, small scattered turnips and meat from the carcasses left by the Yankees and dragged in by the negroes. The new corn left was sufficiently soft to be grated on graters constructed from mutilated tinware.[60]

This family's experience was not an exceptional one. Sherman's soldiers, hardened and trained in hundreds of communities, did their usual thorough job of devastating the farms and homes and wasting the resources of the area. Mrs. Bales stated that "after the Federals had passed, desolation was writ throughout the valley." Judge John Maddox of Rome later said that "all the Yankees left in Chattooga County was a broken-down steer that was not fit to be eaten by man or beast."[61]

Rome's fate was sealed on November 4, 1864, when General Sherman ordered Brigadier General Corse to hold himself in readiness to evacuate the town. The instructions assured Corse that General Sherman would give him as much notice in advance as possible in order "that you destroy in the most effective manner, by fire, or otherwise, all bridges, warehouses, and buildings, especially adapted to armed use, lumber and timber,"[62] and everything that he could not move.

Sherman's order to Corse was one of the many preliminary notices to his commanders that he was now almost ready to undertake a new large-scale movement. On November 8, 1864, through Special Field Orders No. 11 issued from his headquarters at Kingston, the commanding general felt it proper to divulge to the officers and men of the Fourteenth, Fifteenth, Seventeenth and Twentieth Corps the special purpose for which they had been welded into an army. He informed them that the whole army was to cut loose from its present base to undertake a long and difficult march to a new one. All surplus equipment and all men unfit for strenuous duty were to be sent north on the railroad, and where it was impractical to ship surplus material it was to be destroyed. Detailed orders would be issued later, but all units were to stand by for an immediate movement to Atlanta.

On November 10, 1864, General Corse received orders to wreck Rome and proceed with his command to Atlanta.[63] He apparently found his instructions so much to his taste that he gave the job his personal attention. It was he who had been on one occasion even more impetuous than Sherman in his callous disregard of the rights of noncombatants and his contempt for the rules of war. In October he had made a direct request of General Sherman to permit him to punish "one or two regiments of Texas cavalry" who were disrupting Federal communications. This he proposed to do by "burning Cedartown, Van West, and Buchanan . . . for atrocities committed by gangs of thieves having their rendezvous at those places."[64] This had been a little bit too much even for General Sherman, who had dampened Corse's zeal with a telegram the next day: "Wait a little before burning those towns, till we see what Hood is going to attempt."[65] Now in November Hood offered no threat, and Corse could proceed without restraint. The residents of Rome learned to their sorrow on the night of November 10, 1864, just how well deserved was the sobriquet "Corse, the torch,"[66] said to have been given him by Sherman himself. Several witnesses described the scene:

> Never had a scene of such wantonness and misery been presented to Rome. Dry goods boxes and trash were piled high in stores and set off, and the crackling of the timbers furnished a melancholy echo to the wails of women and children. Soldiers ran from place to place with firebrands in their hands, setting the places designated here, and perfectly harmless places there. Necessarily the stores and shops next to the condemned improvements went up in smoke. With hundreds of bayonets bristling the 40 steadfast male Romans could do nothing but watch and allow their souls to fill with regret.[67]

The Union soldiers did their usual thorough job in wrecking Rome. They destroyed, in addition to the stores and shops, two depots, Cunningham's cotton warehouse, the bank, the Etowah Hotel and Cohen's grist mill. They employed impressive and reverberating powder blasts to level the great brick smoke stacks of the Noble Foundry, after which they put the building to the torch. According to eyewitness accounts:

> Only isolated structures escaped, until there was no place much to do business, and less business to do than places. A livery stable caught, and the odor of burning horseflesh could be detected for several blocks. The whinnies of the horses told of their awful plight.[68]

In those little homes which escaped the flames because of their distance from the town, frightened women sat trying to rise above their own fears to comfort their children. One of these women described the peculiar manner in which she sought to retain her sanity. She wrote to her husband at Selma, Alabama, a few days after the soldiers had gone:

> The night the town was burned I was all alone, except for my little children. I cannot describe my feelings. I did not know what to do, so I went to washing, and washed

two or three dozen pieces. . . . I passed the night away somehow and am still alive. But I must not write you all these things.[69]

By nine o'clock on the morning of November 11, 1864, the Federal army had evacuated the wrecked town. Rome had been described by Brigadier General Jacob D. Cox of the Union army as "one of the pleasantest towns we have found in the South,"[70] but it was left a desolate place of sorrow by the Union army. One of those who remained described the ruined town:

> Two days later [after the evacuation] there was not a soldier of either army to be seen. The streets were entirely deserted. Everything was as still and quiet as if no war was in progress. The business section was dead; only a little drug store was left, and that kept by Dr. J. H. Nowlin. The 40 men left behind organized a patrol force for the protection of their homes.[71]

The destruction of Rome could under no circumstances have been dictated by military necessity. It had not been attacked, and all its industry, railroad connections, bridges and buildings which might have been of use to the Confederate army had been destroyed. No excuse can be found which would justify the burning of store buildings and private residences. Their gaunt chimneys stood as monuments to the needless waste of a people's resources by a soldiery long accustomed to expressing its unbridled passions against defenseless citizens.

For several days preceding November 15, 1864, the roads north of Atlanta were congested with the ranks of blue as the various units of the Federal army converged on Atlanta. As they marched, each unit destroyed its assigned section of railroad, effectively isolating northern Georgia from other sections of the Confederacy. Sherman was now prepared to launch his columns into the heart of Georgia "on a worse raid than our Meridian raid was," and he assured a friend, "you may look for a great howl against the brute Sherman."[72]

On November 11, 1864, Captain O. M. Poe, Sherman's Chief Engineering Officer at Atlanta, received the long-awaited order from the General to begin the destruction of the city. Sherman's telegram instructed Captain Poe to begin at once, "but don't use fire until the last moment."[73] The Second Massachusetts Infantry, constituting the Atlanta Post command, was ordered "to protect from accidental or wanton fire and destruction all buildings not designated to be destroyed."[74] Men doubtless took their assignment seriously but found themselves impotent to handle the great surge of troops passing through the town. The soldiers, many of them blackened by the smoke of towns they had burned so recently in northern Georgia, were subjected to an almost irresistible urge to take part in the firing of Atlanta. The post commander felt that his troops deserved praise for what they did accomplish at a time "when the excitement of so great a conflagration was almost overpowering."[75] Captain Poe stated that insofar as the engineer troops were concerned "the work was done in a proper and orderly manner," but a great amount of destruction was done "by lawless persons, who, by sneaking around in blind alleys, succeeded in firing many houses which it was not intended to touch."[76] Captain Conyngham, a war correspondent on Sherman's staff, had no illusions as to who these "lawless persons" were. He recounted that "the first fire burst out on the night of Friday the 11th of November, in a block of wooden tenements on Decatur Street, where eight buildings were destroyed."[77] Fires followed in rapid succession in various parts of the city. Conyngham did not hesitate in stating that "these certainly were the works of some of the soldiers, who expected to get some booty under cover of the fires." Remembering the long experience of Sherman's soldiers in such destruction, it is not difficult to understand the writer's statement that "it was hard to restrain the soldiers from burning it down."[78]

Atlanta was doomed from the start, and on the morning of November 16, 1864, presented a dark picture of smoldering ashes and gaunt walls. The adjutant of the Thirty-second Illinois noted that "when the morning came, it is doubtful whether there were a score of buildings remaining in the city, except in the very outskirts."[79] The city was almost consumed by November 15 according to Lieutenant Colonel Joel C. Martin, who reported that he "reached the ruins of Atlanta" on that date with the

Seventeenth New York Volunteers.[80] Captain George W. Pepper, a staff officer, noted, "Clouds of smoke, as we passed through, were bursting from several princely mansions." On Whitehall Street he noticed that every house of any pretensions was burned.[81] Pepper described the appearance of the dying town as he saw it that same night from his camp on the outskirts:

> In the solemn starlight we could see the billows of smoke rolling up from the city of Atlanta. Such clouds of smoke, and vast sheets of flame, mortal eye has seldom seen. The whole region for miles was lighted up with a strange and indescribable glare.[82]

The destruction of Atlanta was accomplished with even greater efficiency than the Union armies under Sherman's command had demonstrated at Jackson, Meridian and Rome. There were an estimated 3,800 houses within the city limits of Atlanta. When the explosions ceased and the flames died down there remained approximately 400 standing.[83] It is estimated that eleven-twelfths of the city was burned, including shops, depots, mills, dwellings and stores. Several places of business were left standing on Alabama Street.[84] Catholic priest Father O'Reilly succeeded in persuading the soldiers to spare the houses in the vicinity of the Roman Catholic Church. The Protestant Churches apparently had no such persuasive advocates, and the Methodist, Christian and African Churches were all consumed. Colonel Avery, a Confederate officer, rendered inactive by wounds, said that "in and about Atlanta the destruction of houses was four thousand five hundred." He accompanied General Howell Cobb, who commanded the Georgia militia, on one of the first visits to "the destroyed and deserted city and it presented a sad spectacle of ruin and desolation." The Federals were determined to leave the despoiled town a place of pestilence and decay, and had shot their jaded horses and the weaker cattle before leaving Atlanta. Colonel Avery reported that "three thousand carcasses of animals lay in the streets." Sherman's men had shown no more respect for the dead than for the quick, and in the cemetery they had rifled the vaults or coffins from which they had stripped all the silver fittings. A personal representative sent by Georgia's Governor Brown to make an official report on the condition of Atlanta confirmed this robbing of graves in Atlanta's cemeteries. The Union army dumped the bodies from metal caskets, which they used to ship their own dead to the North.[85]

A commission was sent to Atlanta by Governor Brown of Georgia to investigate and make an official report on the extent of the damage. The report of this committee, written by W. P. Howard, its chairman, was published in newspapers throughout the Confederacy.[86] The editorial comments on the report, read by a people already aware of impending defeat, served to cultivate further the seeds of hatred. The people of the South began to see General Sherman as the embodiment of that hatred which the majority of the people of the North felt toward them. *The Columbus* (Georgia) *Times* told its readers without hesitation that Sherman was "a true representative of the North. Each act of his meets with a response in the hearts of that depraved people."[87]

An editorial in *The Canton American Citizen* captioned "Yankee Vandalism in Atlanta" probably more nearly expressed the feelings of Georgians as well as others who felt that all law was being replaced by utter disregard for the sacredness of human life and property. The editorial declared:

> The vandalism of the enemy exceeds belief, and were it not authenticated by an official report, could hardly be credited. The destruction of property, private as well as public, was almost universal. . . . For this barbarous conduct on the part of Sherman there is neither palliation nor excuse. No military necessity, whatever, can be pleaded in extenuation of it. During the whole time the Federals occupied Atlanta, the town was not even threatened by our forces. It was not even menaced with attack. Therefore the burning of a large city and the destruction of millions of dollars of private property, stands forth before the world as an act of monstrous and wanton wickedness, for which no apology can be made. It was done through sheer, unadulterated malice.[88]

VIII

⁀ℜℜ⁀ℜℜ⁀ℜℜ⁀ℜℜ

From Atlanta to the Sea

Special Field Orders No. 120 were issued at Kingston, Georgia, on November 9, 1864. These orders, described by General Sherman as "so clear, emphatic, and well-digested, that no account of that historic event is perfect without them,"[1] were to govern the movements and conduct of the Federal columns in their march through Georgia to the sea. Section IV, dealing with the manner in which the individual brigades should forage on the country, is of particular interest in view of the past performance of these same soldiers in Mississippi and northern Georgia. The opening statement of Section IV said: "The army will forage liberally on the country during the march." However, it was specifically ordered that none but regularly appointed foraging parties were to perform this important function "under the command of one or more discreet officers."[2] Officially designated foraging parties were to operate near the route followed by the army, gathering only such supplies as were necessary to the welfare of their respective commands. The orders were explicit as to the conduct of the rank and file: "Soldiers must not enter dwellings of the inhabitants, or commit any trespass, but during a halt or a camp they may be permitted to gather turnips, potatoes, and other vegetables, and to drive in stock within sight of their camp."[3]

The destruction of property in the country to be penetrated by the troops was treated by Sherman. Enemy property could be destroyed only with the approval of an army corps commander, and these top-rank officers were to be guided by broad principles included in the orders. Where the Federal army moved unmolested and unhindered through the country private property was to be respected:

> . . . but should guerillas or bushwackers molest our march, or should the inhabitants burn bridges, obstruct roads, or otherwise manifest local hostility, then army commanders should order and enforce a devastation more or less relentless according to the measure of such hostility.

Section VI cautioned foraging parties that they should use discretion in seizing supplies from the citizens in order that the burden of the losses should rest more heavily on the rich and better provided than upon the poor in each community. In every case, the relations between Union foragers and civilian populace was to be marked by courtesy on the part of the Federal soldiers. Under no circumstances was threatening or abusive language to be used against the people, and foraging officers were to "endeavor to leave with each family a reasonable portion for their maintenance."[4]

It is difficult to escape the conviction that these orders were issued by Sherman more for the record than for the governing of his troops' actions in the forthcoming campaign. No one knew better than he that the men who were to march under these orders were hardened veterans. No one knew better than he the history of the various regiments and brigades under his command. Many of these men had participated in Sherman's first experiments in total war in the fall of 1862 on the Mississippi River around Memphis. Most of them had enthusiastically carried out his unwritten orders to devastate northern Mississippi. The supplications of terrified women and children and of old men left these soldiers unmoved. Waste, burning, looting were an old story to them. Long had they indulged themselves in unrestricted war against a defenseless people. They had learned long since to ignore the rights of noncombatants and to recognize no law but that enforced by the bright blades of their bayonets. Sherman's men knew their general too well to believe that he intended to subject them to law just at the moment they were to strike deep into the Confederacy's vitals. Finally, the order was completely at variance with Sherman's well-developed philosophy and practices of war.

The men stood in ranks of blue on the outskirts of Atlanta while Special Field Orders No. 120 were read to them. The acrid smoke from the dying city stung their nostrils making a travesty of the carefully phrased instructions. The conduct of both officers and men in Sherman's army would show how they felt toward the restrictions on their behavior contained in the orders for the march. Sherman would permit his own soldiers to throw into his face the phrase "forage liberally," as they passed him carrying their booty from some private home openly in their hands.[5] Even his own corps commanders were confident that Sherman did not intend for his orders to be carried out insofar as the conduct of the soldiers was concerned. Regimental commanders who might have wished to enforce the orders as published finally had to admit defeat in their efforts to prevent straggling "owing to the indifference of line and noncommissioned officers."[6]

On November 15, 1864, the Federal army, clothed in the respectability of Sherman's orders, was put into motion, and like a pent-up flood the waves of blue rolled into the Georgia countryside. Some 60,000 men, selected for their physical fitness, made up the army, divided into two wings, each wing composed of two corps. The cavalry, under command of General Kilpatrick, was to operate independently and wherever needed, subject to General Sherman's orders. The Right Wing, General Oliver O. Howard commanding, marched eastward toward Jonesboro, accompanied by the cavalry. The Left Wing, with General Henry W. Slocum commanding, aimed further to the east via Decatur, Stone Mountain and Madison. General Sherman remained behind until the morning of November 16, 1864, to permit the Fourteenth Corps to complete the destruction around Atlanta. He later described the scene as he turned his back on the ruins of

Atlanta and rode toward the interior of Georgia. Away in the distance could be seen the rear of General Howard's marching columns, an early sun reflected from the gun barrels of the troops. The Fourteenth Corps, with whom he rode, stepped crisply down the road, quickening their pace when a band suddenly filled the air with the strains of "John Brown's Body." There was a holiday spirit in the air—a feeling of recklessness which boded ill for the noncombatants deep in Georgia who had thus far escaped the terrifying sound of the marching feet of an invading army.

Sherman's drive into Georgia, after cutting his lines of communication to the North, was highly dramatized for the people of the Union. It was held up as a feat of great daring and those who dropped out of sight with the Federal armies into the silent fastnesses of Georgia were marked men to be pointed out as local heroes upon their return to their homes on the farms and in the towns of the North and West. General Sherman himself contributed his part to the excellent publicity campaign which has made the story of "the march to the sea" familiar to every schoolboy. His letters to Generals Grant and Halleck made frequent mention of the risks involved in marching through the heart of the enemy's country. Sherman capitalized on the elements of suspense to hold attention by keeping the destination of his army a secret. He later expressed surprise, however, that the march through Georgia had so captured the public imagination. In his estimation, he said, the march was simply "a means to an end" in which he succeeded in moving his base from Atlanta to Savannah. He regarded the movement of his army through South Carolina as ten times as important as that through Georgia.[7]

The march to the sea cannot be fully understood or properly evaluated without some knowledge of the military situation in Georgia in the late fall of 1864. There were no defenders worthy of the name on Georgia's soil. General Hood's withdrawal from the state removed the last organized and effective force of Confederate troops. Georgia was left to be defended by an inadequate state militia, composed largely of boys of sixteen and younger and men of fifty-five and older. General Robert Toombs, in command of the Georgia State Guard, the third regiment of which had helped man the entrenchments during the defense of Atlanta, tried to remain "in front of Sherman as a forlorn observation force to lessen in such slight measure as it could the devastation of the country."[8] The *levy en masse* ordered by Governor Brown on November 19, 1864, making every able-bodied man in the state between the ages of sixteen and fifty-five liable to immediate military service,[9] did not prove effective. The State Guard, recognizing its own impotence in the face of the well-equipped Federal columns, marched hard and courageously on a line parallel to Sherman's route and actually arrived at Savannah before he did. The Confederate cavalry under General Joe Wheeler rode and fought their hearts out in a futile effort to obstruct and delay the Union forces. All the way to Savannah the Confederate horsemen rode the flanks of the blue columns hoping for an opportunity to slip through the protecting screen of General Kilpatrick's Federal cavalry. General Wheeler issued a circular to his command in December 1864 ordering his commanders to have citizens in the line of Sherman's army drive their livestock out of reach. This vain effort to delay the invaders amounted almost to an admission that the Confederate cavalry was powerless to stem the tide.[10] Infantry was needed to oppose infantry, and Governor Brown wrote in bitterness to Confederate Secretary of War Seddon:

> During the period of Sherman's march from Atlanta to Milledgeville, there were not one thousand men, of all the veteran infantry regiments and battalions of Georgians, now in Confederate service, upon the soil of this State. Nor did troops from other States fill their places.[11]

Old Edmund Ruffin, confirmed rebel and bitter critic of the Confederate administration, saw Georgia's plight and recorded in his diary that Sherman's feint on Macon had drawn all available troops—a relatively small number—to that point, which "forces are now in Sherman's rear—and their following on his route will be greatly impeded by his destruction of the roads, bridges, and the provisions of the country."[12]

The press of Georgia at first expressed a disbelief that Sher-

man would attempt a march which one editor branded as "chi-
merical" and "preposterous."[13] Convinced, however, that the
Federal columns were continuing to forge relentlessly ahead, the
newspapers sounded a note of confidence that Georgians would
make every sacrifice, even to destroying their own supplies, to
rout and ruin "the best appointed and most active army of the
United States."[14] The newspapers reflected and probably contributed to the confusion and uncertainty of the Confederate authorities as to just where Sherman would strike.[15] There can be little
question that General Sherman directed his columns in Georgia
with a masterly hand, and his feints, first at Macon, then at Augusta, rendered ineffective what little military strength there was
in the state. Those in command in Georgia consolidated military
strength in defense of the important towns, leaving the devastating columns of the Union army to blast a path of destruction
through the heart of the state.

Both men and officers of Sherman's command remarked on
the absence of any determined Confederate resistance to their
progress through Georgia. A soldier of an Illinois infantry regiment noted in his diary in December that "we have not heard
a rebel gun since the 22nd of last month [November 1864].
They don't trouble our march a particle."[16] An officer on General O. O. Howard's staff stated that General Sherman's orders
required early starts and steady marching in order to cover as
much ground as possible. He declared that this was accomplished
with ease because there was "no need of massing as there is no
enemy to speak of."[17] General Frank P. Blair, commanding the
Seventeenth Corps, in his report on the march to the sea said
that "the opposition from the enemy throughout our entire march
was comparatively nothing."[18] Major General Henry W. Slocum
did not consider the opposition offered the Left Wing of the
Federal army even worthy of mention in his report.[19] The rank
and file of the Union armies, relieved of the dangers of attack
and the fear of sudden death, exhibited "an exuberance and
hilarity of spirit more indicative of a festive excursion than an
exposed and fatiguing campaign."[20]

Major Hitchcock, of Sherman's staff, recounts how the Federal
officers laughed over the stirring proclamations issued by Con-

federate General Beauregard and Georgia's Senator B. H. Hill.[21] Phrased in ringing words, the proclamations called on the citizens of Georgia to strike wherever possible to destroy the invader. They were to "remove all provisions from the path of the enemy," and to delay him as much as possible, "every citizen with his gun, and every negro, with his spade and axe," was to obstruct the invader's progress.[22] General Beauregard urged Georgia's citizens to delay the Federal army in every way possible by setting up obstructions in Sherman's front, flank and rear. The people of Georgia must be confident and resolute, he said, and "trust in an overruling Providence."[23] The Federal soldiers read these appeals in newspapers captured in Milledgeville, and they seem to have had greater influence upon Sherman's actions than upon those of the citizens to whom they were addressed. To render these appeals ineffective Sherman acted immediately through the issuance of Special Field Orders No. 127 from his headquarters at Milledgeville on November 23, 1864. All division, brigade and regimental commanders were warned in the orders to pay more attention to foraging and instructed to "deal harshly with the inhabitants" where obstructions were set up by citizens. Should the citizens attempt to burn corn or forage on the Federal army's route, "houses, barns, and cotton-gins must also be burned to keep them company."[24]

The Union commander realized full well that the only great danger his army faced while deep in Georgia was that of delay. While he had no great concern for supplies and knew he could subsist on the country, his ammunition wagons could transport only a limited amount of cartridges and artillery shells. Had he been delayed and forced to expend his ammunition, he might have been forced to capitulate[25] or at least to suffer heavy casualties. General Sherman therefore made certain that the warning in his orders reached citizens in the communities through which he was to pass. Already the stories of the horrors which attended the march of his troops had gone before him, creating fear and terror which he exploited to its fullest capacity. The citizens of Georgia were in a very real dilemma. Any move on their part to impede the invading army meant utter destruction of all their possessions. They were at the mercy even of their neighbors and would be held responsible for any effort in their communities to resist the enemy. On the other hand, if their homes lay in the path of the invader, their property might still be forfeit if the reports of Sherman's destructiveness were true. There could be no unity of action. Under the pressure of imminent danger, the people of Georgia acted as individuals, each concerned with his own problem, each reluctant to destroy his own property. Perhaps the Federal army would take another road—perhaps the soldiers would take only food and livestock, and supplies of food could be concealed until the army passed. Just as easily livestock could be hidden in the swamps or canebrakes. Thus, held in a paralysis of fear, nurturing a spark of hope that he might be fortunate enough to escape, the Georgian, with few exceptions, did nothing. To their sorrow comparatively few of them in Sherman's path escaped serious losses of one kind or another, and countless others lost everything they had. Again terror played its role in General Sherman's remorseless war against noncombatants.

It was through this defenseless country that the Federal legions marched rather than fought their way to the sea. The reports of private soldiers as well as those of the highest-ranking officers, almost without exception, recount in glowing terms the excellent fare of the Union army on its march. A profusion of vegetables lent variety to ordinary army rations. They surfeited themselves on choice cuts of beef and pork, leaving the balance of the carcasses to rot and poison the air. They dipped their cornbread in ham gravy or in the sorghum and honey to which they helped themselves so plenteously and wastefully. No wonder that the acting medical director could report to General O. O. Howard that the health of the Army of the Tennessee "has been peculiarly gratifying" due, among other factors, he said, to "the abundance of nutritious food, and particularly of vegetables." He reported that less than two percent of the army was unfit for duty during the whole march.[26] The incidence of illness in the other corps of the Federal ranks was likewise surprisingly low, with many commanders pointing out that their commands were more robust at the conclusion of the march than they had been on leaving Atlanta.

Georgia's bumper crop of foodstuff for both men and livestock was not due to accident. As early as February 1864 the newspapers, echoing the policy of the Confederate government, urged Georgians to raise food crops on every foot of available land. "We earnestly implore all owners of and occupants of land; all gardeners, who have the smallest spot of garden to manage" to raise provisions in the spring of 1864, said *The Augusta Weekly Chronicle & Sentinel*.[27] The papers pointed out that the more cereals a farmer grew the larger number of cattle, hogs and other stock he could raise. "Let everyone who has land resolve to plant as much corn as he can plow," continued the editor. In addition, heavy plantings of peas, beans, small grains and peanuts were recommended. Edmund Ruffin, the South's most outstanding agriculturist as well as one of its most ardent rebels, saw no way in which Georgia could hope to starve Sherman out. "Owing to a combination of circumstances," he noted in his diary in November 1864, "Ga. [*sic*], is now more abundantly supplied with provisions than at any previous time, and perhaps as much so as any extensive country can be."[28] Ruffin pointed out that Georgians had reduced, if not almost entirely given up, their planting of cotton and had more than doubled their planting and cultivation of food crops. The extra crops had had the benefit of "a remarkably propitious and fruitful season." The bitter old diarist bemoaned the fact that nearly all this bountiful crop had just been gathered, where it lay at the convenience of the marauding army. The farmers were just beginning to kill and cure their meats for storage in smokehouse and pantry.[29] There was nothing to prevent Sherman's men from feasting off a country rich in good food. The cattle and horses of the Union army fared equally well on the plentiful grain and fodder. General Slocum, commander of the Left Wing, estimated that his troops took five million pounds of grain and six million pounds of fodder, over and above the amount consumed by his large herds of cattle foraging on the march.[30] The quartermaster of the Fourteenth Corps estimated that his corps alone obtained more than a million pounds of fodder and a million and a half pounds of grain.[31]

The first day out of Atlanta the marching columns of blue passed through a countryside already despoiled by foraging parties out of Atlanta. They marched through Decatur, where only a month before the women and children had stood and begged for something to eat of those passing by on the road. For some days these people, faced with a stark hunger, had picked grains of corn from the cracks and seams of the troughs used to feed the Union cavalry horses. Finally they had resorted to scouring the battlefields for Minié balls, trading the lead obtained for supplies of food.[32] The country between Decatur and Stone Mountain had been so devastated that a Decatur woman described it as a "war-stricken section of country where stood chimneys only, standing amid ruins." There appeared to be no living creature left and to the woman "the solitude was terrifying."[33]

At Lithonia, Georgia, the Fourteenth Corps took up the work of railroad destruction and also burned the depot and railroad buildings. While the railroad wreckers heated and twisted rails, other troops "foraged liberally" off of the surrounding country. Major Hitchcock, of Sherman's staff, noted that the soldiers "got potatoes (sweet), fodder, chickens, etc."[34] The thoroughness with which the Union soldiers stripped a community or plantation of its eatables impressed Captain Pepper, a volunteer aide, and he noted that "food in gardens, food in cellars, stock in fields, stock in barns, poultry everywhere, appeared in the distance, disappeared in the presence, and was borne away upon the knapsacks and bayonets of thousands of soldiers."[35]

Kilpatrick's cavalry swept through Jonesboro on the right flank of the Federal columns and viewed again the desolation wrought there by foraging parties in September and October 1864. Although there was some sign of life in the town and some of the residents had returned, there could not have been anything there worth stealing or destroying. Confederate Captain Thomas J. Key had seen the condition of the citizens of Jonesboro in September as the exiles had begun to return "to their houses to find their furniture broken to pieces, their clothing and beds stolen by the Yanks, all their fencing burned, and hogs and cattle eaten." He had seen women coming with containers to draw provisions from the army because they had been "robbed of everything that sustains life."[36]

Following the main road from Atlanta the Fourteenth Corps, still accompanied by Sherman and his staff, marched through Covington, Georgia. Fortunately for the town the troops passed through rapidly, and there was insufficient time for the thorough sacking which otherwise might have been its fate. Sherman himself rode through Covington by a back street, thus avoiding a deputation of citizens who had been appointed to meet him.[37] Going on some mile and a half beyond Covington the corps went into camp on a Judge Harris's plantation. By the time General Sherman and his staff reached the house the advance guard had already discovered a store of molasses and with canteens they were filling themselves with the sweet liquid. Major Hitchcock recounts that one man, cup to mouth, cried out as Sherman passed him, "Forage liberally," to the uncontrollable amusement of his fellows. The General made no comment. Later Sherman sat talking with the Negroes on the Harris plantation, explaining to them his ideas on freedom while the woods and fields roundabout echoed with frequent shots, as the unrestrained soldiers shot down livestock and poultry.[38]

Captain George W. Nichols, one of Sherman's aides-de-camp, in his story of the march referred to "a certain large plantation near Covington" which he said was well stocked before the Union columns reached it, but for which he would not answer after the men of the Fourteenth Corps finished with it.[39] It is highly probable that he referred to the Burge Plantation, one of the larger and richer plantations near Covington. Mrs. Dolly Sumner Lunt Burge lived alone with one daughter on her place, operating it with a labor force of some 100 slaves. Mrs. Burge, born in Maine, was related to Massachusett's Senator Charles Sumner. She had moved to Georgia as a young woman to teach school at Covington, where a short time later she had married Thomas Burge. Upon the death of her husband, before the war, Mrs. Burge had been left to operate his extensive acres. On November 19, 1864, the Federal columns moved down upon her lands, and she was subjected to the treatment which so many of her fellow Georgians would experience. She walked to her gate to see the road filled with blue-uniformed men. They began to stream into the yard. Mrs. Burge hurriedly warned her frightened slaves to hide, and then rushed to the gate to claim a guard for the protection of her property. But she had no opportunity:

> . . . like demons they rush in! To my smokehouse, my dairy, pantry, kitchen and cellar, like famished wolves they come, breaking locks and whatever is in their way. The thousand pounds of meat in my smokehouse is gone in a twinkling, my flour, my meat, my lard, butter, eggs, pickles of various kinds—both in vinegar and brine—wine jars and jugs are all gone. My eighteen fat turkeys, my hens, chickens, fowls, my young pigs, are shot down in my yard and hunted as if they were rebels themselves.[40]

In the midst of this confused scene, punctuated by the shouting of the soldiers and the shooting which accompanied the looting of her home, the woman in her helplessness again appealed to a guard. The guard, whose purpose apparently was largely decorative, had been stationed to fulfill the letter of Sherman's Special Orders No. 120. He informed Mrs. Burge: "I cannot help you, madam; it is orders." As so many helpless citizens had done, and as so many more would do, the woman stood by and watched them drive off her own buggy horse, and "then came old Mary, my brood mare, who for years had been too old and stiff for work, with her three-year-old colt, my two-year-old mule, and her last little baby colt." What hurt Mrs. Burge even more than the loss of her livestock was the treatment accorded her slaves. She described in her diary how shocked she was to find that while she was trying so hard to save her house from fire the Union soldiers "were forcing my boys from home at the point of the bayonet." She was a woman who had dealt kindly with her slaves and felt a sincere sense of responsibility for them, and she was deeply concerned that the soldiers "would force from their homes the poor, doomed negroes."[41]

The marching ranks of blue fairly inundated the Burge Plantation. The marching columns usually left the roads to the wagon trains and spread out to march through the fields on either side where practical to do so.[42] In this manner they marched both in front of and behind the Burge house, like a stream splitting itself upon a rock and reuniting farther along. They swept around the house tearing down the paling fence and treading it and her garden underfoot. They drove their herds of livestock through the backyard and house lot, leaving the earth torn and rutted. That same night the families in the neighborhood of the Burge Plantation also suffered a visit from the invading Union soldiers, and Mrs. Burge wrote that "the heavens from every point were lit up with flames from burning buildings."[43] It was not until the next day that the troops stopped passing, and as the last one dropped out of sight Mrs. Burge noted in her diary that she was "poorer by thirty thousand dollars than I was yesterday morning. And a much stronger Rebel!"[44]

After a foray like the one at the Burge Plantation the ranks of the Federal army took on the appearance of a nondescript mob as the soldiers walked, rather than marched, in irregular groups. They spread out in a fluid line, each individual loaded with whatever loot he had been able to appropriate, more or less setting his own pace. A private in the Seventeenth Corps remarked on the picture Sherman's troops made as they passed through the Georgia countryside. Many of them carried pieces of unskinned hog, impaled on their bayonets while their haversacks bulged with meal or corn. Frying pans, kettles, coffee pots and other cooking utensils hung from belts, knapsacks, or were suspended from the soldier's neck. Cooking utensils were not furnished by the United States to the soldiers,[45] and they were therefore considered as prizes by Federal troops at every point on the march when they could be found. Mrs. Burge had suffered the loss of every utensil in her kitchen, "ovens, skillets, coffee-mills, of which we had three, coffee-pots—not one have I left."[46]

Near the Burge Plantation the Union soldiers stopped at the home of a Mrs. Glass, where they dug up all the fine glassware which she had buried, and assuring her that she had set her last fine table, they smashed it all. Another neighbor, Mrs. Perry, had all her family silverware stolen.[47]

On this same day a part of the Fourteenth Corps reached Sandtown or Newborn, a small settlement of some 12 or 15 houses. Major Hitchcock accompanied General Sherman to see John W. Pitts, a retired merchant, who had settled the village and tried to develop it. Pitts had given away building lots and founded an academy in Newborn as an attraction to settlers. While General Sherman talked with Mr. Pitts, trying to convince him how utterly in the wrong the South was and how hopeless its cause, the Union soldiers were robbing the man right before his eyes of all his grain, fodder, poultry and mules.[48] Those soldiers not engaged in stripping Mr. Pitts of his possessions turned their attention to the settlement, which they proceeded to pillage. Captain Pepper of Sherman's staff described a typical scene, enacted time and again, when the vandals of Sherman's army descended upon helpless communities of noncombatants:

> A halt at high noon beside a village, a besieging of houses by the troops, soldiers emerging from doorways and backyards, bearing quilts, plates, poultry and pigs, beehives attacked, honey in the hands and besmearing the faces of the boys, hundreds of soldiers, poking hundreds of bayonets in the corners of yards and gardens, after concealed treasure; here and there a shining prize, and shouting and scrambling, and a merry division of the spoils. In the background women with praying hands and beseeching lips unheeded.[49]

Major Hitchcock, who was probably as intimately associated with General Sherman on the march as any one of his staff, had tried more than once to soothe his conscience, which troubled him at the conduct of the Union soldiers. On numbers of occasions he had confided to his diary the comforting assurance that as far as he knew there had been no violence, or that at least the men had refrained from burning a house they had looted. At the end of many daily entries in his record of the march he seems to sigh with relief that there had been a minimum of straggling and destruction. At Marietta he had questioned Sherman while he and the general had watched the town go up in flames as to whether Marietta was burned by the general's orders.[50] Sherman denied that he ever ordered the burning of dwellings[51] and had said that he felt that Confederate President Jeff Davis burned them. Hitchcock had not probed too deeply on that occasion for Sherman's real attitude and had attributed the questionable practices which he saw to the inescapable horrors of war.

On November 19, 1864, three days after leaving Atlanta, the Major was forced to admit that Sherman's Special Orders No. 120 were being ignored. He noted in his diary that "the men are foraging and straggling, I am sorry to say, a good deal. At and near every farmhouse we hear constant shooting—of pigs and chickens." Wanderers from the line of march and individual foragers were so disorganizing the army that on the day the Major wrote two men had been killed and three wounded by foragers accidentally shooting each other.[52]

On the first day out of Atlanta, Hitchcock had seen a house wantonly burned by Union soldiers and he had felt out Colonel Charles Ewing, General Sherman's brother-in-law, to ascertain what Colonel Ewing's attitude was toward such conduct. Ewing had agreed that it violated the General's field orders, but nothing could be done, he said, because of the "red tape" involved in trying to correct it. An offender could not be shot unless his sentence was confirmed in Washington, and Ewing said Washington would never approve such punishment. Next Hitchcock questioned Captain Lewis M. Dayton, aide-de-camp and acting Adjutant General to Sherman, to ascertain how the conduct of the Federal troops could be reconciled with "laws of war, etc." The discussion waxed warm with Hitchcock upholding the humane course of action. Dayton stated unequivocally that the Union forces should be free to do whatever they pleased, even to scalping. Hitchcock concluded that Dayton's attitude was unimportant except for the fact that it was *"typical."*[53] Brigadier General Alpheus S. Williams, commanding the Twentieth Corps, apparently had no doubts as to the purpose of the march. He knew what General Sherman meant to do to Georgia and that Special Orders No. 120 did not have to be taken too seriously. In his report on the activities of his command on the march he acknowledged "repeated instances of wanton pillage," but still felt that his men for the most part had conducted themselves well when it was considered that "the nature of the march was calculated to relax discipline."[54] Both General Jeff C. Davis and General Henry W. Slocum expressed the opinion that throughout the whole army the belief was held that General Sherman favored and desired the ruthless destruction of private property in Georgia.[55]

As the four columns of the Federal army penetrated deeper into Georgia they indulged in a carnival of destruction. At Social Circle, which the Twentieth Corps reached on November 18, 1864, they found the railroad depot and storehouse in flames. Lieutenant Colonel Hughes, of the Ninth Illinois Mounted Infantry in advance of the column, had attended to these buildings as well as a large store of cotton which was burning.[56] Rufus Mead, a Federal commissary officer, said that details of officers and men were appointed to see that nothing of value was left undestroyed. He described the country between Social Circle and Madison as "overflowing with sweet potatoes, corn, syrup and hogs," and pointed out that the soldiers wasted as much as they used. No officer complained of the wastefulness, he said. "In fact," Mead wrote, "I think General Sherman didn't intend to leave anything for the Rebs." Although on one occasion Mead was inclined to feel sorry for "some women who cried and begged so piteously for the soldiers to leave them a little [food]," he displayed a spirit of righteous wrath which seemed to grow out of a sense of holiness of the Union Army's mission to chastise the evil people of the South. This feeling is expressed frequently in the diaries and journals kept by both officers and men under Sherman's command and apparently permeated the ranks of the army. It seemed to justify them in their own minds in extinguishing within themselves any small sparks of sympathy remaining after their brutalizing experiences. Upon reflection Mead said that perhaps "extermination" of these helpless people was the only way. "They feel now the effects of their wickedness and who can sympathize very much with them?"[57] His fellow campaigners certainly wasted no time in sympathizing with their victims as evidenced by the trail of suffering and ruin left along the line of march. Mead described the wanton waste of the people's substance—sweet potatoes scattered along the road to rot—the carcasses of hogs with only the forequarters left. Only the hams and better cuts were removed. Beef cattle lay in the fields and along the roadsides, butchered for their livers alone, the stench from their bloated bodies filling the air.[58]

Rolling over the fields and roads of Georgia the Federal army blighted almost everything it touched. The commanding officer of the Eighty-eighth Indiana Infantry reported that his command halted for dinner at a plantation near Shady Dale. Within the comparatively few minutes of the soldier's dinner period they so damaged the property that the owner "estimated his individual loss by our army at $50,000."[59]

Not satisfied with destroying the necessities of life and all the means whereby the residents of Georgia might hope to recover, the Federal troops now resorted to more outrageous forms of vandalism. They seemed to glory in the helplessness of their victims before their bayonets. Their actions speak louder than words to show to what lengths the Union soldiers went not only to leave the Georgians destitute, but also to crown their pillaging and robbery with the complete humiliation of their victims. In Washington County they broke into homes and removed the women's clothing. In the presence of the frightened women the soldiers, with evident delight, dressed the slave women in their mistress's clothes, and thus arrayed, the Negro women rode away on their mistress's finest saddle horses.[60] Foraging parties brought back to the columns in the afternoon mute evidence of the crimes committed against residents living in the lanes and byroads. Stolen horses or mules drew stolen buggies, wagons, sulkies and chaises. These oddly assorted vehicles, representing all the transportation that the helpless people had, were piled high with all kinds of foodstuffs and often topped off with musical instruments, portraits, bed clothing, books, cooking utensils and other loot forced from private homes. The foragers, callous to the suffering and destitution which they had left behind them, returned to their commands frequently in elaborate masquerades to the great amusement of the soldiers. The whole march was regarded by the hardened Federal veterans as a continuous show. They laughed heartily as some bearded Westerner minced along in a filmy wedding dress, an heirloom which he had snatched from a splintered chest during the day. Others wore high silk hats, while still another passed his wagon in review before the column in mock seriousness, stiffly attired in the treasured Revolutionary regimentals of some Georgia family.[61]

The Federal foragers became known as "bummers—a term which is not generally understood in its proper sense of reproach," stated a newspaper correspondent who knew Sherman.[62] The word was coined somewhere along the way and spread throughout the army as applying only to Sherman's troops. Captain Pepper, of Sherman's staff, stated that the word "bummer" came to hold "a recognized position in the army lexicon."[63] One of Sherman's aides-de-camp, Captain George W. Nichols, described a bummer as "a raider on his own account—a man who temporarily deserts his place in the ranks while the army is on the march, and starts out upon an independent foraging expedition. Sometimes he is absent for a few days only, occasionally he disappears for weeks together."[64] These men became to all intents and purposes brigands and desperadoes. Out of sight of their officers there was no discipline and they operated completely free of even the social pressure which might have been exerted by the disapproval of their less depraved associates. They refused to be controlled, and Captain Nichols decided that "conversations with them upon the general impropriety of their conduct"—apparently the only action the officers directed against the "bummer"—were "decidedly useless."[65] Both Pepper and Conyngham, attached to Sherman's staff, describe the "bummer" as a dirty, ragged man, with his face smoked by many pine-knot fires, riding a stolen mule or horse far on the flanks of the marching columns. Captain Conyngham, picturing the bummer for his readers, wrote:

> Think how you would admire him if you were a lone woman, with a family of small children, far from help, when he blandly inquired where you kept your valuables. Think how you would smile when he pried open your chests with his bayonet, or knocked to pieces your tables, pianos, and chairs; tore your bed clothing in three inch strips, and scattered the strips about the yard. . . . Color is no protection from these rough-riders. They go through a negro cabin in search of diamonds and gold watches with just as much freedom and vivacity as they "loot" the dwelling of a wealthy planter. . . . Some of them are loaded down with silverware, gold coin and other valuables. I hazard nothing

in saying that three-fifths (in value) of the personal property of the country we passed through was taken.[66]

The cabins of Negroes and poor whites were robbed by the "bummers" with the same energy and viciousness that marked their treatment of the more imposing plantation houses. Captain Charles E. Belknap, who commanded a brigade foraging party in Sherman's army, described how independent foraging parties clashed and fought over the same prizes. Two or three of such parties "came together about the cabin of a poverty-stricken 'cracker' and the combats that ensued for the possession of the livestock threatened for the time being to destroy the brotherly love said to exist between the various regiments." When these men ran up on a rich find they took all they could haul, "and the torch did away with the balance" to spite other foragers who arrived a few minutes later.[67] Captain Nichols recounted that "one of the excitements of the march" was the searching of homes and grounds to uncover the valuables which the residents of the state had made such frantic efforts to conceal. "Nothing escaped the observation of these sharpwitted soldiers," declared this officer. They keenly watched women and old men for some careless movement or glance which might indicate their secret cache.[68] The soldiers came to know most of the usual hiding places in dooryards, under house steps and flooring. They were very sensitive to new-turned earth, whether in the garden or hog lot. Newly fashioned graves were immediately torn open, yielding a corpse in many instances and in others exposing family silver and valuables. "With untiring zeal the foragers prodded the ground with ramrod and bayonet," wrote Captain Belknap, who apparently saw nothing amiss in this violation of orders by his foraging parties.[69]

While the Federal troops seared a path through the country, the cities and towns of Georgia suffered severely at their hands. On November 19, 1864, the Twentieth Corps entered Madison, situated on the railroad between Atlanta and Augusta. Madison, the county seat of Morgan County, was noted for its comfortable homes and well-tended yards and shrubbery. While one brigade was detailed to destroy the railroad the army crowded into the town. Captain Conyngham said that "the work of pillage went on with a vengeance." His picture of the vandalism gives some idea of the excesses committed by the United States soldiers in Madison:

> Stores were ripped open; goods, valuables, and plate, all suddenly and mysteriously disappeared. I say mysteriously, for if you were to question the men about it, not one of them admitted having a hand in it. . . . If a good store chanced to be struck, the rush for it was immense. Some of those inside being satisfied themselves, would fling bales of soft goods, hardware, harness, and other miscellaneous articles, through the windows. I have seen fellows carry off a richly gilt mirror, and when they got tired of it, dash it against the ground. A piano was a much prized article of capture. I have often witnessed the ludicrous sight of a lot of bearded, rough soldiers capering about the room in a rude waltz, while some fellow was thumping away unmercifully at the piano, with another cutting grotesque capers on the top-board. When they got tired of the saturnalia, the piano was consigned to the flames, and most likely the house with it. All the stores were gutted, and the contents scattered and broken around. Cellars of rich wine were discovered and prostrate men gave evidence of its strength, without any revenue test. A milliner's establishment was sacked, and gaudy ribbons and artificial flowers decorated the caps of the pretty fellows who had done it. Their horses and the negro wenches, too, came in for a share of the decorative spoils.[70]

No mention is made in the report of the commanding officer, General Alpheus S. Williams, of the wanton looting of Madison. The corps commander's report, written from those furnished by division commanders, stated only that "two divisions, with the trains of the corps, moved through Madison and encamped four miles beyond. About six miles of railroad were destroyed by Ward's division."[71]

Milledgeville, the capital of Georgia, was the point which Sherman had selected for the Fourteenth and Twentieth Corps to meet Passing through Eatonton on November 20, 1864, the soldiers burned the factory there, which employed some 30 or 40 women and girls, operating 500 spindles. Some ten miles from Milledge-ville on the night of November 22 General Sherman with the Fourteenth Corps went into camp on a large plantation which one of the Negroes of the place identified as the property of General Howell Cobb of Georgia. Sherman immediately "sent word to General Davis to explain whose plantation it was, and instructed him to spare nothing."[72] Major Hitchcock recorded that the General "told all the darkies to help themselves, as well as the soldiers, to the supplies found here, and ordered the balance burned." The Major said his conscience did not trouble him over the destruction of this "head devil's" property.[73] Major James A. Connolly, Inspector General with the Fourteenth Corps, said that the Twenty-third Missouri was given "permission to burn all the rails and buildings on the plantation tonight."[74] The Missourians did a thorough job, according to an officer of the Thirty-eighth Indiana Infantry, who reported that "when the Corps marched the next morning the place looked as though it had been visited by a very healthy and vigorous cyclone."[75]

The Twentieth Corps moved into Milledgeville on November 22, 1864, followed the next morning by the Fourteenth Corps. The Union forces encountered little or no resistance in entering the city. The Georgia legislature, in session at the time of the alarm, had departed in great haste, using any and every means of conveyance which could be found. General Ira R. Foster, Quarter-master General of Georgia, had acted under Governor Brown's orders to secure the removal of the most valuable properties of the state, largely books of record, valuable documents and furnish-ings at the state house and executive mansion. Many of the old documents and files of letters could not be sorted out and removed because of limited time and were therefore left in their places in the state house. The same was true of the state library, the larger part of which was left to the mercies of the invaders.[76]

The Federal occupation of Milledgeville, by comparison with other places, was very orderly. General Slocum set up his head-quarters at the Milledgeville Hotel while Sherman occupied the governor's mansion. Immediately upon his arrival Slocum had appointed Colonel William Hawley of the Third Wisconsin as Provost Marshal, and during the Federal stay in Milledgeville his regiment and the One Hundreth Seventh New York guarded the city.[77] The residents of Milledgeville for the most part had remained in the city. Guards were posted before dwellings, and there was little destruction of private property. The regard for private property in Georgia's capital was unusual in the light of the past performances of the Union army. Even cotton within the city limits was not burned for fear that it would endanger good buildings and residences. The cotton stored within the city was bonded not to be turned over to the Confederate government. Sherman said that "General Slocum, with my approval, spared several mills, and many thousand bales of cotton, taking what he knew to be worthless bonds, that the cotton should not be used for the Confederacy."[78] All the cotton in the vicinity of Milledgeville that could be reached was burned. Orders were issued and executed to destroy the magazines, arsenals, depots and stores. The penitentiary was fired by some lawless soldiers who said the prisoners had manufactured goods for the Confederate army.[79] Several thousand stands of arms, a lot of old-fashioned rifles and shotguns, thousands of pikes and bowie knives were broken and thrown into the river.

The conduct of Sherman's troops in Milledgeville proved conclusively that when he wanted to control their actions he could effectively do so. An alert, efficient provost guard policing the town had almost eliminated the stragglers with their ever-ready firebrands. Milledgeville proved, at the same time, how quickly the wreckers in the army set about their work where discipline was winked at by officers. The state house and library and other public buildings were made fair game. The scene at the state house, described by Captain Conyngham, was a picture of what the residents of Milledgeville might have been subjected to in the absence of enforced discipline. Captain Conyngham wrote:

> Trophy-hunters, boisterous negroes, who did not know what to do with themselves and their freedom, drunken soldiers, all revelled now about the State House. The library was ransacked by the literati, and archives and books carried off in loads. Minerals, fossils, state bonds, and state money were at a discount.

Stacks of Georgia state money were found in the Treasurer's office. There were millions of dollars there, the most of it not signed. The men loaded themselves with it.[80]

The soldiers deliberately removed documents and letters from the files, scattered them about the floor where they were trampled underfoot. The residents of Milledgeville reported that the soldiers used many of the official papers to kindle their fires.[81] Major Connolly, of General Baird's staff, declared in his diary that it was a "downright shame" that "our soldiers and even some officers have been plundering the state library today and carrying off law and miscellaneous works in armfuls." The Major, apparently indignant, said that "public libraries should be sacredly respected by all belligerents." He did not object to stealing a few "horses, mules and niggers," he assured his diary, "but I will not engage in plundering and destroying public libraries."[82] In the face of such vehemence it is amusing to find Major Connolly on December 8, 1864, quoting historical facts on Georgia's early settlement —he tells of Oglethorpe's arrival, the number of early settlers and other details, noting as his authority: "Hist. Coll. of Georgia— White." The next day he quotes the full title, saying, "In White's 'Historical Collections of Georgia,' I find the names of the original German settlers of this section of Georgia."[83]

The Federal soldiers, although prevented from burning and pillaging, found other ways to show their contempt for the capital city of Georgia. Miss Eliza Frances Andrews, passing through Milledgeville in the spring of 1865, described the capitol building as "shockingly defaced, like everything else in Milledgeville. There don't seem to be a clean or a whole thing in the town." The walls and rooms of the hotel "were black with tobacco spit."[84]

On November 24, 1864, the Fourteenth and Twentieth Corps renewed the march. The Twentieth, accompanied by Sherman, took the direct road toward Sandersville, while the Fourteenth moved by a parallel route toward the same objective. Just outside of Sandersville the Federal troops met a brigade of Confederate cavalry, which retired before the superior Union force. General Sherman said, "I saw the rebel cavalry apply fire to stacks of fodder standing in the fields of Sandersville, and gave orders to burn some unoccupied dwellings nearby."[85] The Confederate cavalry, part of Wheeler's command, were driven through Sandersville, and the Fourteenth Corps marched into the town at almost the same time the Twentieth arrived. Sherman was irritated over the Confederate resistance, particularly their firing on the invading Federal troops from the courthouse. Major Hitchcock, who was with the General, said Sherman informed the people that he ordered their courthouse burned because the Confederates had used it as a fort.[86] The residents felt Sherman's anger in a more personal way, however, as an unofficial order released the vandal soldiers to pillage the town. Rufus Mead, Jr., with a Connecticut regiment, noted in his letter to his family:

> We got into S[andersville] about 9 A.M. and completely ransacked the whole town, only left the citizens unmolested. It was done to retaliate for burning the bridge and resistance of the day before. That is Sherman's motto. The troops plundered and ransacked everything until 3 P.M. when our Div. went to Tenille, burnt the station, tore up track, etc.[87]

A resident of Sandersville described the manner in which the Union soldiers surged into her home, stealing everything they could lay hands on—china, silver, linens, including the cloth on the table, and all food supplies. "From Saturday morning until Monday many inhabitants had neither food nor water," as the soldiers had shot all the hogs, cows and chickens which they could not take with them. "The ground was strewn with food, carpets were drenched with syrup and then covered with meal."[88]

The residents of Sandersville felt the cruel impact of General Sherman's merciless warfare against noncombatant women and children, not because "guerillas" had endangered the Federal army, but because their own troops had dared to resist the enemy. Here Sherman threw away even the guise of justification for his ruthless war on the helpless people of the South. Before, he had been merciless, he said, because that was the only way he could strike at "guerillas." At Sandersville he saw the Confederate cavalry, recognized it as such and denied the right of the Confederate army to resist invasion of its own soil. Unable to catch and crush the small detachment of Wheeler's Confederate horsemen who had so courageously opposed themselves to his massive columns, Sherman made the defenseless citizens the victims of his wrath.

The Left Wing now pushed rapidly on through Tenille Station, tearing up railroad and destroying everything of value in the vicinity. They passed through Davisboro, which they left in ruins, and made camp at Louisville, Georgia. On November 29, reinforced by Baird's division, General Kilpatrick's cavalry moved rapidly from Louisville toward Waynesboro, in a feint on Augusta. This move served two purposes in that it confirmed the Confederates in their belief that the whole Union strength was being directed against Augusta, and it also permitted Kilpatrick to destroy sections of the railroad between Augusta and Millen. General Kilpatrick took the opportunity to blast the country between Sparta and Gordon so thoroughly that it was referred to as the "burnt country." A traveler through that section wrote:

> There was hardly a fence left standing all the way from Sparta to Gordon. The fields were trampled down and the road was lined with carcasses of horses, hogs and cattle, that the invaders, unable to consume or to carry away with them, had wantonly shot down to starve out the people and prevent them from making their crops. The stench in some places was unbearable. . . . The dwellings that were standing all showed signs of pillage.[89]

The Right Wing, under General O. O. Howard, was moving on the right in the general direction of Millen, destroying the railroad as it marched. A part of this army wrecked Irwinton, Georgia. An officer of an Illinois regiment wrote on November 25, 1864, that "the boys had a great time last night." The citizens had tried to bury their valuables, and Federal troops in holiday spirit spread out to uncover the treasure. "Hundreds of them were armed with sharpened sticks probing the earth, 'prospecting.' " After this exhibition the Illinois soldier describes the monotony of having to listen to the reading of orders against pillage, loot and arson. "We fell in at retreat, and had General Order No. 26 read to us I guess for the 20th time."[90]

On November 30, 1864, the Federal soldiers burned all of the business district of Louisville, the former capital of Georgia, and began to move in the direction of Millen. General Blair's Seventeenth Corps arrived there on December 3, 1864, after destroying the railroad from Ogeechee River down to Millen. They were ordered to make their destruction at this point even "more devilish than can be dreamed of,"[91] and they proceeded to wreck the railroad thoroughly and burn the imposing depot to the ground. Then, acting on their own, the soldiers destroyed the hotel and storehouses, leaving the little railroad town in charred ruins.[92]

While the Seventeenth Corps wrecked Millen the other Federal columns were close by awaiting Sherman's command to drive directly to Savannah. Using Millen as a pivot the army swung around from its easterly course and moved southward on parallel routes. General Jeff C. Davis with the Fourteenth Corps followed the Savannah road; Slocum's Twentieth Corps marched down the middle between Davis and Blair's Seventeenth Corps, which followed the railroad out of Millen. South and west of the Ogeechee River the Fifteenth Corps, accompanied by the Right Wing Commander, General O. O. Howard, drove southward to Eden's Station under orders to cross toward Savannah at that point. Each corps commander was to judge the progress of the other columns by the towering smoke from the fires set by the troops. General Slocum was to dress on Blair's Seventeenth Corps, whose whereabouts, Captain Dayton of Sherman's staff told him, he could locate "by the smokes."[93] Sherman assured General Howard that "Blair can burn the bridges and culverts, and also enough cotton gins and barns to mark the progress of his head of column."[94]

On December 8, 1864, at a point about nine miles from Savannah an incident occurred which focused Sherman's attention and that of his staff officers on the rules of civilized warfare—a subject which had not troubled them up to this time. The Confederates had buried eight-inch shells in the roadway and attached friction matches so that they would explode when stepped on. One of the mines exploded, blowing off the foot of Lieutenant Tupper, Adjutant of the First Alabama Cavalry (Federal), and wounding several other men.[95] Sherman, who had long since scrapped the laws of civilized war, had little enough grace to say that "this was not war, but murder."[96] Major Hitchcock and Captain Nichols, Sherman's staff officers, forgot with equal ease the cruelties of the Union troops and expressed indignation that the Confederates would descend to such evil practices in war. Appeals to the rules of war fell easily from these officers' lips when their enemy failed to observe them to the letter. The torpedoes were "murderous instruments of assassination," declared Major Hitchcock, which were "contrary to every rule of civilized warfare."[97] According to these officers, the rules of war permitted the use of torpedoes only before breastworks or in a breach made in a line of works. Used under such circumstances they could be expected and precautionary measures adopted. Captain Nichols, in spite of the terrible events he had witnessed on the march, could say that "the laws of war do not justify an attempt of the kind that had been so disastrous today."[98]

Sherman immediately ordered the provost guard to send forward a detail of Confederate prisoners, who, "armed with picks and spades," were made to "march in close order along the road, so as to explode their own torpedoes, or to discover and dig them up."[99] The rules of war agreed upon by civilized nations in the nineteenth century provided that no prisoner of war should be exposed to unnecessary risk of life or limb. Having once laid down his arms and submitted himself to his captor, the person of the prisoner was considered inviolate. Sherman did not hesitate to place the Confederate prisoners in jeopardy of life and limb nor did it seem to occur to him that he was dealing in "murder and not war." He had convinced himself as far back as his Memphis days that he was justified in using every weapon that he could devise or command to make war terrible for the South. Had he not crowded out his conscience long since, Sherman might have remembered the railroad cuts south of Atlanta on the Atlanta and West Point Railroad. They were loaded with torpedoes which had been concealed under brush at his order in August 1864.[100] This did not prevent his retaliation against the helpless Confederate prisoners, who, in spite of their pleadings, were forced to carry out their hazardous assignment.

The Federal army encountered little opposition until it was within 15 miles of Savannah, and only token resistance was offered then. The roads were obstructed by timbers which the Confederates had felled across them, and there were occasional earthwork artillery emplacements. These were brushed aside without difficulty and by December 10, 1864, the Confederates had been driven within their lines in the defenses before Savannah. Sherman now disposed his force for the investment of the city. The Fourteenth Corps took its position on the extreme left, touching the Savannah River; the Twentieth Corps was next, its right flank in contact with the Seventeenth Corps, and the Fifteenth Corps occupied the extreme right. The last act in the march to the sea was about to be played.

On December 13, 1864, General William B. Hazen, with the Second Division of the Fifteenth Corps, assaulted and overwhelmed Fort McAllister, a Confederate defense point which had stood in the way of Sherman's communication with the Union naval units lying off Savannah. With this fort eliminated, the Federal army made contact with the navy and could then be supplied, by means of light-draft vessels, with heavier artillery and ammunition, as well as the supplies needed for a siege. Sherman expected a long siege and sent for heavy guns, which he ordered Generals Howard and Slocum to place in position "to bombard Savannah."[101] On December 17, 1864, Sherman dispatched, under flag of truce, a formal demand for the surrender of the city, assuring Confederate General William J. Hardee, who commanded the Savannah garrison, that he would make no effort to restrain the Federal troops if he was forced to take Savannah by assault. On the following day General Hardee refused to surrender the city, and Sherman, still hoping to avoid a frontal assault, embarked for Port Royal, South Carolina, to secure General John S. Foster's cooperation in blocking the only exit from Savannah left open to the Confederates. Although investing the city on three sides, Sherman had been unable to cut the Union Causeway, a wagon road running from the east bank of the Savannah River toward Hardeeville, South Carolina. It was through this avenue that the Confederate garrison quietly evacuated Savannah on December 20, 1864. Sherman on the way back from Port Royal was informed by messenger that the Federal army had marched into the city on December 21, 1864, without firing a shot.

The march to the sea was finished. The military results of the campaign were very important, and the North considered it eminently successful. It raised the spirits of the North and further depressed the South. By marching almost unopposed through the inner citadel of the Confederacy the national army proved the growing weakness of the South and showed both sides that the end of the war was near at hand. The fall of Atlanta, the South's transportation center, together with the march through the most productive part of the state cut off Georgia's supplies from Lee's army in Virginia and further reduced the area of the Confederacy under Southern control.

It would be difficult to arrive at an accurate estimate of the material damages suffered by the state of Georgia. Certainly no complete records were kept of the amount of private property destroyed. Sherman attempted to make an estimate of the damages done by his army in his report to General Halleck when he set the figure "at $100,000,000; at least $20,000,000 of which has inured to our advantage, and the remainder is simple waste and destruction." This estimate was based on the "damage done to the State of Georgia and its military resources," and included the loss of corn, fodder, foodstuff, cattle, hogs, sheep and "more than 10,000 horses and mules."[102] The destruction of railroads accounted for millions of dollars in loss. Nearly 300 miles of track were ripped up from Atlanta to Savannah, while bridges, trestles and stations were destroyed by fire. Culverts and masonry piers were battered down or blown up. Rolling stock was destroyed, and locomotives run off into fields, where they were later occupied as homes by poor people.[103] Cotton burned by the Union army also represented tremendous loss to the people of the state.[104] It would be difficult to calculate the value of the countless numbers of cotton gins and presses, together with corn and flour mills, which were destroyed. Their potential value to a poverty-stricken people far exceeded their actual value at the time of their destruction.

In his estimate of the staggering material losses inflicted on the state of Georgia Sherman completely failed to consider the greatest and most lasting damage of all—that inflicted upon the sensibilities of the defenseless, noncombatant population of the state.

From Atlanta to the sea the pathway left by the Union army was one vast sheet of misery, a misery which "was as great as it was unnecessary."[105] Not only were the citizens of Georgia despoiled of their goods and property, but their homes were violated, their most intimate possessions were either stolen or destroyed before their eyes. They suffered the humiliation and helplessness that resulted from an inability to defend themselves against the malicious strength of the invaders of their soil. They looked on while the national troops stripped them of all they possessed and crowned their vandalism by taking away even the citizens' hopes for the future by deliberately destroying their farming implements and with them the future crops of food and fibers.[106] The loss of slave labor posed a problem to women and children left alone on the farms and plantations. Thousands of slaves followed the Federal columns in response to the exhortation of the soldiers, only to be abandoned at Savannah.[107]

Sixty thousand hardened, undisciplined men were loosed on a country inhabited largely by women, children and old men. These men, long separated from feminine associations and accustomed to enforcing their wills upon helpless people at bayonet point found at their mercy the Georgia women, for the most part in entirely unprotected homes. The insults offered these women and the crimes committed against them by the unrestrained soldier of Sherman's army have been passed over largely in silence.[10] Even the most lawless wrecker in the Union army did not seem to want this atrocious crime against defenseless women charged against him. The women of the South likewise suffered in silence the insults offered them. They realized that their complaints would go unheeded, and their charges would only serve to further humiliate the injured women themselves as well as their families. The Union army because of its conduct in Georgia had left itself open to charges of offenses against women, and thereby added to its unsavory reputation. Such damages as these could not be computed in terms of dollars and cents.

War with all its horrors had been brought to the doors of the citizens of Georgia. An invading army, without any claim of military necessity, had thrown away every inclination toward mercy for weakness and helplessness. The Federal troops ha resorted to the sheer brutality of overpowering strength to despoil a people of their material resources and to injure irreparably their finer sensibilities. Material damages could be repaired, but spiritual wounds left scars of hate which would be sensitive for generations yet unborn.

IX

South Carolina

On the very day that the Federal troops occupied Savannah, Sherman turned his eyes toward his next objective, South Carolina. His overall plan since leaving Atlanta had contemplated action against the state which the North regarded as the instigator of secession and rebellion. Sherman concluded his report of the fall of Savannah to General Grant by assuring Grant that he "could go on and smash South Carolina—all to pieces."[1] He proposed to accomplish this by marching on Columbia, the capital of South Carolina, via Branchville and Orangeburg, breaking up as much railroad en route as possible. He pointed out to Grant that by ignoring both Charleston and Augusta he could accomplish the same thing in South Carolina that he had in Georgia—the division of the Confederate forces. In following this strategy Sherman assured Grant that "I feel confident that I can break up the whole railroad system of South Carolina and North Carolina, and be on the Roanoke, either at Raleigh or Weldon, by the time spring fairly opens." Except for the effect on Southern morale, Sherman did not consider the capture of Charleston particularly important. "Charleston is now a mere desolated wreck," he pointed out to Grant, "and is hardly worth the time it would take to starve it out."[2] The morale of the South could be made to suffer even more grievously by operating in the interior, and Sherman was convinced that the breaking up of the interior lines of railroad would lead inevitably to the abandonment of both Charleston and Wilmington.

The march of the Federal army through South Carolina actually began on February 1, 1865, although several brigades had crossed over into the state early in January. The organization of the army and the manner of marching were similar to that which had been employed in Georgia. Sherman's army of 60,000 men was again divided into two wings with General O. O. Howard commanding the Right Wing, made up of General John A. Logan's Fifteenth Corps and the Seventeenth Corps under General Frank P. Blair's command. The Left Wing was under the command of General H. W. Slocum with Generals Jeff C. Davis and A. S. Williams commanding the Fourteenth and Twentieth Corps respectively. The cavalry, numbering about 4,000, continued under the command of General Judson Kilpatrick.

The army was accompanied by a train of 2,500 wagons and 600 ambulances, carrying ammunition and coffee, salt and bread —supplies which could not be gotten out of the country. In addition, each corps carried along its indispensable pontoon bridges. The Federal troops, as they had done in Georgia, divided into several columns and marched by different roads to specified rendezvous points. This splitting of forces mystified the Confederate generals in South Carolina and at Augusta, as it had in Georgia, and again caused them to separate their small forces. In consequence, Sherman's army marched through the middle, encountering little or no effective opposition from the Confederate troops. Confederate Generals Joe Wheeler, Wade Hampton and Hardee withdrew their forces consistently and burned the bridges behind them as the impetus of Sherman's heavy columns carried the invading Federal troops relentlessly farther and farther into South Carolina.

Goldsboro, North Carolina, was Sherman's objective, because it was the junction point for two railroads to the coast at Wilmington and New Bern. Over these roads at Goldsboro Sherman's army could expect to receive reinforcements for further action against

Lee near Richmond. It was toward this goal that Sherman directed the Federal columns. He described the route to Grant:

> . . . straight on Columbia, feigning on Branchville and Augusta. We destroyed in passing, the railroad from the Edisto nearly up to Aiken; again from Orangeburg to the Congaree [River]; again from Columbia down to Kingsville on the Wateree [River], and up toward Charlotte as far as the Chester line; thence we turned east on Cheraw and Fayetteville.[3]

It was only after they crossed the Cape Fear River that the Union troops encountered any hard fighting. At Bentonville, North Carolina, General Joseph E. Johnston made his desperate attack on what he hoped was an isolated Federal corps. This battle was fought on March 19–21, 1865, and ended in defeat for the Confederates. The Southern cause was now hopeless since Sherman was joined at Goldsboro by General John M. Schofield's troops from New Bern and a force under General Alfred H. Terry which had marched from Wilmington.

Although in many ways the march through the Carolinas might be considered simply a continuation of the march through Georgia, the Federal troops found it far different. Many officers and men had referred to the campaign in Georgia as an excursion. They had found it very pleasant to march through the country, eating heartily, little burdened by either fighting or working. From the moment they left Savannah, however, all this was changed. The country they now entered was low and swampy, and heavy rains had flooded the lowlands and swollen the streams out of their banks. The march which had been so easy in Georgia, where the roads were in the general direction of the larger streams and the country was well adapted to the movement of an army, now became both difficult and hazardous. The direction of the Federal army's march carried them across the quagmires and swamps, and forced them to cross great rivers at flood stage. The marching columns were for days at a time in water, often knee deep. The soldiers toiled day in and day out to force the artillery and wagons through mud and water which reached to the axles. The chief engineering officer reported that the route which the Federal army followed "involved an immense amount of bridging of every kind known in active campaigning, besides some 400 miles of corduroying."[4] The laying down of corduroy, according to the chief engineer, "involved the severest labor," particularly in the absence of fence rails, which were used whenever available. Saplings were chopped down and placed in closely matted form to prevent the vehicles from sinking into the deep mud. After one division had crossed, those following had to corduroy the road all over again. In addition to the hard labor of laying down roadway "the Right Wing built fifteen pontoon bridges, having an aggregate length of 3,720 feet. The Left Wing built about 4,000 feet, thus making a total of 7,720 feet, or nearly one mile and a half."[5]

There had been no enemy worthy of the name to oppose the march from Atlanta to Savannah. The Federal columns had been free of the fear of meeting veteran Confederate troops, and there had been no important garrisons on either flank to threaten their progress. On crossing into South Carolina Sherman's army knew that in front of them was a Confederate force under General Hardee which might be formidable in opposing their crossing of the larger rivers. To the east lay the Confederate garrisons at Charleston, Georgetown and Wilmington, whose actions were unpredictable. There was every reason for the Federal army to expect that as large a part of Hood's army as possible would be rushed to Augusta to strike them from the left.[6]

The Confederates set up road blocks and built breastworks behind the swampy river crossings. These positions should have delayed the Union troops and cost them dearly in dead and wounded, but to the surprise of the Federal commanders, the Confederates continued to evacuate their positions after making only a halfhearted fight. Although there were more casualties among the Union troops in South Carolina than there were in Georgia, the blue columns rolled on, flanking and pushing before them the disorganized Southern forces.

The veteran soldiers of Sherman's corps followed the same practices of devastation and destruction in South Carolina that they had in Georgia, with one outstanding exception—they destroyed and wrecked South Carolina with a thoroughness and deliberation that arose out of pure hatred for that state. It was not an impersonal feeling directed against the enemy in general, but rather a personal hatred felt by the soldiers in the ranks as well as the officers of the invading army. Such an intensity of feeling was directed against South Carolina that there can be but little doubt that it had been nurtured and tended throughout the months that these men had hoped they would reach that state. Threats had been muttered by some of the Federal soldiers as to what they would do to the home of secession, others openly threatened to vent their malice on the people of that state. Captain Conyngham noted the vindictive attitude of the troops and he wrote that "there can be no denial of the assertion that the feeling among the troops was one of extreme bitterness towards the people of the State of South Carolina. It was freely expressed as the columns hurried over the bridges at Sister's Ferry, eager to commence the punishment of 'original secessionists.' " Even soldiers who had been somewhat conservative in house burning in Georgia were heard to utter threats against South Carolina. "Officers openly confessed their fears that the coming campaign would be a wicked one," continued Captain Conyngham. He described this feeling toward the people of the hated state as "universal."[7] A Connecticut commissary officer had forecast before the march from Savannah that the South Carolinians' "day of reckoning must come." He declared that they had been safe, "but we will follow them and make them repent yet in sackcloth & ashes for their high handed iniquity."[8] Captain Julian Hinkley, of the Third Wisconsin Infantry, had said on beginning the march from Atlanta that he hoped the Federal army's destination was Charleston. "I wanted the people of South Carolina who had started the war to feel its effects and to reap their share of the horrors."[9] Major Connolly, of General Absolom Baird's staff, wrote his wife of the attitude of the Union soldiers and how they demonstrated their hatred. "The army burned everything it came near in the State of South Carolina," he said, because "the men 'had it in' for the State and they took it out in their own way."[10]

Men and officers were not the only ones to exhibit their intentions to wreak a particularly cruel vengeance on South Carolina. The feeling reached into high places. As early as December 18, 1864, when Sherman's plans for the Carolina campaign were in the discussional stage, Major General Halleck, Chief of Staff, had written Sherman: "Should you capture Charleston, I hope that by *some accident* the place may be destroyed, and, if a little salt should be sown upon its site, it may prevent the growth of future crops of nullification and secession."[11] General Sherman was fully aware of the attitude of his men, and having observed their wasteful and destructive path through Georgia, he realized only too well what lay in store for South Carolina. "The truth is," Sherman informed General Halleck, "the whole army is burning with an insatiable desire to wreak vengeance upon South Carolina. I almost tremble at her fate, but feel that she deserves all that seems in store for her."[12] He later admitted that he "saw and felt that we would not be able longer to restrain our men as we had done in Georgia."[13] In the light of the Federal soldiers' lack of discipline in Georgia, this statement on Sherman's part boded ill for South Carolina and her people.

The people of South Carolina were fully aware of the fate which lay in store for them when Sherman's wreckers and looters were loosed upon them. As early as December 1864 a petition signed by citizens at Columbia was submitted to Confederate Secretary of War James A. Seddon. It was respectfully requested "that at least one corps of our army be sent from Virginia to save the States of Georgia and South Carolina from being laid waste by the enemy."[14] Georgia had fallen by the way and South Carolina now faced the enemy alone. *The Charleston Daily Courier* left no doubt in its readers' minds as to how the North felt toward them. On January 4, 1865, *The Daily Courier* on the front page reproduced, under the caption "What Is In Store For South Carolina," portions of an editorial from *The Philadelphia Inquirer*. The tone of the Northern editorial reflected almost the same thirst for vengeance as that expressed by the veteran soldiers of the army. The editor had written:

> The shout which went up from Sherman's western boys when their faces looked Charlestonward, on their march, rings louder than ever in his ears. It was an ominous battle cry, "Lead us into South Carolina! Take us to Charleston!" Ransom knows and Jeff Davis knows what will be the fate

of that accursed hotbed of treason, whenever the Union
forces are ordered to cross its threshold.

This was a strange hatred which directed its venom not against
armies but against the noncombatants of South Carolina and their
personal property. The people of the North were, in effect, issuing
an open invitation to the Union army to sack and pillage the
country. The editor of *The Inquirer* wanted South Carolinians to
feel the consequences of what he branded as "her own diabolical
acts," and he continued:

> She will yet feel them, we trust, to the largest measure. It
> is but justice, and Heaven will surely mete it out, and force
> her to drink to the dregs the bitter cup which she placed to
> the lips of the Nation. When that day shall come the world
> will approve her punishment, and to the sentence of right-
> eous retribution will say, Amen!"[15]

The next issue of *The Daily Courier* informed South Carolinians
that every citizen must do his duty in the crisis. The Federal army
had seemingly accomplished what the press of the state had de-
rided as foolhardy. It had driven through Georgia in record time
and now stood poised to strike into the heart of South Carolina.
The editor solemnly warned the citizens of the state:

> Subjugation involves for us every evil it is possible to con-
> ceive of. The enemy may have been lenient toward others,
> but toward the people of Charleston and of the state he will
> show no mercy. For us he has reserved the vials of his
> fiercest wrath. We shall have to drink the cup of bitterest
> woe to the dregs—wring them out and drink them.[16]

The next few days were filled with feverish activity as telegrams
passed from Confederate General Hardee at Charleston to President Davis at Richmond. General Hardee urged that as many men
as possible be sent to reinforce the Charleston garrison. President
Davis telegraphed General Beauregard to forward the badly needed
men only to receive Beauregard's reply on January 9, 1865, that
the condition of the "common roads and breaks in railroads"

would delay their arrival.[17] On January 25, 1865, General Hardee's request became more urgent as he telegraphed for 3,000 men. Three days later Confederate General D. H. Hill forwarded an urgent wire from Augusta to General Beauregard that the Federal columns were advancing rapidly upon that city, and he had to have reinforcements at once.[18] The harassed general at Augusta in early February tried to send all available forces to the many points where they were thought to be needed and to provide artillery, arms and horses. On February 5, 1865, he forwarded a telegraphic appeal to Governor Joseph E. Brown of Georgia and Governor W. J. Magrath of South Carolina to rally their states in the crisis and send every available man forward to defend their soil.[19] Confederate disorganization was again playing into Sherman's hands.

Confusion resulting from the threatened invasion by Sherman's army of destroyers was not confined to the military alone. The citizens of South Carolina, fearing both for their personal safety and for the safety of their property began to move themselves and their families and as much of their property as possible to places where they felt the enemy could not reach them. The trains from Charleston to Columbia were loaded with valuable furniture, clothing and even fine stocks of wines and liquors, sent by frantic Charlestonians to friends and relatives in Columbia or other towns to the north of Columbia for preservation. Many refugees from Charleston and the surrounding country, fleeing from the seacoast town and that part of the state which it seemed clear would feel the heavy hand of the invader, crowded the overburdened railroad. Other citizens sought refuge at Camden or Cheraw or one of the other towns north of Columbia, where it was thought there would be comparative safety from the dreaded march of the Union troops. In the rural areas the scene was much the same, as the larger planters, particularly, picked up their families and removed them into the towns which they thought might offer protection. *The Augusta Constitutionalist* commented on the great number of fugitives from South Carolina who poured into Augusta in January 1865. They arrived in throngs, bringing with them their families, flocks, herds, cattle and servants. This group was made up largely of planters from the neighboring Barnwell District who were fleeing "the wrath to come."[20] A South Carolina diarist paints a vivid picture of the excitement caused by the invading Federal army, as citizens madly sought safety. He wrote:

> The march of General Sherman which began in Jan. 1865 created consternation in the Districts of Barnwell & Beaufort & Orangeburg & hundreds of families left their comfortable homes, driving their cattle & hogs before them in hopes of saving them from the enemy. Unfortunately, not knowing which route Gen. Sherman meant to take, many of these families took the very road pursued by the federal army & crowded into Orangeburg, then into Lexington, Richland district, only to be overtaken at last, by the Federals.[21]

Sherman's troops, with their experiences in Georgia still fresh in mind, wasted no time in setting about their work of destruction in South Carolina. Captain Conyngham noticed the intensity of the men and their determination to destroy everything possible in the state. Almost as soon as the first troops had crossed the Savannah River, Conyngham stated, "I first saw its (hatred's) fruits at Rarysburg, where two or three piles of blackened brick and an acre or so of dying embers marked the site of an old revolutionary town; and this before the column had fairly got its 'hand in.' " So impetuous were the Union soldiers that they forced General Sherman to abandon his headquarters at McBride's Plantation to keep it from burning down around his head.[22] Captain Dexter Horton, marching with the Left Wing, entered terse descriptions of two small towns encountered early on the march. On February 7, 1865, he wrote: "Passed through Robertsville. All burned to the ground." The next day he said of the small town of Brighton: "All their inhabitations burned all along the road." The Fourteenth Corps, he said, were securing a plentiful supply of forage out of the area.[23] Captain Horton gave testimony to the thoroughness of the devastation of the country through which his column marched when he complained of the unpleasantness of "smoke from woods, fences, homes etc." blown by heavy winds into the men's faces.[24] One of Sherman's volunteer aides said that "whenever a view could be had from high ground, black columns of smoke were seen rising here and there within a circuit of twenty or thirty miles." This officer stated that houses were burned as they were found and "solid built chimneys were the only relics of plantation houses after the fearful blast had swept by. The destruction of houses, barns, mills, etc., was almost universal. Families who remained at home occasionally kept the roof over their heads."[25]

Doubtless much of the looting and pillaging and the burning of private property on the flanks of the Union columns was perpetrated by Kilpatrick's cavalry. General Kilpatrick had a bad reputation for wanton destruction even among men as accustomed to such conduct as were Sherman's soldiers. Union General Jacob D. Cox said of Kilpatrick that his "notorious immoralities and rapacity set so demoralizing an example to his troops that the best disciplinarians among his subordinates could only mitigate its influence."[26] Kilpatrick had boasted of what he would do to South Carolina before the march started. At a party for his officers he had told them that in later years travelers in South Carolina would ask who had so desolated the country and left so many chimneys without houses. The answer, he assured his commanders, would be Kilpatrick's cavalry.[27]

At the village of Lawtonville a Connecticut officer noticed that there were "only 2 or 3 out of 20 or more houses left."[28] This was the fate of nearly all the towns on the route traveled by Sherman's army. The villages of Hardeeville, Grahamville, Gallisonville, McPhersonville, Barnwell, Blackville, Midway and the towns of Orangeburg and Lexington were successively given over to the torch and left in ruins.[29] Captain Conyngham described Orangeburg, a pretty town of about 2,000 population, as it looked the morning after it was burned. "It was a sad sight," he said, "to witness the smoking ruins of the town, the tall, black chimneys looking down upon it like funeral mutes, and to see old women and children, hopeless, helpless, almost frenzied, wandering amidst the desolation."[30] In the northern part of the state the towns of Winnsboro, Camden and Cheraw were looted and plundered thoroughly before being burned by the vindictive Union troops. A Union soldier passing through Cheraw noted that it "has been quite a business place, I judge, but now all the stores, shops, etc.

are in ashes while the houses on another street still remain."[31] At Liberty Hill, South Carolina, a refugee from Charleston described the vindictiveness of Sherman's soldiers as they swarmed over the home in which she was visiting. After robbing the home of everything of value, the soldiers went down into the cellar, where they "pour kerosene oil, molasses, and feathers together, then stir them up with their bayonets." Such concoctions were usually poured into pianos or spread upon the rugs throughout the house. This witness described the sounds made by the soldiers as similar to those made by carpenters at work, as drawers were torn open, the tops of chests pried off, and all jewelry, silverware and other personal possessions were stolen.[32] At Camden the Union soldiers broke into and plundered all the stores. What they could not take with them they threw into the streets for the Negroes, who were invited and encouraged to help themselves. The soldiers then broke up into small squads and spread out through the town to indulge in private looting of residences. Many families were thus stripped of everything they had in the world.[33] At Winnsboro the homes of the citizens were ruthlessly looted of their valuables, and in some cases defenseless women "were cursed and threatened to be shot" if they did not deliver up their keys.[34]

While the towns and villages of South Carolina were being sacked and burned the people in the rural districts through which the Federal soldiers passed were being subjected to an even more vicious treatment. Not only were they forced to turn over their last morsels of food to the Union troops and to stand by while their farming implements were broken up and their livestock either driven off or shot, but now they were robbed outright by Sherman's soldiers. They demanded money and valuables from the noncombatant residents in the country and did not hesitate to resort to violence to force the people to surrender whatever they had of value. Sherman's aide, Captain Pepper, declared that the North could never conceive of the extent to which the Union soldiers had resorted to "deliberate and systematic robbery for the sake of gain. Thousands of soldiers have gathered by violence, hundreds of dollars each, some of them thousands, by sheer robbery." This officer described the brutality of Sherman's pillagers toward those who would not divulge the hiding place of their money and valuables. Old men were strung up and permitted to dangle at death's door, then lowered and questioned again. This process was repeated until the victim capitulated or the soldiers were satisfied that he had nothing of value. Another method was to compel a man to "double-quick" one or two miles until he dropped from exhaustion.[35]

The robbery of citizens was not confined simply to the stealing of money and jewelry, but was extended by the avaricious troops to any item of value which they could carry off and hope to sell or send home. They stole "plate and silver spoons, silk dresses, elegant articles of toilet, pistols, indeed whatever the soldier can take away," declared an officer who observed them at their sordid business. This officer likewise recorded the fiendish delight the soldiers derived from their destructive actions—destruction without any purpose whatsoever, except for the sheer joy of spreading misery and heartache. "Pianos were cut to pieces with axes, elegant sofas broken and the fragments scattered around the grounds, paintings and engravings pierced with bayonets or slashed with swords, rosewood centre-tables, chairs, etc., broken to pieces and burned for fuel in cooking the food taken from the cellar or meathouse."[36] A Federal major confessed to his wife that before Sherman's army had reached the halfway mark on the march through South Carolina he was

> perfectly sickened by the frightful devastation our army was spreading on every hand. Oh! It was absolutely terrible! Every house except the church and the negro cabin was burned to the ground; women, children and old men turned out into the mud and rain and their houses and furniture first plundered and then burned.[37]

There seemed to be an almost fanatical zeal in the terrible manner in which the Federal troops deliberately and maliciously reduced the citizens of South Carolina to hopelessness and poverty. This attitude was noted by one who witnessed the march through the broken state. "Many of our foragers, scouts, and hangers-on of all classes, thought, like Cromwell, that they were doing the work of the Lord, in wantonly destroying as much property as possible." He had noted something of this attitude in

Georgia, he wrote, but "it was only in South Carolina that it was brought to perfection."[38] This attitude was demonstrated in the new heartlessness exhibited by the soldiers. This writer, a Federal staff officer, had come upon a retired plantation house which had just been fired:

> The soldiers were rushing off on every side with their pillage. An old lady and her two grandchildren were in the yard alarmed and helpless! The flames and smoke were shooting through the windows. The old lady rushed from one to another beseeching them at least to save her furniture. They only enjoyed the whole thing, including her distress."[39]

General Sherman's own aide-de-camp observed women crying for help and heard them wail in grief as their homes were looted and burned, and was unmoved by it.[40]

The burning and looting of private homes was the rule rather than the exception in South Carolina. It is stated in a report made by a committee of reputable South Carolina citizens that "for eighty miles along the route of his [Sherman's] army, through the most highly improved and cultivated region of the State, according to the testimony of respectable and intelligent witnesses, the habitations of but two white persons remain."[41]

The crowning act of vandalism was the burning of Columbia on the night of February 17, 1865, by Sherman's troops. A great controversy has raged ever since the destruction of South Carolina's capital city as to who was responsible for the tragedy. Sherman and many of his officers contended that the general conflagration resulted from burning cotton bales fired by Confederate General Wade Hampton upon his evacuation of the city. There are just as many witnesses who insist that the cotton fires had been completely extinguished early in the day before the first fires burst out in separated sections of Columbia that night. No one can follow the record of Sherman's lawless troops in South Carolina without the conviction that Columbia was a doomed city even before it was taken. Its destruction was entirely in agreement with General Sherman's program in South Carolina, and his troops, having looted and pillaged their way to Columbia, had no restrictions placed upon their urge to plunder and burn the city. Sherman had assured General Halleck that, if his army took Charleston, it would not be necessary to sow salt on the site, because, he said, the Fifteenth Corps would be the one to enter Charleston first, "and, if you have watched the history of that corps, you will have remarked that they generally do their work pretty well."[42] When Sherman decided to pass Charleston by and march on Columbia instead, the Fifteenth Corps were among the troops who marched into Columbia.

The question of who issued the orders for the burning of South Carolina's capital is not important. Orders neither for nor against the sacking of the town, the robbery of its citizens and its final reduction to ashes were required by Sherman's trained wreckers. All they needed was the indifference of their commanding officers. Without the restrictions imposed by orderly military procedure, they did their most effective work of devastation and ruin. They were given a free rein in the streets of Columbia, many units being dismissed upon their arrival in the city and the men left to forage alone or in groups. As the Seventeenth Army Corps marched through Columbia, they were in good order, according to one witness, and they could have been used to prevent other soldiers of the advance guard from pillaging and sacking store buildings. The plundering of the stores was carried on within sight of the Seventeenth's marching column.[43] Sherman himself was aware of the actions of his troops, as he had seen them plundering houses and had heard citizens' complaints about their lawlessness. He had walked about the city the same afternoon before the fires started at night, and the temper of the soldiers could not have escaped him.[44]

The fires burst out with the coming of darkness on the night of February 17, 1865. Most witnesses agree that the flames broke out in opposite sides of the city as if timed by some prearranged signal. Twenty fires broke out almost at once, and while the alarm was being given, a similar alarm was sounded from Cotton Town, in the northernmost limit of the city. Simultaneously new fires lit up the night from Main Street, in the center of the business area. The fire equipment could not be used as the hose had been cut by drunken Federal soldiers earlier in the day. It was agreed by many witnesses that a stiff wind did fan the flames and spread them, but many buildings and homes would have been saved by the gaps between them and the fires. The reveling Federal soldiers, in their element in the fire, smoke and cinders, refused to let the citizens fight the flames. When the crippled fire engines were brought out the soldiers turned them over in the streets and further cut up the water hose. When the fires did not spread rapidly enough the soldiers started them anew with "some inflammable material," stated James G. Gibbes, a prominent Columbian. "I suppose it to be turpentine, with which they made fire balls." It was in this way that Gibbes's father's fireproof home was burned after it had escaped the general conflagration.[45] The sworn statement of a member of Columbia's fire department declared, "The fires were the work of incendiaries and not of accident." From 30 years' experience in fire fighting, the deponent declared that "the fires occurred in twenty or thirty different places at the same time, and so far from each other that they could not have been connected."[46]

From early in the evening of February 17, 1865, until nearly daybreak of February 18 the flaming city presented an appalling sight. Among the falling embers and clouds of flame-shot smoke the frenzied people of Columbia sought to save what little they could of their possessions. The sick and helpless were hurriedly removed to the streets to save them from fiery graves. Even though the South Carolina College buildings were being used by both sides as a hospital, two attempts were made by the soldiers to set them on fire. On one of these occasions the patients were moved out of the buildings into an open area in the middle of the campus, and more than 20 of them died as a result of exposure and fright.[47] The streets of Columbia presented a frightful picture of dancing shadow and flame. The residents, unprepared for fire because of Sherman's assurance that private property would be respected, toiled in desperation to save a little clothing and some of their valuables. An eyewitness described the scene, as "both officers and men drunk to excess, were seen staggering from house to house, frantic with excitement, cursing the rebels for starting this war." As rapidly as valuable articles were rescued by the distraught homeowners they were snatched up and confiscated by the waiting soldiers. Under cover of the confusion and excitement of the roaring fires, soldiers in the uniform of the United States openly entered and looted houses as rapidly as they could break into them ahead of the flames.[48] One soldier became so surfeited with the unrestrained robbery and pillage of the citizens that he entered in his diary for the day that "I think the city should be burned, but would like to see it done decently."[49] A newspaper correspondent with Sherman's army presented a graphic picture of that terrible night as he observed it:

> . . . the streets were soon crowded with helpless women and children, some in their night clothes. Agonized mothers, seeking their children, all affrighted and terrified, were rushing on all sides from the raging flames and falling houses. Invalids had to be dragged from their beds, and lay exposed to the flames and smoke that swept the streets, or to the cold of open air in backyards.
>
> The scene at the convent [Sisters of Charity] was a sad one indeed. The flames were fast encompassing the convent and the sisters, and about sixty terrified young ladies huddled together on the streets. . . . The superioress of the convent had educated General Sherman's daughter Minnie. He had assigned a special guard of six men; so they felt secure, and were totally unprepared for the dreadful scene that ensued. Some Christian people formed a guard around the agonized group of ladies, and conducted them to the park.

This writer was impressed with the indifference of the troops who were supposed to police the town. Amid the shouts and screams of the unfortunate residents, "a troop of cavalry, I think the 29th Missouri," rode the streets, "but I did not once see them interfering with the groups that rushed about to fire and pillage the houses."[50]

A Union officer who had been a prisoner of the Confederates at Columbia declared that "the sights of that awful night will never fade from my memory." He tried to fathom the depths of the citizens' hopelessness. For many of them this loss of all they possessed was the last bitter stroke of misfortune. He pointed out their plight:

Most of the citizens of Columbia had sons or relations in the Rebel army. Half of them were dead, the army itself was flying everywhere and in the blackness of this terrible night their fortunes were all lost, their homes were all burning up. Many wandered about wringing their hands and crying; some sat stolid and speechless in the streets watching everything they had go to destruction. A few wandered about wholly demented.[51]

The excitement and confusion of the raging fires served to cover conduct on the part of the undisciplined Federal soldiers which was even more terrible than that of looting or pillaging the citizens' homes. Many of the soldiers began to attack women in the shadows and out-of-the-way places. Negro women were the most common victims of the bestiality of the troops. They had come with the crowds of Negroes, who were urged by the soldiers to carry off as many valuables as they could. A reputable Columbian observed:

> . . . that soon after the pillage began the frightened negro women sought earnestly protection & places of refuge, against the lustful soldiery & even abandoned their little property to get under the protection of some efficient guard. The bodies of several females were found on the morning of Saturday [February 18], stripped naked & with only such marks of violence upon them as would indicate the most detestable of crimes. . . . I would cast a veil over this part of the history of the fall of Columbia.[52]

A teacher at a college near Columbia noticed the change in the attitude of the Negro men. Although Sherman's soldiers loaded them down with all the booty they could carry, they became "thoroughly disgusted" and vowed vengeance for the base treatment their women had been subjected to.[53]

By the morning of February 18, 1865, the fires had almost burned out, and the streets of the city had been cleared of riotous Federal troops. The capital of South Carolina was a desolate, smoking ruin. Captain Conyngham viewed the wrecked city and wrote:

All the business portion, the main streets, the old capitol, two churches, and several public and private buildings were one pile of rubbish and bricks. Nothing remained but the tall spectre-looking chimneys. The noble looking trees that shaded the streets, the flower gardens that graced them, were blasted and withered by fire. The streets were full of rubbish, broken furniture, and groups of crouching, despondent, weeping, helpless women and children.[54]

The material destruction caused by the fire "involved eighty-four out of one hundred and twenty-four blocks, or squares, and these contained over five hundred edifices, including five churches, five banking houses, two hotels, the convent, foundries, factories and depots."[55] In addition the old state house and the buildings at the fair grounds were left in ruins. Among the most lasting losses were the legislative library, containing 25,000 volumes, "and the priceless collections of manuscripts, books, paintings and statuary of the Drs. O'Connell and Robert W. Gibbes, stored at St. Mary's College, and at the mansion of the last named. Dr. Gibbes's historical collection was particularly rich and rare."[56]

The condition of the residents in Columbia was indeed pathetic. The acting mayor, James G. Gibbes, reported that the city was crowded with refugees from other sections of South Carolina even before it was burned, and after the fire "it would be impossible to find shelter for one-tenth of the homeless." He pointed out that there was no transportation—the railroads were destroyed and there were no horses and conveyances—so that the homeless and hungry could not be moved to other places. Every store and shop had been destroyed, and there were not enough provisions to support the people for two days. Nothing could be expected from the surrounding country, which had been swept clean by Sherman's wasteful foragers.[57] Many of the homeless left Columbia on foot to seek food and shelter. The wife of Confederate General Joseph E. Johnston wrote a friend referring to the sad plight of these people, "Many leaving with little bundles of clothes—and many compelled to remain, for they had nothing but God to look to for shelter."[58]

A committee of citizens waited on General Sherman on Sunday morning, February 19, to seek relief for the starving people of Columbia. A member of this committee was impressed with Sherman's attitude and appearance as he faced those who had just been impoverished by his army. "Sherman alone appeared flushed with victory & made no effort to conceal his exultation. He occasionally made remarks bordering on the facetious which were strangely out of place or harmony with his suffering and sorrowful auditory." Sherman's attitude was all the more noticeable when contrasted with the appearances of Generals Howard, Blair and Woods, who were also present and had the grace to look "serious & even saddened as if ashamed of the mischief they had been compelled to do."[59]

Sherman acquiesced in the Mayor's request for relief for the hungry and agreed to leave a small supply of undestroyed provisions, some salt, and to turn over several hundred head of cattle. The committee was aware of the fact that these cattle were the stolen property of South Carolinians, and McCarter noted in his journal that "we had to learn the humiliating lesson of being suppliant, for a morsel of our own bread & for our own meat."[60] Five hundred sixty head of cattle were driven into the South Carolina College enclosure, where they were found to be the refuse of the Union army's herds. They were so emaciated and weak that they could hardly have been driven farther. The citizens decided to butcher them as rapidly as possible, but even so, 160 of them died before they could be killed for beef.[61] The general distress of the citizens of Columbia was attested to by the citizen's committee appointed to take testimony on the extent of the destruction. The evidence showed "that for about three months daily rations, consisting generally of a pint of meal and a small allowance of poor beef for each person, were dealt out at Columbia, to upwards of 8,000 sufferers."[62]

The Federal soldiers moved out of Columbia on February 20, 1865, and continued their march northward. By March 6 both wings of the army crossed the Pee Dee River and marched for Fayetteville, North Carolina, which place they reached on March 11, 1865. The whole track of the Federal route from Columbia to the North Carolina line was marked with fire and ruthless destruction. Immediately upon crossing into North Carolina the conduct of the Federal troops underwent a pronounced change. Captain George W. Nichols noted in his diary on March 8, 1865, at Laurel Hill, North Carolina, that "the conduct of the soldiers is perceptibly changed. I have seen no evidence of plundering; the men keep their ranks closely; and more remarkable yet, not a single column of the fire or smoke which a few days ago marked the positions of heads of column, can be seen upon the horizon."[63] General Manning F. Force was also impressed with the improved conduct of the soldiers. "When we crossed the boundary line into North Carolina," he said, "destruction ceased. Not a house was burned, and the army gave to the people more than it took from them." These same ruthless men who had so heartlessly despoiled and devastated South Carolina continued their march to Raleigh and Washington, after the surrender of Lee and Johnston, in such an exemplary manner that General Force said: "Not a man strayed from the ranks, not so much as a chicken was taken, not a fence rail was burned."[64] General H. W. Slocum, according to a staff officer, felt that North Carolina had made more sacrifices for the Union and felt more friendly toward the North, and for that reason "should be protected from their friends." In his General Orders No. 8, issued at Sneedsboro, North Carolina, on March 7, 1865, General Slocum reminded his men and officers that North Carolina was one of the last states to pass the ordinance of secession and that there was a strong Union sentiment among the great majority of its citizens. In conclusion the order expressed the hope that "every effort will be made to prevent any wanton destruction of property, or any unkind treatment of citizens."[65]

The changed conduct of Sherman's troops after crossing into North Carolina proves conclusively that discipline could be enforced when it suited Sherman's purposes to enforce it. The curbing of the lawlessness of his men, trained for years to burn, pillage and destroy, only brings into clearer focus the enormity of the crimes Sherman deliberately perpetrated upon the helpless, noncombatant population of the South. The prostrate state of South Carolina, broken, impoverished, hopeless, was filled with a deep and abiding bitterness. They had been forced to submit to superior strength while every indignity and outrage had been heaped upon their persons. They had witnessed the destruction of their homes, their agricultural implements, their barns, gin houses and mills. Helplessly they had seen the Union soldiers wantonly waste the last scrap of their provisions and shoot down their livestock when they could find no use for the animals. South Carolinians were numbed by the ferocity of the destruction visited upon them, not only because it violated all the laws of war, but because it was so completely unnecessary to accomplish their surrender.

Sherman's practice of total war against the people of the South had led him to wage a war almost of annihilation against those whom he professed he was bringing back into the Union of States. Since the whole purpose of the conflict was to bring back into the fold those states which had attempted to withdraw, good policy and common sense required that it be accomplished with as little cause for future hatred as possible. The people of Mississippi, Georgia and South Carolina returned to their places in the Union of States, but the same results could have been obtained without the wanton destruction, the outrages and indignities which were visited upon them. All other causes of estrangement would pass away and be forgotten long before the crime committed by Sherman against a people's spirit would be forgiven.

Epilogue

The peace at Appomattox brought no peace to the South. All sections of the Confederacy felt the blight of war and the shock of grief over loved ones who never returned. The defeat which the South suffered was all the bitterer because the Confederate States had fought long and courageously against odds that weighted the scales against them with every passing day. The loss of the South's manhood, young and middle-aged alike, represented an irreplaceable asset—the sheer manpower necessary to rebuild the section. Families were disrupted, separated, and many of those lost in the countryside were never reunited with their relatives. Aside from the incalculable losses in personal property, people of the South lost in the newly freed slaves not only a labor force but a property investment of several billion dollars. Cotton, the currency of the South, valued at more than 25 million dollars was confiscated or burned. Investments in the bonds and money of the Confederacy resulted in the total loss of capital badly needed for the vital job of restoration and rehabilitation. Fields were ruined; houses, barns and agricultural implements were burned and destroyed. Livestock was killed or confiscated. General Grant recognized the need for animals to help make a crop and permitted Confederate soldiers to take horses and mules with them when they returned to their homes. Most of these were so undernourished and weakened by the heavy strain placed on them in the closing months of the war that they never lived to reach the weed-grown fields of the deep South.

Greater than the loss of property, however, was the depression and hopelessness of the people of the South. Bitterness and deep anger replaced the sense of sacrifice, action and dedication which had characterized their determination to win the war at any cost. These feelings were intensified at the end of the war by the realization that so much of the widespread destruction which had been visited upon the civilian population by a vindictive enemy had been unnecessary for a Union victory. Bitterness and hatred would have been expected in the hearts of returning veterans who had taken part in many desperate actions on many blood-soaked battlefields. However, in the case of the South, military action taken against women, children and old people caused anger and resentment to permeate the lives of those at home. General Sherman himself realized the intensity of the feelings of women and children as his troops destroyed everything they held dear. He had written Mrs. Sherman in June 1863: "I doubt if history affords a parallel to the deep and bitter enmity of the women of the South. No one who sees them and hears them but must feel the intensity of their hate."

It is generally conceded that those who have been defeated, and then humiliated, remember war far longer than those who were the victors. The memories of the defeated are nurtured within the family and told and retold. Mothers especially exercise a lasting influence over the thoughts and attitudes of their children. The women referred to by Sherman, whose husbands, sons and brothers were away defending their country, passed along to their children and kept alive the sense of humiliation and hatred which grew out of their helplessness at the hands of an undisciplined soldiery. It was not difficult to tell and retell the stories of needless destruction of even the primitive tools needed to mitigate the long, painful period of poverty and restoration. It was not difficult to keep alive resentment and anger against those whose military forces occupied the defeated South for 12 years and against those who, among many indignities visited on the people, promoted and supported the corrupt Black-dominated legislatures. There was a widespread feeling among the people of the former Confederacy that the North as a whole felt a deep sense of malice toward them. Many businessmen, as they struggled to regain a measure of economic stability, were convinced that Northern businessmen deliberately burdened the South, placing it in a colonial relationship with the North. Freight-rate differentials which worked to the disadvantage of Southern industry were eliminated only as recently as the late 1940s.

The acts of terror committed against the civilian populace of the South by Sherman's troops indeed planted seeds of hatred which bore bitter fruit and postponed a sense of unity and understanding between the people of the United States far longer than might otherwise have been the case.

NOTES
BIBLIOGRAPHY
INDEX

Notes

PREFACE

1. These instructions, issued as General Orders No. 100, April 24, 1863, are in *The War of the Rebellion: A Compilation of the Official Records of the Union and Confederate Armies* (129 vols. and index, Washington, 1880–1901), Ser. III, Vol. III, pp. 148–164. This collection cited hereafter as *Official Records*.

INTRODUCTION

1. Sherman to Mrs. Sherman, April 15, 1859, in M. A. DeWolfe Howe (ed.), *The Home Letters of General Sherman* (New York, 1909), p. 159. Hereafter referred to as *Home Letters*.

CHAPTER I.   Louisiana to Bull Run

1. David French Boyd, "General W. T. Sherman as a College President," in *The American College* (New York, 1909–1910), II, 3.
2. *Ibid.*, pp. 3–4. Boyd explains that there was at the time a Sherman who was prominent in Georgia educational circles.
3. *Ibid.*, p. 2.
4. William T. Sherman, *Memoirs of General William T. Sherman* (2 vols.; New York, 1875), I, 148. Hereafter referred to as *Memoirs*.
5. Boyd, *op. cit.*, p. 6.
6. *Home Letters*, pp. 183–184.

7. *Ibid.*, p. 186.
8. *Memoirs*, I, 155.
9. *Ibid.*, pp. 155–156.
10. *Ibid.*, p. 156.
11. *Home Letters*, p. 177.
12. *Ibid.*, p. 195.
13. Boyd, *op. cit.*, pp. 6–7.
14. *Memoirs*, I, 161–162.
15. This salary was greater than that paid governors of states in 1860.
16. Boyd, *op. cit.*, pp. 7–8.
17. *Memoirs*, I, 166.
18. Sherman to Mrs. Sherman, September 18, 1858. *Home Letters*, p. 153.
19. *Memoirs*, I, 166.
20. Rachel Thorndike (ed.), *The Sherman Letters* (New York, 1894), p. 92. (Hereafter referred to as *Sherman Letters.*) It is interesting to note that Ellen Sherman had written John Sherman soliciting his help in securing employment for Tecumseh. The letter, undated, is found in the W. T. Sherman Papers, Division of Manuscripts, Library of Congress, and doubtless caused Senator Sherman to bestir himself in his brother's behalf. The W. T. Sherman Papers show that Ellen Sherman wrote frequently to John Sherman concerning her husband, and she appeared to consider John the stronger and more dependable of the two brothers.
21. *Memoirs*, I, 167.
22. *Ibid.*, pp. 167–168. Sherman describes the meeting and how it affected him.
23. This attitude will be observed throughout Sherman's wartime correspondence and was intensified after the charge of insanity was made.
24. *Memoirs*, I, 168.
25. John Sherman to W. T. Sherman, April 12, 1861. *Sherman Letters*, p. 110.
26. *Idem.* It is difficult to understand on what basis John told Sherman that he was a great favorite with the army. Comparatively speaking, Sherman's army experience was limited and of short duration. True he was a West Point graduate, but the highest rank he attained was that of quartermaster captain.
27. *Ibid.*, p. 112.
28. *Memoirs*, I, 171.
29. *Ibid.*, pp. 171–172. The italics appear in Sherman's *Memoirs*, but not in the original letter found in the W. T. Sherman Papers.
30. W. T. Sherman to John Sherman, April 1861 (exact date not given). *Sherman Letters*, pp. 111–112.
31. This theme can be noted throughout Sherman's correspondence, particularly in the early months of the war. See *Home Letters*, pp. 211–212; and *Sherman Letters*, p. 127, as examples.

32. W. T. Sherman to John Sherman, April 22, 1861. *Sherman Letters,* p. 113.
33. *Memoirs,* I, 175 and 177.
34. Sherman to Thomas Ewing, Jr., May 23, 1861. *Home Letters,* p. 197.
35. Sherman to Thomas Ewing, Jr., June 3, 1861. *Ibid.,* p. 198.
36. Sherman to Mrs. Sherman, June 8, 1861. *Ibid.,* p. 199.
37. Sherman to Mrs. Sherman, July 16, 1861. *Ibid.,* pp. 200–201.
38. Sherman to Mrs. Sherman, July 28, 1861. *Ibid.,* p. 208.
39. *Ibid.,* p. 209.
40. August 3, 1861. *Ibid.,* pp. 211–212.
41. William F. G. Shanks, *Personal Recollections of Distinguished Generals* (New York, 1866), p. 26.
42. Sherman to Mrs. Sherman, undated letter, apparently written in August 1861. *Home Letters,* p. 214.
43. Sherman to Mrs. Sherman on July 28, 1861, and August 3, 1861. *Home Letters,* pp. 209–211. Sherman to John Sherman, August 19, 1861. *Sherman Letters,* p. 126. This is also indicated in *Memoirs,* I, 200, as Sherman, even in retrospect, attempted to work out the enemy's moves.
44. Sherman to General Stephen A. Hurlbut, July 10, 1862. *Official Records,* Ser. I, Vol. XVII, Pt. II, pp. 88–89.

CHAPTER II. Kentucky Command—Specter of Oblivion

1. *Memoirs,* I, 192–193. Also see Sherman to John Sherman, August 19, 1861, *Sherman Letters,* p. 126.
2. Sherman to John Sherman from Fort Corcoran, August 19, 1861. *Sherman Letters,* p. 127.
3. Sherman to Garrett Davis, October 8, 1861. *Official Records,* Ser. I, Vol. IV, p. 297.
4. Sherman to John Sherman, October 26, 1861. *Sherman Letters,* pp. 133–134.
5. Sherman describes his feelings, *Memoirs,* I, 200–210. Sherman to President Lincoln, October 10, 1861, *Official Records,* Ser. I, Vol. IV, p. 300. Sherman to President Lincoln, October 14, 1861, *Ibid.,* pp. 306–307. Sherman to the Secretary of War, October 20, 1861, *Ibid.,* pp. 312. *Official Records,* Ser. I, Vol. IV, pp. 255–302, paints an unmistakable picture of the utter disorganization of Union efforts in Kentucky. These pages are filled with constant appeals for troops and arms.
6. Sherman to Adjutant General Lorenzo Thomas, October 22, 1861. *Official Records,* Ser. I, Vol. IV, pp. 313–314. An excerpt from this letter is also found in *Sherman Letters,* p. 133. In *Memoirs,* I, 204–205, Sherman gives the complete text.
7. Sherman to John Sherman, October 5, 1861. *Sherman Letters,* pp. 132–133. It is characteristic of General Sherman's letters to shift from one subject to another without reason. The ellipses here indicate omission of unrelated matter.

8. *Memoirs,* I, 200.

9. Sherman complained on November 6 that the Confederates received prompt, accurate reports as to Union strength and movements, whereas "we can procure information only by circuitous and unreliable means." W. T. Sherman to Adjutant General Lorenzo Thomas, November 6 1861, W. T. Sherman Papers.

10. William Preston Johnston, *The Life of General Albert Sidney Johnston* (New York, 1879), pp. 306–398, gives a graphic account of the problems facing the Confederate forces in Kentucky, with official correspondence, etc.

11. *Ibid.,* p. 316. General Johnston's information apparently was none too accurate, since he referred to "perfectly equipped" Union forces.

12. *Ibid.,* p. 315.

13. *Idem.*

14. *Ibid.,* p. 366. On October 26, 1861, Sherman had written his brother informing him that the Confederates "have already invaded the state with five times my forces." *Sherman Letters,* p. 134. Sherman to John Sherman, October 26, 1861. See Stanley F. Horn, *The Army of Tennessee; A Military History* (Indianapolis, 1941), p. 56 ff.

15. Sherman to Adjutant General Lorenzo Thomas, November 6, 1861 W. T. Sherman Papers.

16. W. P. Johnston, *op. cit.,* pp. 316 and 351.

17. *Memoirs,* I, 200.

18. Mrs. Sherman to John Sherman, November 10, 1861. W. T. Sherman Papers. This letter was written from Louisville and Mrs. Sherman says "I was alarmed by the receipt of a dispatch from Capt. Prince. . . 'Send Mrs. Sherman & youngest boy down to relieve Gen. Sherman mind from the pressure of business—no occasion for alarm.'" The dispatch was sent to Thomas Ewing and opened by Mrs. Sherman in her absence.

19. *Idem.*

20. *Idem.*

21. Lloyd Lewis, *Sherman, Fighting Prophet* (New York, 1932), pp. 196 197. Lewis gives in detail some of the specific charges made against Sherman by correspondents.

22. Immediately before and after Vicksburg Sherman was even bitterer toward reporters, whom he charged with giving valuable information to the enemy through news reports, even down to the location of specific batteries of guns. He barred them from accompanying his troops, and court-martialed one who disobeyed.

23. Albert D. Richardson, *The Secret Service; the Field, the Dungeon and the Escape* (Hartford, 1866), p. 247.

24. Shanks, *op. cit.,* pp. 22 and 53, gives a good picture of the impression Sherman made on those who observed him at this time.

25. *Ibid.,* p. 33. Sherman's version is substantially in agreement with the

version of how the story became public property. See *Memoirs*, I, 202–214. Also A. D. Richardson, *op. cit.*, p. 247. Richardson was a correspondent for *The New York Tribune*, and he subscribes to Sherman's story as to how the report originated.

26. *Memoirs*, I, 204. On the day that Sherman took the command from General Anderson he wrote a citizen of Paris, Kentucky: "I am forced into the command of this department against my will, and it would take 300,000 men to fill half the calls for troops." Sherman to Garrett Davis, October 8, 1861. *Official Records*, Ser. I, Vol. IV, p. 297.

27. *Memoirs*, I, 204. In his *Memoirs*, I, 206–214, Sherman introduces evidence to show that what he said was in no sense unreasonable. There is included a statement by Major General Thomas J. Wood, U.S.A., who was present at the interview and who stated that there was present in the room a reporter of *The New York Tribune*. This ties in with Shanks's version, presented on p. 52.

28. See excerpts from Sherman's letter to John Sherman in April 1861 (exact date not given). *Sherman Letters*, pp. 111–112.

29. *Memoirs*, I, 193. Sherman tells of this interview with Mr. Lincoln at the time he was ordered to Kentucky. Sherman assured the President that he did not desire promotion, and the President had agreed to the unusual request.

30. Mrs. Sherman to John Sherman, November 10, 1861. W. T. Sherman Papers.

31. Sherman to John Sherman, November 21, 1861. *Ibid.*

32. *Idem.*

33. Series of telegrams between Sherman and General Halleck, General Pope and General Halleck, all dated November 28, 1861. *Official Records*, Ser. I, Vol. VIII, pp. 391–392. L. Lewis, *op. cit.*, p. 199, states that Ellen Sherman probably demanded a furlough for her husband. *Memoirs*, I, 215, reproduces the order to return to St. Louis.

34. General Henry W. Halleck to Sherman, December 18, 1861. *Official Records*, Ser. I, Vol. VIII, pp. 445–446. Halleck frankly told Sherman that much of the harsh criticism pointed at Sherman resulted from loose talk.

35. *Memoirs*, I, 215–216.

36. *Idem.*

37. Ellen Sherman to John Sherman, December 12, 1861. W. T. Sherman Papers.

38. *Memoirs*, I, 217. Henry W. Halleck to Thomas Ewing, February 15, 1862. It is not unlikely that Halleck was impressed by Sherman's excellent political connections in Washington. Also it cannot be overlooked that Ellen Sherman had taken it upon herself to write directly to President Lincoln on January 10, 1862, asking the President to vindicate her husband. She pointed out that his subordinate position under Halleck only served to endorse the charges that General Sherman

was mentally ill. Ellen Sherman to President Lincoln, January 10, 1862. W. T. Sherman Papers.

39. Ellen Sherman to John Sherman, December 16, 1861. W. T. Sherman Papers.
40. *Idem.* The underscoring is Mrs. Sherman's.
41. *Memoirs,* I, 214.
42. See *ante,* p. 37, footnote 26.
43. Ellen Sherman to John Sherman, December 16, 1861. W. T. Sherman Papers.
44. Ellen Sherman to John Sherman, December 17, 1861. *Ibid.*
45. Sherman to Thomas Ewing, December 12, 1861. *Ibid.* See also *Memoirs,* I, 214–215.
46. Ellen Sherman to John Sherman, December 17, 1861. W. T. Sherman Papers.
47. *Memoirs,* I, 214–215.
48. Sherman to John Sherman, early January 1862 (exact date not given). *Sherman Letters,* p. 138.
49. Sherman to John Sherman, January 4, 1862. W. T. Sherman Papers.
50. Sherman to John Sherman, January 8, 1862. *Ibid.*
51. W. F. G. Shanks, *op. cit.,* p. 43. Sherman refers to the opportune arrival of Buell at Shiloh with "fresh Kentucky troops," in a letter to Mrs. Sherman, April 11, 1862. *Home Letters,* pp. 221–222. In *Memoirs,* I, 244–247, Sherman tends to disparage Buell's effect in deciding the battle. He admits that Buell's force made it possible to sweep the field and consolidate the victory.
52. Sherman to John Sherman, approximate date January 6, 1862. *Sherman Letters,* p. 138.
53. Sherman to Thomas Ewing, December 31, 1864. *Home Letters,* p. 321. This letter says that his men would march to certain death at his order. Sherman to Mrs. Sherman, January 5, 1865. *Ibid.,* p. 326. Sherman tells her of the childlike faith of his soldiers, who "think I know everything," and who think there is no place where he has not been. It was suggested more than once that Sherman courted his men for their affections through lax discipline.

CHAPTER III.   Shiloh—Renewed Confidence and a New Friend

1. John Sherman to General Sherman, February 15, 1862. *Sherman Letters,* p. 140.
2. Boyd, *op. cit.,* p. 4.
3. W. F. G. Shanks, *op. cit.,* p. 37.
4. Ulysses S. Grant, *Personal Memoirs* (2 vols.; New York, 1885), I, 315. See Grant to Sherman, February 19, 1862. *Official Records,* Ser. I, Vol.

VII, p. 638. Grant thanks Sherman for the encouraging letter Sherman sent upriver to him.

5. General Halleck had written Sherman in February 1862 that new movements were planned, and he added: "You will not be forgotten in this." Halleck to Sherman, February 17, 1862. *Official Records*, Ser. I, Vol. VII, p. 629. See Halleck to Sherman, February 25, 1862, *ibid.*, pp. 667–688; and Halleck's order to Sherman for steamboats, February 27, 1862, *ibid.*, p. 670.

6. Sherman to Mrs. Sherman, April 11, 1862. *Home Letters*, p. 221.

7. W. F. G. Shanks, *op. cit.*, p. 59. General Halleck recommended Sherman to the Secretary of War for promotion for "Saving the day on the 6th, and contributed largely to the glorious victory of the 7th." Dated April 13, 1862. W. T. Sherman Papers.

8. Sherman to Mrs. Sherman, May 26, 1862. *Home Letters*, p. 226.

9. Grant, *Memoirs*, I, 338. Also see *ibid.*, pp. 339 and 343, which further show how impressed Grant was with the way Sherman conducted himself. Doubtless this laid the basis for his later confidence in Sherman's abilities.

10. A. D. Richardson, *op. cit.*, pp. 243–244. This war correspondent for *The New York Tribune* contrasts the attitudes of Grant and Sherman to criticism. Grant "silently smoked and waited," while Sherman "was foolishly sensitive to every word of criticism."

11. John Sherman to General Sherman, February 15, 1862. *Sherman Letters*, p. 140.

12. A. D. Richardson, *op. cit.*, p. 248. See *Memoirs*, I, 225. Sherman recounts "that single battle had given me new life, and I was in high feather."

13. Sherman to Mrs. Sherman, April 24, 1862. *Home Letters*, p. 225.

14. Sherman to Thomas Ewing, April 27, 1862. *Ibid.*, pp. 225–226. Senator Ewing did defend Grant, as indicated by clippings, sent Sherman by Mrs. Sherman, of articles appearing in a Louisville paper, *Home Letters*, pp. 226–227. George C. Gorham, *Life and Public Services of Edwin M. Stanton* (2 vols.; Boston and New York, 1889), I, 311, says it is not known how these attacks against Grant started. They were similar to efforts to hurt his name after his victory at Fort Donelson. This author further points out that it was Halleck's immediate duty to investigate the charges and either relieve Grant of command or clear his name. Halleck did nothing at all.

15. Sherman to Mrs. Sherman, June 6, 1862. *Ibid.*, p. 227.

16. *Idem.*

17. Sherman to Mrs. Sherman, June 6, 1862. *Home Letters*, p. 228.

18. *Idem.*

19. *Ibid.*, p. 229. Shanks states that Sherman's dislike for newspapermen was affected and that with all of his feigned dislike for them, he prob-

ably owed more to the press than any other officer in the Union army. W. F. G. Shanks, *op. cit.,* pp. 48 and 50. It is more likely that as Sherman came more and more into public favor he realized how well newspapermen could enhance his reputation.

20. *Memoirs,* I, 254. It is well to remember that Sherman's estimate of the situation was written in retrospect, as was Grant's in his *Memoirs,* quoted in the following pages.

21. The orders referred to were officially designated as Special Orders No. 30 and are interesting in the extravagant phraseology used by Sherman to convince his men that Corinth was, in every sense, a great victory and that the rebels had not had the courage to face them in battle. Quoted in full, *Sherman Letters,* pp. 151–154.

22. From a note in pencil written on the same sheet with copies of Special Order No. 30, General Sherman to John Sherman, May 31, 1862. *Sherman Letters,* pp. 154–155.

23. Grant, *Memoirs,* I, 385; Sherman, *Memoirs,* I, 255; Sherman to Mrs. Sherman, June 6, 1862, *Home Letters,* p. 228. Such incidents as this point to the personal basis on which Sherman's and Grant's friendship rested. G. C. Gorham, *op. cit.,* I, 308–312, indicates that General Halleck not only ignored Grant, but, by inference, permitted the War Department to believe that Grant was guilty of negligence and misconduct.

24. Grant, *Memoirs,* I, 383.

25. *Ibid.,* p. 381.

26. *Memoirs,* I, 257–258.

27. Grant, *Memoirs,* I, 397. Halleck to Grant, July 31, 1862, *Official Records,* Ser. I, Vol. XVII, Pt. II, p. 142.

CHAPTER IV.   Memphis Commander—The Theory of
Collective Responsibility

1. Grant, *Memoirs,* I, 394.

2. *Ibid.,* p. 395.

3. *Memoirs,* I, 265. Sherman to John Sherman, September 3, 1862, *Sherman Letters,* p. 160.

4. Sherman to Mayor Park, July 27, 1862. *Memoirs,* I, 270–271. Also appears in *Official Records,* Ser. I, Vol. XVII, Pt. II, p. 252.

5. Complete text of the letter from Sherman to Secretary Salmon P. Chase, August 11, 1862, *Memoirs,* I, 266–268. Sherman stopped payment for cotton in gold on the grounds that it was exchanged for munitions. See his letter to Colonel John A. Rawlins, Grant's Assistant Adjutant General, July 30, 1862. *Official Records,* Ser. I, Vol. XVII, Pt. II, p. 140. He was later ordered from Washington to resume payment in gold, with the implication that he had exceeded his authority in suspending such payments without official sanction. Halleck's orders stated that the question would be submitted to the Secretary of War. Halleck to

Grant, August 2, 1862. *Official Records,* Ser. I, Vol. XVII, Pt. II, p. 150.

6. *Idem.*

7. Other Union commanders were aware of this situation. Brigadier General John A. Logan, in a dispatch to a subordinate, warned: "I am of the opinion that the enemy will have support from nearly all of the citizens of that country." Logan to Hogg, July 30, 1862. *Official Records,* Ser. I, Vol. XVII, Pt. II, p. 136.

8. Sherman to Grant, August 17, 1862. *Official Records,* Ser. I, Vol. XVII, Pt. II, p. 178. In *ibid.,* p. 205, Sherman reported to Grant an attack on a lieutenant and a detachment ten miles from Memphis—an attack which Sherman said was made by civilians.

9. E. N. Gilpin, "The Last Campaign—A Cavalryman's Journal," reprint from the *Journal of U.S. Cavalry Association,* Vol. 18, No. 68, April 1908, p. 626, gives an account of Forrest's sortie into Memphis itself, disguised as a wagon driver, where the only thing that prevented his capturing Sherman was that Sherman was delayed in returning to his headquarters.

10. Thomas Jordan and J. P. Pryor, *The Campaigns of Lieutenant-General Forrest and Forrest's Cavalry* (New York, 1868), pp. 364–365. Forrest's cavalry was composed of small commands, raised locally, varying in size from groups of 25 to 200 men. On p. 363 there is reference to a group called the West Tennessee Partisans.

11. John Allen Wyeth, *Life of General Nathan Bedford Forrest* (New York, 1899), p. 180 ff. An interesting account of the ruses resorted to by Forrest to cause Union commanders to overestimate his strength. Forrest's raid into West Tennessee in December 1862 was carried out with about 1,500 effectives, but was estimated at between 3,000 and 7,000 men. See also John Watson Morton, *The Artillery of Nathan Bedford Forrest's Cavalry* (Nashville and Dallas, 1909), pp. 49–50. Morton was Forrest's chief of artillery and describes how the General lighted a series of fires at night, marched his men as infantry, caused drums to be beat at intervals, to build up an impression of great force. *Ibid.,* p. 137, Forrest divided his force into three parties to confuse the enemy. Doubtless Generals Price and Van Dorn used similar tactics.

12. Sherman to John Sherman, August 26, 1862. *Sherman Letters,* p. 160.

13. Sherman to John Sherman, September 22, 1862. *Ibid.,* p. 162.

14. Henry Wager Halleck, *International Law or, Rules Regulating the Intercourse of States in Peace and War* (New York, 1861), p. 387, paragraph 9, ruled that in cases where it could be shown that a prisoner's name appeared on a muster role, or that he held a commission, he could not be treated as a guerilla, but was entitled to treatment as a prisoner of war. Apparently inquiries had been sent to Washington for a definition of the term "guerilla," as Halleck called on Dr. Francis Lieber, as early as August 6, 1862, for a ruling on the

term. Dr. Lieber's reply was inconclusive, more concerned with historical background, and concluded with the statement that Halleck's own
definition, found in *International Law,* was dependable. *Official Records,*
Ser. III, Vol. II, p. 301. Lieber's reply, *ibid.,* pp. 301–309.

15. Sherman to Mrs. Sherman, July 31, 1862. *Home Letters,* p. 230.
16. John Sherman to Sherman, May 19, 1862. *Sherman Letters,* pp. 150–151.
17. Letter written by Sherman to the editor, the whole text of which is
given by Sherman in his *Memoirs,* I, 276–278. The newspaper is identified simply as the *Bulletin,* and is dated September 21, 1862. It does not
appear in the *Official Records* with his other Memphis correspondence.
The letter is very detailed, pointing out, among other things, that he
could not punish his whole command, but would have to have identifica-
tion of guilty individuals, and further that local insults to Union soldiers removed the incentive for officers to punish the men. It is
interesting to note that Grant did punish whole commands, as well as
the officers in charge, where uncalled-for damage to private property
was discovered. He fined the men through deductions from their pay,
and dishonorably discharged the officers. See Court-Martial Order,
Official Records, Ser. I, Vol. XVII, Pt. II, pp. 331–332, also p. 350.
18. Sherman to Colonel C. C. Walcutt, September 24, 1862. *Official
Records,* Ser. I, Vol. XVII, Pt. II, pp. 235–236.
19. Here Sherman's thinking follows closely the reasoning of Carl von
Clausewitz, the author of the famous treatise *On War.* Clausewitz, who
stated that "war does not carry in itself the elements for a complete
decision and final settlement," points out that the people of the enemy
nation must be brought into complete submission, otherwise "the war
may break out afresh, either in the interior, or through assistance given
by Allies." See pp. 173–174, Joseph I. Green (Colonel), *The Living
Thoughts of Clausewitz* (New York, 1943).
20. It is interesting to note that Sherman was not the only Union officer
who felt the impact of the vicious stabs of roaming Southern horsemen.
On August 21, 1862, Grant had reported to Halleck that "guerillas"
had captured two steamers on the Tennessee River and sunk another.
Official Records, Ser. I, Vol. XVII, Pt. II, p. 182. General Dodge reported to Grant, August 23, 1862, that he had taken 900 shotguns and
500 rifles from guerillas and citizens. *Ibid.,* p. 184. General Grant later
reported to Halleck (September 5, 1862) that the capture and sinking
of the steamers was accomplished through the connivance of the boat's
captains with Southerners. *Ibid.,* p. 202.
21. Sherman to Grant, September 4, 1862. *Official Records,* Ser. I, Vol.
XVII, Pt. II, p. 201.
22. Sherman to John Sherman, October 1, 1862. *Sherman Letters,* p. 166.
23. Sherman to John Sherman, October 1, 1862. *Sherman Letters,* p. 166.
24. Sherman wrote General Halleck on September 17, 1863, after Vicksburg, advocating his method of war, which he described as "war, pure

and simple: to be applied directly to the civilians of the South." Sherman's letter reflects his anger over criticism of his methods in the North, and he charges the politicians with cowardice. *Memoirs,* I, 340–341. Northern criticism of Sherman's activities offer an attractive field for further investigation.

CHAPTER V. Experiments in Terror

1. Special Order No. 254, issued at Memphis, September 27, 1862. *Official Records,* Ser. I, Vol. XVII, Pt. II, p. 240.
2. H. W. Halleck, *op. cit.,* p. 296. Paragraph 10 outlines the accepted attitude of the middle of the nineteenth century toward vindictive retaliation, or *retorsio facti,* saying in part: "We have no right . . . to put prisoners and hostages to death, and to destroy private property, merely because our enemy has done this to us; for no individual is justly chargeable with the guilt of a personal crime for the acts of the community of which he is a member."
3. *Ibid.,* p. 427. Chapter XVIII, paragraph 3.
4. Adam Badeau, *Military History of Ulysses S. Grant* (New York, 1885), p. 19. Badeau knew Sherman personally.
5. Sherman to Grant, October 4, 1862. *Official Records,* Ser. I, Vol. XVII, Pt. II, pp. 261–262.
6. It is impractical here to try to document this statement, as Sherman mentions in too many places just how terrible the destruction is—he deplores the necessity for it. In other places he says it will shorten the war and is, in effect, a blessing in disguise. This impression becomes stronger after an examination of the official orders issued throughout Sherman's career. These orders bear little resemblance to the operations they were supposed to cover, insofar as the conduct of his troops against noncombatants was concerned.
7. See Grant's letter to Sherman, October 29, 1862. *Official Records,* Ser. I, Vol. XVII, Pt. II, p. 307. In this letter he expresses his hearty approval of the expelling of families from Memphis, and recommended that if Sherman had to feed Memphis's destitute, he should collect for sums so spent through an assessment on the better-provided citizens.
8. The extent to which Halleck influenced Sherman in the formation of his philosophy cannot be evaluated here. That he later approved Sherman's actions in Georgia and South Carolina there can be no doubt. See his congratulatory letter to Sherman at Savannah, quoted in full in Sherman's *Memoirs,* II, 222–223. It appears at this time that Halleck's influence, if any, was negative rather than positive. The question of Halleck's influence offers an interesting field for further investigation.
9. A. Badeau, *op. cit.,* p. 17. Grant on being appointed commander-in-chief of the Union Armies insisted, as one of his first acts, that Sherman be given command of the Military Division of the Mississippi, the second most important position in the army. Sherman's name was still

largely unknown in the East. W. F. G. Shanks, *op. cit.,* p. 19, said of Sherman's nervous organization: "He furnishes the motive power, but he frequently requires to be controlled and directed." A. D. Richardson, in *op. cit.,* p. 249, noted that Sherman was "a most valuable lieutenant for a general of . . . judgment, like Grant or Thomas. With one of them to plan or modify, he is emphatically the man to execute."

10. This letter well illustrates a characteristic which Shanks observed and which he described: "His nervousness is not less perceptible in his writings than in his conversation and manners." And further he said: "His ideas are never elaborated in his letters, though given more fully than in his conversations." W. F. G. Shanks, *op. cit.,* pp. 27–28.

11. Sherman to Grant, October 4, 1862. *Official Records,* Ser. I, Vol. XVII, Pt. II, pp. 260–261.

12. U. S. Grant, *op. cit.,* I, 396. Grant states that Memphis was the only part of his department not connected with headquarters by telegraph, and communication with that place was difficult, often requiring three or four days.

13. Sherman to Grant, October 18, 1862, and Sherman's Special Order No. 283, dated October 18, 1862. *Official Records,* Ser. I, Vol. XVII, Pt. II, pp. 260–261.

14. *Idem.*

15. Sherman to Grant, October 9, 1862. *Official Records,* Ser. I, Vol. XVII, Pt. II, p. 273.

16. Sherman to Colonel John A. Rawlins, Grant's Assistant Adjutant General, October 21, 1862. *Ibid.,* p. 285

17. H. W. Halleck, *op. cit.,* p. 778. This matter is fully developed by the author, showing that occupation of a town does not admit of occupation of the surrounding country if the enemy continues to offer resistance.

18. *Ibid.,* pp. 779–780, quotes in support Chief Justice Taney: "By the law and usages of nations, conquest is a valid title *while the victor remains exclusive* possessor of the conquered country." (The italics are Halleck's.)

19. Sherman to Grant, October 4, 1862. *Official Records,* Ser. I, Vol. XVII, Pt. II, p. 261. Sherman implies that his anger arose from the endangering of lives.

20. Sherman to Grant, September 4, 1862. *Ibid.,* p. 201. Sherman informed Grant of, among other things, the arrival at Memphis of a lot of shot and shell, and he feared it would cause the boats to be fired on. Sherman wrote Grant on October 4, 1862, that he had "two good roads to the river front so that steamboats can land our stores there." *Ibid.,* p. 260.

21. Sherman to Grant, October 18, 1862. *Ibid.,* p. 280.

22. *Idem.*

23. Special Order No. 283, dated October 18, 1862. *Idem.* This order is particularly interesting when contrasted with Sherman's stand on Sep-

tember 21, not quite a month before this, as he expressed it in a newspaper article, a viewpoint completely orthodox, in which Sherman had stated that he would enforce the law against pillage, "waste or destruction of cornfields, etc.," near Memphis.

24. Sherman to Grant, October 21, 1862. *Ibid.*, p. 285.

25. General Order No. 60, issued by General Grant at Memphis, July 3, 1862. *Ibid.*, p. 69. The orders indicate that Grant had his troubles while in command at Memphis and might account in part for his sympathetic attitude toward Sherman's harsh measures at Memphis. Grant was still conscious of "guerilla" activity at Corinth. In August 1862 he urged General Halleck to send him cavalry to combat them. Grant to Halleck, August 20, 1862. *Ibid.*, p. 182.

26. In H. W. Halleck, *op. cit.*, pp. 298–300, paragraphs 12 and 13, the question of collection for damages is fully discussed.

27. Sherman to Halleck, July 11, 1862. *Official Records*, Ser. I, Vol. XVII, Pt. II, p. 90.

28. Special Order No. 130, issued by Sherman to accomplish collection for damages through loss of mules. *Ibid.*, p. 96.

29. Sherman to General Hurlbut, July 10, 1862. *Ibid.*, pp. 88–89.

30. H. W. Halleck, *op. cit.*, p. 461. Chapter XIX, Paragraph 18, states positively there can be no excuse for failure to preserve order in an army: "He who cannot preserve order in his army has no right to command it." And further from the same authority: ". . . it has become a recognized maxim of war that the commanding officer who permits indiscriminate pillage, allows the taking of private property without strict accountability, whether engaged in offensive or defensive operations, fails in his duty to his own government and violates the usages of modern warfare . . ."

31. Section V, General Order No. 94, November 23, 1862. *Official Records*, Ser. I, Vol. XVII, Pt. II, pp. 358–359. Grant had instructed Sherman to subsist his troops off the countryside, but to issue receipts in every instance for property so used. Grant to Sherman, November 10, 1862. *Ibid.*, p. 336.

32. Section V, Special Order No. 285, issued at Memphis, October 22, 1862. *Ibid.*, pp. 289–290.

33. Later events proved that Sherman could enforce discipline when he felt it necessary. In a letter to Thomas Ewing he refers to the admirable conduct of his troops around Savannah. *Home Letters*, pp. 321–322. Also, it cannot be regarded as an accident that, after the destructive march through South Carolina, the same troops yielded to the customary restraints of disciplined forces immediately upon leaving South Carolina and entering North Carolina. See Samuel M. Bowman and Richard B. Irwin, *Sherman and His Campaigns* (New York, 1866), p. 353.

34. W. F. G. Shanks, *op. cit.*, pp. 42–43. Although this criticism sounds

harsh, Shanks admired Sherman very much and considered him one of the outstanding generals of the war. He did not refuse to see Sherman's faults, as well as his virtues. So many who have written on General Sherman have been obviously biased in seeing only virtues. Alfred H. Burne, *Lee, Grant and Sherman* (New York, 1939), pp. 137–138, analyzes Sherman's military abilities and sums up that Sherman never won a victory, never employed his whole force, and that his whole campaign was one of caution.

35. Henry Hitchcock, *Marching with Sherman, Passages from Letters and Campaign Diaries of Henry Hitchcock,* edited by M. A. DeWolfe Howe (New Haven, 1927), p. 134. Entry for December 3, 1864. The general orders referred to are the oft-discussed and much-pointed-to General Orders No. 120, dated November 9, 1864, issued by Sherman several days before the march across Georgia was begun. They are all that could be asked in the way of conforming with the laws of war, governing the conduct of an orderly army invading enemy territory. (The italics are Hitchcock's.)

36. H. W. Halleck, *op. cit.,* Chapter XIX, paragraph 18, states that the officer in command is at all times responsible for the discipline of his subordinate officers and men, and those in subordinate command cannot be held accountable for the conduct of the army.

37. H. Hitchcock, *op. cit.,* pp. 124–125. Entry of December 1, 1864. (The italics are Hitchcock's.)

38. *Ibid.,* p. 131. Entry of December 3, 1864.

39. *Memoirs,* II, 184.

40. *Ibid.,* p. 254.

41. M. D. Vattel, *The Law of Nations* . . . (Translated from the French), (Northhampton, Mass., 1820), p. 435, Book III, Chapter X, paragraph 173, states that only enormous offenses by an enemy could justify their punishment through pillage and destruction of their property. H. W. Halleck, *op. cit.,* p. 465, Chapter XIX, Paragraph 23, condemns punishment administered under the pretense of necessity.

CHAPTER VI.   Devastation of Mississippi

1. Sherman to Mrs. Sherman, July 5, 1863. *Home Letters,* pp. 269–270.

2. Sherman to Mrs. Sherman, January 28, 1863. *Home Letters,* pp. 237–238. John Sherman to Sherman, February 16, 1863. W. T. Sherman Papers. In these letters Senator Sherman appealed to his brother to face adversity with courage for the sake of his wife and children. Sherman to John Sherman, February 18, 1863. *Ibid.* The General complained he had had enough of attacks on his ability, and he stated, "I have had my share and wish no more." In a letter of February 26, 1863, Senator Sherman lost patience with the General's weakness and charged him with ingratitude. He warned General Sherman against resigning. *Ibid.* Sherman went to great lengths to explain his failure at Chickasaw

Bayou, as shown by the large number of letters dating from January 1863 on the subject found in the W. T. Sherman Papers. Admiral David D. Porter wrote a letter supporting Sherman. See David D. Porter, *Incidents and Anecdotes of the Civil War* (New York, 1865), p. 128 ff.

3. Eric William Sheppard, *Bedford Forrest, the Confederacy's Greatest Cavalryman* (New York, 1930), pp. 75–76.

4. *Ibid.,* p. 89.

5. Grant to Sherman, July 13, 1863. *Official Records,* Ser. I, Vol. XXIV, Pt. III, p. 507.

6. Sherman to Mrs. Sherman, July 5, 1863. *Home Letters,* p. 270.

7. Grant to Sherman, May 12, 1863. Grant to McClernand, May 12, 1863. *Official Records,* Ser. I, Vol. XXIV, Pt. III, p. 300.

8. Grant to Sherman, May 14, 1863. *Ibid.,* p. 312.

9. Special Orders No. 105, May 14, 1863. *Ibid.,* p. 312.

10. Sherman to General Joseph A. Mower, May 15, 1863. *Ibid.,* p. 314.

11. Sherman to General Mower, May 15, 1863. *Ibid.,* p. 315.

12. General Grant to War Department, December 25, 1862. *Official Records,* Ser. I, Vol. XVII, Pt. I, p. 478. See also Grant to Halleck, January 5, 1863, *ibid.,* p. 481; and Grant to Halleck, January 4, 1863, *ibid.,* p. 480.

13. General Orders No. 7, December 18, 1862. *Ibid.,* p. 619.

14. Jenkins Lloyd Jones, *An Artilleryman's Diary,* Wisconsin History Commission: Original Papers, No. 8. Wisconsin History Commission (Madison, 1914), p. 43. Entry for April 2, 1863.

15. Benjamin F. Stevenson, *Letters from the Army* (Cincinnati, 1884), p. 180. Dr. Stevenson to his wife, January 28, 1863.

16. *Memoirs,* I, 289.

17. P. L. Rainwater (ed.), "Letters of James Lusk Alcorn," *Journal of Southern History,* Vol. III (May 1937), pp. 201-202. Reprinted by permission of the managing editor. Letter dated December 18, 1862. (Italics are the letterwriter's.)

18. *Memoirs,* I, 320.

19. Sherman to Mrs. Sherman, May 6, 1863. *Home Letters,* pp. 259–260.

20. *Idem.*

21. General Blair to Sherman, May 29, 1863. *Official Records,* Ser. I, Vol. XXIV, Pt. II, p. 436.

22. General W. H. Jackson to Major A. P. Mason, Assistant Adjutant General, June 7, 1863. *Ibid.,* p. 440.

23. Brigadier General John Adams to Captain Henry Robinson, Assistant Adjutant General, June 5, 1863. *Ibid.,* p. 442.

24. General Adams to Captain Robinson, June 6, 1863. *Idem.*

25. General Orders No. 52, July 4, 1863. *Official Records,* Ser. I, Vol. XXIV, Pt. III, p. 475.

26. Joseph E. Johnston, *Narrative of Military Operations* (New York,

1874), p. 514. This letter, dated June 24, 1863, also informed Secretary Seddon that if forced to give up Jackson the Confederacy would lose Mississippi.

27. *Memoirs,* I, 331.
28. General Orders No. 56, July 10, 1863. *Official Records,* Ser. I, Vol. XXIV, Pt. III, p. 496.
29. Memorandum Orders, July 14, 1863. *Ibid.,* p. 510.
30. Hurlbut to Halleck, July 14, 1863, enclosing General Dodge's letter. *Ibid.,* p. 411.
31. Hurlbut to Halleck, July 14, 1863, 2:30 P.M. *Ibid.,* p. 512.
32. Sherman to Colonel Charles R. Woods, July 15, 1863. *Ibid.,* p. 516.
33. General Johnston reported to President Davis on July 9, 1863, that inadequate transportation rendered him inactive. *Official Records,* Ser. I, Vol. XXIV, Pt. I, p. 199. In Johnston's letter to Davis of July 13, 1863, the General expressed regret over having to give up a point as vital as Jackson was to the Confederacy.
34. Sherman to Lieutenant Colonel A. Rawlins, Assistant Adjutant General, July 28, 1863. *Official Records,* Ser. I, Vol. XXIV, Pt. II, p. 536.
35. Sherman to Admiral David D. Porter, July 19, 1863. *Ibid.,* Pt. III, p. 531.
36. Benson J. Lossing, *The Pictorial Field Book of the Civil War in the United States of America* (3 vols., Hartford, n.d.), III, 146. See footnote 2 for the eyewitness account. The eyewitness quoted was a correspondent of *The Chicago Times,* and the account is found in James Wilford Garner, *Reconstruction in Mississippi* (New York, 1901), p. 12.
37. *Idem.* Lossing visited the site in the spring of 1866.
38. Sherman to Porter, July 19, 1863. *Official Records,* Ser. I, Vol. XXIV, Pt. III, p. 531.
39. J. W. Garner, *op. cit.,* p. 12.
40. *Idem.* Ewing was General Sherman's brother-in-law.
41. *Ibid.,* pp. 12–13, quoting a correspondent of *The Chicago Times.* The report appeared in *The New York World,* August 14, 1863.
42. Edgar L. Erickson (ed.), "With Grant at Vicksburg. From the Civil War Diary of Captain Charles E. Wilcox." *Journal of the Illinois State Historical Society,* Vol. XXX (April 1937–January 1938), p. 501.
43. Sherman to Grant, July 28, 1863. *Official Records,* Ser. I, Vol. XXIV, Pt. II, p. 536.
44. *Idem.*
45. Colonel Woods to Captain Sawyer, Assistant Adjutant General, July 20, 1863. *Ibid.,* p. 619.
46. Sherman to Grant, July 14, 1863. *Ibid.,* p. 526.
47. J. W. Garner, *op. cit.,* p. 17.
48. *Idem.* Information from *The New York Evening Express,* September 21, 1863.

49. Colonel R. V. Richardson to General Pemberton, May 3, 1863. *Official Records,* Ser. I, Vol. XXIV, Pt. I, p. 550.
50. General Hurlbut to Lieutenant Colonel Rawlins, Assistant Adjutant General, April 25, 1863. *Ibid.,* p. 558.
51. Colonel George E. Bryant to Captain Randall, Assistant Adjutant General, April 25, 1863. *Ibid.,* p. 558.
52. Colonel Edward Hatch to Captain Weir, Acting Assistant Adjutant General, June 26, 1863. *Ibid.,* Pt. II, p. 496.
53. Brigadier General J. Z. George to Captain W. A. Goodman, Assistant Adjutant General, June 26, 1863. *Ibid.,* p. 506.
54. Major R. S. Carter to General Joseph E. Johnston, July 25, 1863. *Ibid.,* p. 661.
55. General E. O. C. Ord's Report of Operations of the Thirteenth Corps in the Jackson Campaign, July 27, 1863. *Ibid.,* p. 576.
56. General W. H. Jackson to Colonel B. S. Ewell, Assistant Adjutant General, July 20, 1863. *Ibid.,* p. 660.
57. Sherman to Grant, July 28, 1863. *Ibid.,* p. 537.
58. Sherman to Mrs. Sherman, July 5, 1863. *Home Letters,* p. 270. Sherman says: "We have ravaged the land, and have sent away half a million negroes, so that this country is paralyzed and cannot recover its lost strength in twenty years."
59. Sherman to Grant, from Jackson, July 18, 1863. *Sherman Letters,* p. 213.
60. Sherman to John Sherman, August 3, 1863. *Sherman Letters,* p. 213.
61. Sherman to Grant, letters of July 19 and 21, 1863. *Official Records,* Ser. I, Vol. XXIV, Pt. II, p. 530.
62. *Idem.*
63. Sherman to Grant, July 21, 1863. *Ibid.,* p. 531.
64. Sherman to Grant, July 21, 1863. *Ibid.,* p. 530. Correspondence between Jackson Citizen's Committee and Sherman, and the citizen's agreement to use the supplies for relief only, July 16–21, 1863. *Ibid.,* pp. 539–540.
65. *Idem.* July 23, 1863.
66. Grant to Sherman, July 28, 1863. *Ibid.,* Pt. III, p. 557.
67. Grant to Sherman, July 29, 1863. *Ibid.,* p. 559.
68. Assistant Adjutant General Sawyer to Colonel John M. Corse, August 9, 1863. *Ibid.,* p. 584.
69. Grant's General Orders No. 50, August 1, 1863. *Ibid.,* p. 570.
70. Sherman to Mrs. Sherman, June 27, 1863. *Home Letters,* pp. 268–269.
71. *Idem.*
72. The Diary of Edmund Ruffin, 1856–1865, 10 Vols., Division of Manuscripts, Library of Congress. Ruffin's diary contains a good collection of newspapers of the day. This reference is taken from the complete first and second pages of *The Richmond Daily Dispatch* of August 25, 1863.

The Augusta Chronicle editorial was reprinted by the Richmond paper. It may be found between the daily entries of August 23 and 24, 1863.

73. *Ibid.,* entry of June 22, 1863. Complete front page and second page of *The Richmond Daily Dispatch,* June 22, 1863.

74. *Idem.* In *The Richmond Daily Examiner* for July 6, 1863, is a reprint from *The New York Herald* recounting the exemplary conduct of the Confederate armies in Pennsylvania. See also Susan Leigh Blackford, III (ed.), *Letters from Lee's Army* (New York, 1947), pp. 181, 184, 186, and 188; Francis W. Dawson, *Reminiscences of Confederate Service, 1861–1865* (Charleston, 1882), p. 92. Dawson was an Englishman who held the rank of captain in Lee's army. This book was limited to 100 copies; the copy quoted here is in the Rare Book Collection, Library of Congress. Dawson refers particularly to Lee's personal interest in seeing that the army conducted itself properly.

75. Bell Irvin Wiley, *The Life of Johnny Reb, The Common Soldier of the Confederacy* (Indianapolis, 1943), p. 135.

76. General Joseph E. Johnston to President Davis, July 11, 1863. *Official Records,* Ser. I, Vol. XXIV, Pt. I, p. 200.

77. Johnston to Davis, July 23 [22?], 1863. *Ibid.,* p. 209.

78. Johnston's report to Secretary of War, November 1, 1863. *Ibid.,* p. 246.

79. Major R. S. Carter to General Johnston, July 25, 1863. *Ibid.,* Pt. II, p. 661.

80. General James R. Chalmers to General Johnston, July 30, 1863. *Ibid.,* Pt. III, p. 1038.

81. Jno. W. C. Watson to General Johnston, August 4, 1863. *Ibid.,* p. 1044.

82. General James R. Chalmers to Assistant Adjutant General Ewen, July 22, 1863. *Ibid.,* p. 1024.

83. B. F. Stevenson, *op. cit.,* p. 254. To his wife, dated September 10, 1863.

84. J. L. Jones, *op. cit.,* p. 106. Entry of October 9, 1863. Grant had been authorized by General Halleck in August to enlist and organize into regiments deserters and citizens of Mississippi. Halleck to Grant, August 3, 1863. *Official Records,* Ser. I, Vol. XXIV, Pt. III, p. 571.

85. Special Orders No. 147. July 24, 1863. *Official Records,* Ser. I, Vol. XXIV, Pt. III, p. 548. No information was found to prove that this order was actually enforced.

86. *Idem.*

87. Grant's General Orders No. 50, issued at Vicksburg, August 1, 1863. *Ibid.,* p. 571.

88. Sherman to Lieutenant Colonel John A. Rawlins, Assistant Adjutant General, August 4, 1863. *Ibid.,* p. 575.

89. *Memoirs,* I, 339–340. Sherman to General Halleck, September 7, 1863. This letter was written at General-in-Chief Halleck's request. Halleck stated that Lincoln wanted the opinion of his generals in the field on the question of reconstruction in Louisiana, Mississippi and Arkansas, as well as on the prospects for ultimate and complete success in the

war. Generals Grant and McPherson were asked to write similar letters.

90. John K. Bettersworth, *Confederate Mississippi: The People and Policies of a Cotton State in Wartime* (Baton Rouge, 1943), pp. 280–281, quoting from a letter of Anne Martin to Emmie Crutcher, September 16, 1863, Philip Crutcher Collection, Mississippi Archives.

91. *Memoirs,* I, 357.

92. J. L. Jones, *op. cit.,* p. 110.

93. *Ibid.,* p. 111.

94. *Ibid.,* p. 116. This was in country near Chickasaw, Alabama.

95. *Ibid.,* p. 121.

96. Circular issued at Sweetwater, Tennessee, December 8, 1863. *Official Records,* Ser. I, Vol. XXXI, Pt. III, pp. 357–358. The rich Sweetwater Valley lies to the south of Knoxville between the latter town and Chattanooga.

97. Sherman to Grant, December 11, 1863. *Ibid.,* p. 382.

98. Sherman to General Jeff C. Davis, December 11, 1863. *Ibid.,* p. 377.

99. *Ibid.,* pp. 588–589. See headings of correspondence on these pages.

100. *Ibid.,* pp. 590–591. Also p. 689 shows headquarters of Mississippi Cavalry, Loring's Division, etc.

101. *Ibid.,* pp. 322–338, which abounds in correspondence between Union commanders trying to stop the raids and attacks of Confederate forces.

102. General Tuttle's report to General Hurlbut, December 3, 1863. *Ibid.,* pp. 322–323. General Grierson to Hurlbut, December 3, 1863. *Ibid.,* p. 325. Assistant Adjutant General Lomar to General Chalmers, October 25, 1863, advising that supplies be sent from Meridian to Brandon. *Ibid.,* p. 589. General Stephen D. Lee's orders to Chalmers to raid and destroy the railroad. *Ibid.,* pp. 704–705.

103. General Chalmers to Assistant Adjutant General Colonel B. S. Ewell, October 21, 1863. *Ibid.,* p. 574.

104. Diary of William Owner, December 20, 1860 to May 12, 1867, 9 vols., Division of Manuscripts, Library of Congress. Very little is known about Owner. It is obvious that he resided in Washington, D.C. His diary shows that he was opposed to Lincoln and "Black Republicans." In his own handwriting he gives his diary this title: "Notes & Incidents of the B[lack] R[epublican] War to subjugate the South and Steal Niggers." Owner particularly hated the inhuman warfare waged against the South by Northern armies. He was also a severe critic of Lincoln's administration. It must be assumed that he secured his information from newspapers or official dispatches reaching Washington.

105. Sherman to Commanding Officer, Eastport, November 23, 1863. *Official Records,* Ser. I, Vol. XXXI, Pt. III, p. 238.

106. General Richardson reports 500 head of cattle. *Ibid.,* p. 540. General Loring reports quantities of grain between Big Black and Yazoo Rivers. *Ibid.,* p. 579. Commissary reports approximately 500 head of cattle at Meridian. *Ibid.,* p. 580. General Johnston reports hogs may

be found near the river. *Ibid.,* p. 630. Major Dameron reports hogs being driven east through Alabama. *Ibid.,* p. 674. Commissary chief reports efforts to collect everything possible to prevent Union from using. *Ibid.,* p. 675.

107. *The Canton* (Mississippi) *Tri-weekly Citizen,* Sunday, January 17, 1864. Sherman always referred to these attacks as "guerilla" assaults. General Ross was regularly commissioned as an officer of cavalry. After such an attack as this he usually drew his guns off, only to set them up at another vantage point.

108. *Ibid.,* January 20, 1864. This issue of *The Tri-weekly Citizen* recounted that it had learned from Union papers that "Briarfield," Jefferson Davis's plantation, was to be converted into a Negro camp.

109. Autograph Draft of W. T. Sherman's Memoirs, Division of Manuscripts, Library of Congress. These are taken from letters and reports prepared for, but not included in the published *Memoirs.* See *Memoirs,* I, 388–389, in which Sherman says that by striking east from the river he could set free for other purposes a large body of men in local garrisons. Also he hoped to destroy the rebel cavalry commanded by General Forrest.

110. *Augusta Daily Chronicle and Sentinel,* February 6, 1864.

111. *Memoirs,* I, 391.

112. Stephen D. Lee, "Sherman's Meridian Expedition and Sooy Smith's Raid to West Point," *Southern Historical Society Papers,* Vol. VIII, January to December 1880, Richmond, Va., No. 2, 1880, pp. 54–58. See also William M. Polk, *Leonidas Polk, Bishop and General* (2 vols., New York, 1915), II, 327 ff.

113. Wirt Armistead Cate (ed.), *Two Soldiers, The Campaign Diaries of Thomas J. Key, C.S.A., and Robert J. Campbell, U.S.A.* (Chapel Hill, 1936), p. 235.

114. *Idem.*

115. Report of Captain Andrew Hickenlooper of expedition to Meridian, March 25, 1864. *Official Records,* Ser. I, Vol. XXXII, Pt. I, p. 216.

116. *Idem.*

117. *Mobile Daily Advertiser and Register,* February 16, 1864.

118. Autograph Draft of W. T. Sherman's Memoirs, containing copies of letters from him to military officers. This report is found among letters prepared to be published in Sherman's *Memoirs,* but not appearing in the final draft. This report directed to General Grant's Chief of Staff Brigadier General John A. Rawlins, March 7, 1864.

119. *Idem.*

120. W. T. Sherman Papers. General William Sooy Smith to General W. T. Sherman, February 26, 1864. Also in *Official Records,* Ser. I, Vol. XXXII, Pt. I, p. 253.

121. *Memoirs,* I, 392. *The Sherman Letters* contain no letters as to what occurred on the Meridian campaign.

122. Sherman to Lieutenant Commander E. K. Owen, Mississippi Squadron, January 30, 1864. *Official Records*, Ser. I, Vol. XXXII, Pt. I, p. 185.

123. *New York Times*, March 27, 1864, found in J. W. Garner, *op. cit.*, p. 13, footnote 5.

124. *Ibid.*, p. 14, quoting from letter of Adjutant of 32nd Ohio Volunteers in *New York Daily News*, March 21, 1864.

125. *Idem.*, footnote 2 refers to *New York World*, March 14, 1864, and *New York Herald*, March 15, 1864.

126. *Mobile Daily Tribune*, March 5, 1864. Extracts from a private letter published in a column captioned "From up the Road."

127. From northern news reprinted in *Canton American Citizen*, April 4, 1864.

128. *Ibid.*, April 25, 1864.

129. Stephen D. Lee, *op. cit.*, Vol. VIII, pp. 59–60. The seriousness of the loss of wagons and teams can be properly appreciated only by those who realize the vital importance of these implements to those who till the soil. (The italics are Lee's.)

130. *Montgomery Daily Advertiser*, February 28, 1864.

131. *Idem.*

132. *Idem.*

133. J. W. Garner, *op. cit.*, p. 14.

134. *Idem.*

135. Captain L. M. Rose's report on his part in the Meridian campaign, March 8, 1864. *Official Records*, Ser. I, Vol. XXXII, Pt. I, p. 222.

136. *Mobile Daily Advertiser and Register*, February 27, 1864. The various newspapers in the South requested that persons receiving letters giving information on events of the war submit them to the editor for printing. In the absence of any organized news service this served to keep readers posted. Names of the writers as well as the receivers of such letters were usually omitted.

137. J. W. Garner, *op. cit.*, p. 14.

138. *Mobile Daily Advertiser and Register*, February 27, 1864.

139. *Idem.* General S. D. Lee estimated that the Union forces at Enterprise numbered about 8,000 men. *Official Records*, Ser. I, Vol. XXXII, Pt. I, p. 364.

140. *Montgomery Daily Advertiser*, February 27, 1864. Private letter, names of writer and addressee omitted. This letter was reprinted from *The Mobile Register*.

141. Brigadier General W. Q. Gresham to Captain C. Cadle, Jr., Assistant Adjutant General, March 5, 1864. *Official Records*, Ser. I, Vol. XXXII, Pt. I, p. 248.

142. *Montgomery Daily Advertiser*, February 27, 1864. Reprint of private letter appearing in *The Mobile Register*.

143. Colonel E. F. Winslow to Adjutant of Seventeenth Army Corps, February 29, 1864. *Official Records*, Ser. I, Vol. XXXII, Pt. I, p. 251.

144. *Canton* [Mississippi] *American Citizen,* May 25, 1864.
145. General Sherman's report of operations in Mississippi, March 7, 1864. *Official Records,* Ser. I, Vol. XXXII, Pt. I, p. 177.
146. General Orders No. 1, December 23, 1863. *Official Records,* Ser. I, Vol. XXXI, Pt. III, p. 858.

CHAPTER VII.   Atlanta and Northern Georgia

1. Lewis, *Sherman,* pp. 409–411. Lewis presents a graphic picture of reaction in the North.
2. *Memoirs,* II, 110.
3. David P. Conyngham, *Sherman's March Through the South* (New York, 1865), p. 192. Conyngham, a reporter for *The New York Herald,* joined Sherman at Chattanooga and served as a volunteer aide-de-camp all the way to Bentonville, N. C. He met Sherman's estimate of what a good war correspondent should be—in uniform and exposed to the same dangers as those about whom they wrote. Conyngham appears to have been a good reporter, with only the bias to be expected of one so intimately associated with the leading actor in the great drama of war.
4. W. A. Cate, *op. cit.,* p. 119. "The Diary of Thomas J. Key, C.S.A.," entry for August 23, 1864.
5. D. P. Conyngham, *op. cit.,* pp. 192–193.
6. *Ibid.,* p. 218.
7. *Idem.*
8. Papers of Rufus Mead, Jr., May 25, 1861, to May 3, 1865, Division of Manuscripts, Library of Congress. A collection of unpublished letters written by Mead to his family in Connecticut. Mead writes in an excellent, clear hand, expresses himself well. From all indications he was well educated and interested in local politics in his own state, as well as in national affairs. This quotation is from his letter of September 8, 1864.
9. Sherman to General Hood, September 12, 1864. *Memoirs,* II, 120. Telegram to General Halleck, *ibid.,* p. 101.
10. Hood to Sherman, September 12, 1864. *Ibid.,* p. 122.
11. Sherman to Halleck, September 20, 1864. *Ibid.,* p. 118.
12. *Montgomery Daily Advertiser,* September 15, 1864.
13. Editorial from *Macon Telegraph* reproduced in *Mobile Daily Advertiser and Register,* September 15, 1864.
14. Hood to Sherman, September 9, 1864. *Memoirs,* II, 119.
15. Mayor Calhoun and city councilmen to Sherman, September 11, 1864. *Ibid.,* pp. 124–125.
16. Sherman to Mayor Calhoun, September 12, 1864. *Ibid.,* pp. 126–127. This letter was published in Samuel M. Bowman, *Sherman and his Campaigns.* Also *Harper's Pictorial History of the Great Rebellion,*

Part Two (New York, 1868), p. 620, reproduces both the Mayor's and Sherman's letters, crediting Bowman's account.

17. Rufus Mead, Jr., Papers. Letter to his family, September 19, 1864, from Atlanta.

18. Matthew Page Andrews (compiler), *The Women of the South in War Times* (Baltimore, 1924), pp. 303–304.

19. Report 108, Journal of Brigadier General Francis A. Shoup, Chief of Staff, entry of September 22, 1864. *Official Records,* Ser. I, Vol. XXXIX, Pt. I, p. 805. Seven hundred of those expelled from Atlanta, widows, wives and children of Confederate soldiers, were picked up along the railroad from Atlanta to Macon by Governor Brown's orders and sent to Dawson, Georgia. General Ira R. Foster, Quartermaster General of Georgia, had caused over 100 houses to be erected to shelter the refugees. Here, at Exile Camp, as it was called, these people were fed and cared for at the state's expense. From a letter written by General Foster found in Isaac W. Avery, *The History of the State of Georgia from 1850 to 1881* (New York, 1881), pp. 310–311.

20. Hood to Governor Joseph E. Brown, September 13, 1864. *Official Records,* Ser. I, Vol. XXXIX, Pt. II, p. 833.

21. George W. Pepper, *Personal Recollections of Sherman's Campaigns in Georgia and the Carolinas* (Zanesville, Ohio, 1866), p. 239. Little information can be found further to identify Captain Pepper. He says of himself on page 11 that he was commissioned by Governor Todd of Ohio in the fall of 1863 and that he joined Sherman near Chattanooga. Although he states that he acted as war correspondent "for two or three prominent journals," nowhere does he identify them by name.

22. The Confederates employed Sherman's own method of railroad destruction against him. Near Acworth, Georgia, they heated and twisted the rails and filled the railroad cuts with brush, dirt and stone. See William Pitt Chambers, "My Journal," in *Publications of the Mississippi State Historical Society,* Centenary Series, Vol. V (1925), p. 339.

23. Sherman's report to General Halleck, January 1, 1865. *Official Records,* Ser. I, Vol. XXXIX, Pt. I, p. 583.

24. Report of Colonel James L. Selfridge, Forty-sixth Pennsylvania Infantry, December 26, 1864. *Ibid.,* pp. 653–654.

25. Report of Major Patrick Griffith, December 26, 1864. *Idem.*

26. Report of Colonel Ezra Carman, Thirteenth New Jersey Infantry, December 27, 1864. *Ibid.,* p. 655.

27. Report of Colonel James S. Robinson, Eighty-second Ohio Infantry, December 28, 1864. *Ibid.,* p. 661.

28. *Ibid.,* pp. 661–662.

29. Report of Brigadier General Adpheus S. Williams, commanding Twentieth Army Corps, January 9, 1865. *Ibid.,* p. 650.

30. Sherman to General Slocum, October 23, 1864. *Ibid.,* Pt. III, p. 406.

31. General Sherman to Brigadier General Louis D. Watkins, October 29, 1864. *Ibid.*, p. 494.

32. Sarah Blackwell Temple, *The First Hundred Years, A Short History of Cobb County in Georgia* (Atlanta, 1935), p. 333.

33. Sherman to General Kenner Garrard, *Official Records,* Ser. I, Vol. XXXVIII, Pt. V, p. 76.

34. Sherman to Halleck, July 9, 1864. *Official Records,* Ser. I, Vol. XXXVIII, Pt. V, p. 92.

35. S. B. Temple, *op. cit.,* p. 334, quoting *The Cincinnati Commercial,* date of issue not given.

36. General Thomas to Sherman, July 10, 1864. *Official Records,* Ser. I, Vol. XXXVIII, Pt. V, p. 104.

37. S. B. Temple, *op. cit.,* p. 333.

38. Sherman to General Thomas, July 10, 1864. *Official Records,* Ser. I, Vol. XXXVIII, Pt. V, p. 104.

39. Oscar Osburn Winther (ed.), *With Sherman to the Sea, The Civil War Letters, Diaries and Reminiscences of Theodore F. Upson* (Baton Rouge, 1943), p. 119. Entry dated July 12, 1864, at Marietta, Georgia.

40. S. B. Temple, *op. cit.,* p. 335. No effort is made to prove or disprove the truth of the stories. The author states simply that "the strength with which these stories persist through the years in the county necessitates the mention of them." *Idem.*

41. Captain Syria M. Budlong, Acting Assistant Adjutant General, to Colonel Thomas T. Heath, October 30, 1864. *Official Records,* Ser. I, Vol. XXXIX, Pt. III, p. 513.

42. Journal of Second Division, September 9–November 14, 1864. *Official Records,* Ser. I, Vol. XXXIX, Pt. I, p. 635. Not otherwise identified, probably of the Fourth Corps, ordered north from Atlanta to join General Thomas.

43. Captain S. M. Budlong, Acting Assistant Adjutant General, to Commanding Officer Foraging Escort, October 30, 1864. *Ibid.,* Pt. III, p. 513.

44. Report of Lieutenant Colonel Thomas Morgan, Seventy-fourth Indiana Infantry, November 11, 1864. *Ibid.,* Pt. I, p. 647.

45. *Idem.*

46. See *ante,* Chapter V, footnote 2, p. 68.

47. Sherman to General John E. Smith, November 8, 1864. *Official Records,* Ser. I, Vol. XXXIX, Pt. III, p. 703. Cassville was burned earlier by order of General John E. Smith.

48. L. M. Dayton, Aide-de-camp, to General Jeff C. Davis, November 9, 1864. *Ibid.,* p. 717.

49. L. M. Dayton, Aide-de-camp, to General Jeff C. Davis, November 11, 1864. *Ibid.,* p. 744.

50. Abstract from Journal of Brigadier General Jacob D. Cox, entry of November 3, 1864. *Ibid.,* Pt. I, p. 794.

51. Michael H. Fitch, *Echoes of the Civil War as I Hear Them* (New

York, 1905), p. 232. The author was a brevet colonel of volunteers serving with Wisconsin troops.

52. H. Hitchcock, *op. cit.*, pp. 53–54. Sunday, November 13, 1864.

53. "Diary of Major James A. Connolly," in *Illinois State Historical Society Publications,* No. 35 (1928), p. 399. Entry of Monday, November 14, 1864.

54. *Ibid.,* p. 398. Entry for Sunday, November 13, 1864.

55. *Idem.*

56. Sherman to General John M. Corse, October 10, 1864. *Official Records,* Ser. I, Vol. XXXIX, Pt. III, p. 184.

57. General Corse to Sherman, October 15, 1864. *Ibid.,* p. 292.

58. George Magruder Battey, Jr., *A History of Rome and Floyd County* (Atlanta, 1922), Vol. I, p. 202. It is highly probable that Sherman was with the troops who passed down the Chattooga Valley. He entered Rome October 12, 1864, and returned there October 28, 1864. *Ibid.,* p. 178.

59. *Ibid.,* pp. 202–203.

60. *Idem.*

61. *Idem.*

62. Major Henry Hitchcock, Assistant Adjutant General, to General John M. Corse, November 4, 1864. *Official Records,* Ser. I, Vol. XXXIX, Pt. III, p. 628.

63. Sherman to General Corse, November 10, 1864. *Ibid.,* p. 729.

64. General Corse to Sherman, October 2, 1864. *Ibid.,* p. 31.

65. Sherman to General Corse, October 3, 1864. *Ibid.,* p. 53.

66. G. M. Battey, *op. cit.,* p. 179.

67. *Ibid.,* p. 178. The story of Harry Wimpee, Wm. M. Hardin and others who witnessed the burning of Rome.

68. *Idem.*

69. *Ibid.,* p. 200. From a letter written by Mrs. Robert Battey to her husband, November 17, 1864.

70. Journal of General Jacob D. Cox, entry for October 12, 1864. *Official Records,* Ser. I, Vol. XXXIX, Pt. I, p. 791.

71. G. M. Battey, *op. cit.,* p. 198.

72. Sherman to General A. J. Smith, November 2, 1864. *Official Records,* Ser. I, Vol. XXXIX, Pt. III, p. 596.

73. Sherman to Captain O. M. Poe, November 11, 1864, from Kingston, Georgia. *Ibid.,* p. 741.

74. Report of Colonel William Cogswell, Second Massachusetts Infantry, December 26, 1864. *Ibid.,* Pt. I, p. 652.

75. *Idem.*

76. Report of Captain O. M. Poe, October 8, 1865. *Official Records,* Ser. I, Vol. XLIV, p. 60.

77. D. P. Conyngham, *op. cit.,* pp. 236–237.

78. *Idem.*

NOTES

79. Fenwick Y. Hedley, *Marching Through Georgia* (Chicago, 1890), p. 257.
80. Report of Lieutenant Colonel Joel C. Martin, December 30, 1864. *Official Records,* Ser. I, Vol. XXXIX, Pt. I, p. 640.
81. G. W. Pepper, *op. cit.,* p. 239.
82. *Ibid.,* p. 240.
83. *City of Atlanta, A Descriptive, Historical and Industrial Review of the Gateway City of the South.* World Fair Series of Great American Cities (Louisville, 1892–1893), p. 29. From a brief history of Atlanta by Colonel Isaac Wheeler Avery of the Confederate army. Colonel Avery of the Eighth Georgia was injured at the battle of New Hope Church in 1864. For a number of years after the war he was the editor of *The Atlanta Constitution,* and for a short time he owned *The Atlanta Herald.* He was the author of the *History of Georgia from 1850 to 1881* (New York, 1881). From *Dictionary of American Biography,* Allen Johnson and Dumas Malone (eds.), (New York, 1928—), Vol. I, p. 444.
84. I. W. Avery, *op. cit.,* p. 307.
85. *Idem.*
86. Editorial in *Columbus* (Georgia) *Times* reprinted in the *Canton* (Mississippi) *American Citizen,* December 23, 1864. The full report of W. P. Howard on Atlanta was published on the front page, *ibid.,* December 26, 1864. The report appeared in *The Augusta Chronicle and Sentinel,* December 16, 1864. The Diary of Edmund Ruffin for December 27, 1864, contains a clipping of the report, which doubtless came from a Richmond paper. Ruffin subscribed to many newspapers, but seemed to prefer those printed in Richmond.
87. *Idem.*
88. *Ibid.,* December 26, 1864.

CHAPTER VIII.   From Atlanta to the Sea

1. *Memoirs,* II, 174.
2. *Official Records,* Ser. I, Vol. XXXIX, Pt. III, p. 713.
3. *Idem.*
4. *Idem.*
5. *Memoirs,* II, 181. Sherman recounts a particular instance on a plantation about four miles east of Covington. He said, "A soldier passed me with a ham on his musket, a jug of sorghum molasses under his arm, and a piece of honey in his hand." These were items which could hardly have been secured except through trespass upon private property. As the soldier passed Sherman he remarked "carelessly to a comrade: 'Forage liberally on the country,' quoting from my general orders." It is interesting to note that this occurred on the second day after leaving Atlanta. There were other instances of this kind. Sherman

236

states that he "reproved the man" for foraging on his own, but does not indicate that he questioned the man's leaving his place in the ranks.

6. Report of Colonel James L. Selfridge, Forty-sixth Pennsylvania Infantry, December 26, 1864. *Official Records,* Ser. I, Vol. XLIV, p. 226.

7. *Memoirs,* II, 220–221.

8. Ulrich B. Phillips, *The Life of Robert Toombs* (New York, 1913), pp. 250–251.

9. *Confederate Records of the State of Georgia* (6 vols., Atlanta, 1909–1911), II, 799 ff.

10. Confederate State Papers, Miscellaneous, 1862–1864, Division of Manuscripts, Library of Congress. This printed circular dated in the field December 4, 1864, also served to arouse deep resentment of Georgia citizens against Wheeler's cavalry, whom many charged with being as ruthless as the invaders.

11. *Confederate Records of the State of Georgia,* III, 697–698. Governor Brown to James A. Seddon, Secretary of War, C.S.A., January 5, 1865.

12. The Diary of Edmund Ruffin, entry of November 24, 1864.

13. *Macon Intelligencer,* November 18, 1864, reprinted in *The Mobile Daily Tribune,* November 22, 1864.

14. *Montgomery Daily Advertiser,* from an editorial in the issue of November 24, 1864. News item in *The Mobile Daily Tribune,* November 22, 1864, declared that Sherman could be starved into surrender if Georgians would remove all supplies from his front.

15. *The Columbus* (Georgia) *Times* stated on November 21, 1864, that Sherman's main force was marching on Augusta. Reprinted in *Montgomery Daily Advertiser,* November 23, 1864. *Mobile Advertiser and Register,* November 22, 1864, carried in headlines that the Federals were moving on Augusta. *The Macon Intelligencer* of November 18, 1864, in a reprint in *Mobile Daily Tribune* of November 22, 1864, was confident that Macon was the objective of the Union army.

16. Charles W. Wills, *Army Life of an Illinois Soldier, Including a Day by Day Record of Sherman's March to the Sea, Letters and Diary of the Late Charles W. Wills,* compiled and published by his sister (Washington, 1906), p. 330. Entry of December 1, 1864. Wills was a private and then sergeant of the Eighth Illinois Infantry. Later he served as Lieutenant and Battalion Adjutant of the Seventh Illinois Cavalry, and finally was Captain, Major and Lieutenant Colonel of the 103rd Illinois Infantry.

17. Diary of Captain Wimer Bedford, Division of Manuscripts, Library of Congress. Entry dated November 29, 1864. Bedford was apparently Assistant Adjutant General to General O. O. Howard. The diary is in two small, leatherback pocket-sized books, in ink. The diarist appears to have been more interested in preserving field orders and describing troop movements than in observing incidents along the march.

18. Report of Major General Frank P. Blair, Jr., December 31, 1864. *Official Records*. Ser. I, Vol. XLIV, p. 148.

19. Report of Major General Henry W. Slocum, commanding Left Wing, January 9, 1865. *Ibid.*, p. 158.

20. Report of Brigadier General Mortimer D. Leggett, Third Division, Seventeenth Corps, December 31, 1864. *Ibid.*, p. 152.

21. H. Hitchcock, *op. cit.*, p. 108. Entry for November 28, 1864.

22. Full text of B. H. Hill's appeal is in *The Mobile Daily Tribune*, November 26, 1864. Original sent to the Georgia papers and picked up as reprints by others.

23. *Mobile Daily Tribune*, November 23, 1864. General Beauregard's proclamation, datelined at Corinth, Mississippi, November 18, 1864.

24. Special Field Orders No. 127, November 23, 1864. *Official Records*, Ser. I, Vol. XLIV, p. 527.

25. *Confederate Records of the State of Georgia*, II, 820. Governor Brown in his address to the House and Senate on February 15, 1865, stated that this was the only manner in which Sherman could have been stopped. He charged the Confederate government with failure to supply troops necessary to destroy the Federal army in Georgia.

26. Report of Assistant Surgeon David L. Huntington, December 25, 1864. *Official Records,* Ser. I, Vol. XLIV, p. 79. This was a remarkably low incidence of disability due to illness. In both the Union and Confederate armies the number of men rendered unfit for duty by diseases due to dietary deficiencies was alarmingly high.

27. *Augusta Weekly Chronicle & Sentinel,* February 3, 1864.

28. Diary of Edmund Ruffin, entry for November 27, 1864.

29. *Idem.*

30. Report of Major General Henry W. Slocum, January 9, 1865. *Official Records,* Ser. I, Vol. XLIV, p. 159.

31. Report of Brevet Major General Jeff C. Davis, December 31, 1864. *Ibid.*, p. 167.

32. M. P. Andrews, *op. cit.*, pp. 306, 324–325. From the narrative of Mary A. H. Gay, who lived at Decatur.

33. *Ibid.*, p. 307.

34. H. Hitchcock, *op. cit.*, p. 64.

35. G. W. Pepper, *op. cit.*, p. 260.

36. W. A. Cate, *op. cit.*, pp. 131–132. From the diary of Thomas J. Key, C.S.A., September 10, 1864

37. H. Hitchcock, *op. cit.*, p. 69. November 18, 1864.

38. *Idem.* Major Hitchcock does not further identify Judge Harris, except to state that he is a "prominent man hereabouts."

39. G. W. Nichols, *The Story of the Great March from the Diary of a Staff Officer* (New York, 1865), pp. 59–60.

40. [Dolly Sumner Lunt (Mrs. Thomas Burge)], *A Woman's Wartime Journal, An Account of the Passage over a Georgia Plantation of*

Sherman's Army on the March to the Sea, as Recorded in the Diary of Dolly Sumner Lunt (Macon, 1927). Entry for November 19, 1864.

41. *Idem.* The driving off of slaves was not the general practice of Sherman's soldiers. If anything, Sherman discouraged Negroes who tried to follow his columns. He did try to use all able-bodied Negro men in his labor corps and as wagoners. In such cases they could not take their families with them. In this particular instance it is likely that the slaves were forced to leave as a means of further damage to the plantation. Doubtless many of those who so desired returned to their homes within a few days.

42. George Sharland, *Knapsack Notes of General Sherman's Grand Campaign Through the Empire State of the South* (Springfield, Ill., 1865), pp. 19–20. Sharland, a soldier in the Seventeenth Army Corps, described at some length the method followed in marching. He said that the "army proper marches through the farms and fields either to right or left of the road. In this way they can form a guard for the wagon trains against sudden assaults."

43. D. S. Lunt, *op. cit.* Entry for November 19, 1864.

44. *Ibid.* Entry for November 29, 1864. All references to entries of November 19 and 20 are to be found between pages 34–46.

45. G. Sharland, *op. cit.,* p. 39.

46. D. S. Lunt, *op. cit.* Entry for November 19, 1864.

47. *Ibid.,* p. 54. Entry of December 22, 1864.

48. H. Hitchcock, *op. cit.,* pp. 74–75. November 19, 1864.

49. G. W. Pepper, *op. cit.,* p. 261.

50. H. Hitchcock, *op. cit.,* p. 53. Diary entry of November 13, 1864.

51. See *ante,* p. 165. Sherman's outright request of General Watkins was that he "burn ten or twelve houses." There are many other orders to burn houses to punish communities in which attacks had been made on Union troops.

52. H. Hitchcock, *op. cit.,* p. 75. Entry of November 19, 1864.

53. *Ibid.,* p. 62. November 16, 1864 (Hitchcock's italics).

54. Report of Brigadier General A. S. Williams, January 9, 1865. *Official Records,* Ser. I, Vol. XLIV, p. 212.

55. H. Hitchcock, *op. cit.,* p. 86. November 23, 1864.

56. D. P. Conyngham, *op. cit.,* p. 245. This Colonel Hughes also captured a Confederate surgeon and seized three thousand dollars in gold at Social Circle.

57. Papers of Rufus Mead, Jr. From a letter to his family from Savannah, December 28, 1864. Mead accumulated notes and then wrote long letters giving brief accounts of each day's occurrences. The tendency of soldiers and officers in Sherman's army to attempt to justify the crimes they saw perpetrated in the South follow a remarkably consistent pattern. Nearly all those who kept journals and diaries convinced themselves that the people of the South were guilty of crimes,

and there existed no necessity to extend to them the ordinary decencies of consideration.

58. *Idem.* J. T. Trowbridge, who traveled through the ruined states of the South in 1865, tells of Union soldiers shooting down whole droves of hogs, from which they removed the hindquarters only. His book is an account of conversations with the soldiers of both armies, farmers, Negroes and others. J. T. Trowbridge, *A Picture of the Desolated States and the Work of Restoration, 1865–1868* (Hartford, Connecticut, 1868), p. 478.

59. Report of Lieutenant Colonel Cyrus E. Briant, undated but doubtless rendered in December 1864. *Official Records,* Ser. I, Vol XLIV, p. 171.

60. Ella Mitchell, *History of Washington County* (Atlanta, 1924), p. 67.

61. L. Lewis, *op. cit.,* pp. 445–446.

62. W. F. G. Shanks, *op. cit.,* p. 44.

63. G. W. Pepper, *op. cit.,* p. 275. General Leggett, of the Seventeenth Corps, officially recognized the "bummer" in his Special Field Orders No. 163, December 1, 1864. " 'Bummers' are entitled to a position on ranks, and must be provided with it." *Official Records,* Ser. I, Vol. XLIV, p. 597.

64. G. W. Nichols, *op. cit.,* pp. 240–241.

65. *Ibid.,* p. 242.

66. D. P. Conyngham, *op. cit.,* pp. 313–314.

67. Charles E. Belknap, "Recollections of a Bummer" (Washington, 1898), p. 4. Captain Conyngham also describes battles between bummers of different corps. D. P. Conyngham, *op. cit.,* p. 312.

68. G. W. Nichols, *op. cit.,* p. 115.

69. C. E. Belknap, *op. cit.,* p. 6.

70. D. P. Conyngham, *op. cit.,* pp. 246–247.

71. Report of Brigadier General Alpheus S. Williams, Commanding Twentieth Army Corps, January 9, 1865. *Official Records,* Ser. I, Vol. XLIV, p. 207.

72. *Memoirs,* II, 185–186. Howell Cobb held a commission as major general in the Confederate army. He was well known, having served as Speaker of the U.S. House of Representatives and Secretary of the Treasury under President Buchanan.

73. H. Hitchcock, *op. cit.,* p. 84. Entry of November 22, 1864.

74. "Diary of Major James A. Connolly," p. 406. Entry of November 22, 1864.

75. Henry Fales Perry, *History of the Thirty-eighth Regiment Indiana Volunteer Infantry* (Palo Alto, Calif., 1906), p. 186.

76. See I. W. Avery, *op. cit.,* pp. 307–311, for an interesting, detailed account of Milledgeville on the eve of its occupation by Federal troops.

77. Julian Wisner Hinkley, *Service with the Third Wisconsin Infantry* (Madison, Wisc., 1912), p. 148.

78. *Memoirs,* II, 190. Nichols says that few troops were marched through Milledgeville proper. This could account in some measure for the preservation of the town from destruction. G. W. Nichols, *op. cit.,* p. 57.

79. Captain Conyngham said that the soldiers wanted to release the convicts "for the benefit of Georgia society." D. P. Conyngham, *op. cit.,* p. 255. He is obviously in error, as the prisoners had been released, with the exception of life termers, by Governor Brown's orders before Sherman's troops reached Milledgeville. See I. W. Avery, *op. cit.,* pp. 308–309.

80. D. P. Conyngham, *op. cit.,* p. 254.

81. I. W. Avery, *op. cit.,* p. 309.

82. "Diary of Major James A. Connolly," p. 408. Entry of November 23, 1864.

83. *Ibid.,* pp. 430–431. Entries for December 8 and 9, 1864.

84. Eliza Frances Andrews, *The War-Time Journal of a Georgia Girl 1864–1865* (New York, 1908), pp. 162–164.

85. *Memoirs,* II, 191.

86. H. Hitchcock, *op. cit.,* p. 99. Entry for November 27, 1864. See also report of Colonel Orlando M. Poe, Chief Engineer, dated December 26, 1864, in which he recounts destruction of the courthouse, "a very substantial brick building," at General Sherman's order. *Official Records,* Ser. I, Vol. XLIV, p. 57. Hinkley in his history of the Third Wisconsin said that two of Wheeler's cavalrymen were killed in the skirmish through Sandersville, and adds: "Our Indians seemed to think it was not exactly right to leave the dead bodies with their scalps on. They soon fell into the civilized custom of making war, however, and did not afterwards express any desire to take scalps." J. W. Hinkley, *op. cit.,* p. 151.

87. Papers of Rufus Mead, Jr., letter of December 28, 1864.

88. E. Mitchell, *op. cit.,* pp. 66–67.

89. E. F. Andrews, *op. cit.,* p. 32.

90. C. W. Wills, *op. cit.,* p. 327. Entry of November 25, 1864. General Order No. 26 was issued by General O. O. Howard from Gordon, Georgia, on November 22, 1864, and warned that any man caught in burning or pillaging a house would be shot. *Official Records,* Ser. I, Vol. XLIV, p. 521.

91. L. M. Dayton, Aide-de-camp, to General Frank P. Blair, December 2, 1864. *Official Records,* Ser. I, Vol. XLIV, p. 606.

92. H. Hitchcock, *op. cit.,* pp. 132–134. Entry for December 3, 1864.

93. L. M. Dayton to General H. W. Slocum, December 2, 1864. *Official Records,* Ser. I, Vol. XLIV, p. 609.

94. Sherman to General O. O. Howard, December 5, 1864. *Ibid.,* p. 628.

95. Lieutenant Tupper is not further identified. He was adjutant to Colonel George E. Spencer, who commanded the First Alabama Cavalry.

This cavalry conducted itself so outrageously toward the citizens of Georgia that General Frank P. Blair, to whose corps it was attached, issued a stinging reprimand to Colonel Spencer. On November 20, 1864, General Blair informed Colonel Spencer that "the outrages committed by your command . . . are becoming so common, and are of such an aggravated nature that they call for some severe and instant mode of correction." Blair, who was lax with his own corps, promised that unless the Alabama Cavalry stopped its pillaging of houses he would "place every officer in it under arrest and recommend . . . dishonorable dismissal from the service." C. Cadle, Jr., Assistant Adjutant General, Seventeenth Corps, to Colonel George E. Spencer, November 20, 1864. *Official Records,* Ser. I, Vol. XLIV, pp. 504–505.

96. *Memoirs,* II, 194.

97. H. Hitchcock, *op. cit.,* p. 161. Entry of December 9, 1864.

98. G. W. Nichols, *op. cit.,* p. 86. Entry of December 9, 1864.

99. *Memoirs,* II, 194.

100. T. F. Upson, *op. cit.,* pp. 123–124. Upson describes the manner in which the rails were heated and twisted. As for the deep cuts, "We fill with brush and tree tops and put shells in them that will explode if the Johnny's try to clean them out." In his *Memoirs,* II, 105, Sherman proved that he was familiar with this practice when he wrote: "We filled up many deep cuts with trees, brush and earth, and commingled with them loaded shells, so arranged that they would explode on an attempt to haul out the bushes."

101. *Memoirs,* II, 203.

102. Sherman to Halleck, January 1, 1865. *Official Records,* Ser. I, Vol. XLIV, p. 13.

102. Sherman to Halleck, January 1, 1865. *Official Records,* Ser. I, Vol. XLIV, p. 13.

103. Tom S. Gray, "The March to the Sea," *Georgia Historical Quarterly,* XIV (1930), 135–136.

104. Although little cotton was planted in 1864, apparently a considerable amount remained in barns and warehouses. The owners of the cotton found it difficult to get their cotton out. General Slocum's Left Wing reported the burning of 17,000 bales, and the Right Wing destroyed over 3,000 bales. See Report of General H. W. Slocum, January 9, 1865. *Official Records,* Ser. I, Vol. XLIV, p. 159. General O. O. Howard's report, *ibid.,* p. 76.

105. John Spencer Bassett, *A Short History of the United States, 1492–1929* (New York, 1935), p. 539.

106. J. T. Trowbridge, *op. cit.,* p. 464. Actual starvation stalked many families in the section of Georgia traversed by Sherman's army.

107. Jacob D. Cox, *The March to the Sea, Franklin and Nashville* (New York, 1882), p. 37. *The Charleston Daily Courier,* January 31, 1865, quotes refugees from Savannah who stated that Negro women and

children from the interior of Georgia were huddled together in a pen outside Savannah, where they were suffering from cold and exposure. Little, if any, food and clothing were supplied them by the Union army. The soldiers apparently lost all interest in them after their arrival in Savannah. The same issue of *The Daily Courier* printed an appeal from Union General Rufus Saxon dated January 6, 1865. General Saxon, calling himself military governor of South Carolina, solicited the charity of the North to save hundreds of Negroes who were threatened with death by exposure and disease. He described the slaves at the end of the march: "They have arrived on the coast after long marches, and severe privations, weary, famished, sick and almost naked."

108. Apparently some news of the treatment of Southern women had reached the North since William Owner of Washington, D.C., described in his diary the destruction carried out by the national troops in Georgia and added, "But greater wrong than those enumerated has been perpetrated—women, pure and spotless, have been violated." Diary of William Owner, December 20, 1864. Colonel Isaac W. Avery states that "several well authenticated cases of rape occurred" in Milledgeville. I. W. Avery, *op. cit.,* p. 312. *The Augusta Chronicle and Sentinel* of December 8, 1864, referred to "the inexplicable and atrocious insults offered to the defenseless women of our land," quoted in James Ford Rhodes, *History of the United States* (8 vols.; New York, 1904), Vol. V, footnote, p. 25. General Jacob D. Cox said that "murders, rapes, and other heinous personal offenses were nearly unknown." J. D. Cox, *op. cit.,* p. 41.

CHAPTER IX. South Carolina

1. Sherman to Grant, December 22, 1864. *Official Records,* Ser. I, Vol. XLIV, p. 7.
2. Sherman to Grant, December 24, 1864. *Memoirs,* II, 225.
3. Sherman to Grant, March 12, 1865. *Memoirs,* II, 297.
4. Report of Brevet Brigadier General Orlando M. Poe, Corps of Engineers, U. S. Army, Chief Engineer, October 8, 1865. *Official Records,* Ser. I, Vol. XLVII, p. 173. Each of the four columns built approximately 100 miles of corduroyed road.
5. *Idem.*
6. Henry Van Ness Boynton, *Sherman's Historical Raid. The Memoirs in the Light of the Record. A Review Based Upon Compilations from the Files of the War Office* (Cincinnati, 1875), pp. 208–209. Boynton was the Washington correspondent for *The Cincinnati Gazette* and a severe critic of Sherman's *Memoirs,* which he charges are inaccurate and unfair. Even so, Boynton was forced to admit that the march through South Carolina was a remarkable feat.
7. D. P. Conyngham, *op. cit.,* p. 310.

8. Papers of Rufus Mead, Jr., January 4, 1865.
9. J. W. Hinkley, *op. cit.*, p. 146.
10. "Major [James A.] Connolly's Letters to his Wife, 1862–1865," in Illinois State Historical Society Publications, No. 35 (1928), p. 379.
11. General Halleck to Sherman, December 18, 1864. *Memoirs*, II, 223. (The italics are General Halleck's.)
12. Sherman to Halleck, December 24, 1864. *Ibid.*, pp. 227–228.
13. *Ibid.*, p. 254.
14. Petition of Citizens at Columbia, S.C., to Honorable James A. Seddon, Secretary of War (C.S.A.), December ———, 1864. Exact date unknown. *Official Records,* Ser. I, Vol. XLIV, p. 1011.
15. Reprinted in *The Charleston Daily Courier,* January 4, 1865. The reference is to Confederate Major General Robert Ransom, Jr., commanding the Second Subdistrict of South Carolina with headquarters at Charleston.
16. *Ibid.,* January 5, 1865.
17. Alfred Roman, *The Military Operations of General Beauregard in the War Between the States* (2 vols.; New York, 1884), p. 628, in the Appendix to Chapter XLIII.
18. *Ibid.,* p. 634.
19. *Ibid.,* pp. 636–637, in the appendix to Chapter XLIV. Governor Brown of Georgia withdrew all Georgia militia from Beauregard's command on February 24, 1865. See *ibid.,* p. 647.
20. *The Augusta Constitutionalist* quoted in *The Charleston Daily Courier,* January 20, 1865.
21. [   ] McCarter's Journal, 1861–1866. 2 Vols., Division of Manuscripts, Library of Congress, Vol. II, pp. 68–69. Little is known of McCarter. On page 24 of volume I he states that he is a citizen of South Carolina. He lived in both Charleston and Columbia, and knew the country and the people of prominence in South Carolina. He refers to the Confederate army as "our army." The tone of his journal indicates that he did not approve of secession, and after the beginning of the war he favored peace at any cost.
22. D. P. Conyngham, *op. cit.,* pp. 310–311. Where Conyngham refers to Rarysburg he probably meant Furysburg, which is in the vicinity of Hardeeville and is referred to by Sherman in his *Memoirs,* II, 241.
23. Clement Eaton (ed.), "Diary of an Officer in Sherman's Army Marching Through the Carolinas," *Journal of Southern History,* IX (1943), p. 243. Entries for February 7 and 8, 1865.
24. Entry for February 17, 1865. *Ibid.,* p. 244.
25. G. W. Pepper, *op. cit.,* pp. 336–337.
26. J. D. Cox, *op. cit.,* p. 40.
27. *Ibid.,* pp. 175–176. Footnote on p. 175 states that this report is found in the "ninety-second Illinois," commonly attributed to Colonel Smith D. Atkins, one of Kilpatrick's brigade commanders.

28. Papers of Rufus Mead, Jr., reference to February 6, 1865, found in Mead's letter of March 30, 1865, to his family.

29. Yates Snowden (ed.), *History of South Carolina* (5 vols.; Chicago and New York, 1920), II, 801.

30. D. P. Conyngham, *op. cit.,* p. 323. Conyngham recounts that the Union soldiers claimed that cotton was on fire when they entered the town. He does not give much weight to the claim, however, since he realized that Orangeburg's destruction was in keeping with Sherman's policy.

1. Papers of Rufus Mead, Jr., letter to his family dated March 30, 1865, covering events of the march from February 3, 1865.

2. M. P. Andrews, *op. cit.,* p. 253. From the reminiscences of Mrs. C. P. Poppenheim. The events referred to occurred on February 23, 1865. These troops were probably part of the Fifteenth Army Corps.

3. *Camden Journal and Confederate* of March 10, 1865, as quoted in Thomas J. Kirkland and Robert M. Kennedy, *Historic Camden* (2 vols.; Columbia, S.C., 1926), II, 164.

4. E. A. Pollard, *Southern History of the War* (2 vols.; New York, 1866), II, 450.

5. G. W. Pepper, *op. cit.,* pp. 330–331.

6. *Ibid.,* p. 332.

7. "Major [James A.] Connolly's Letters to his Wife," p. 380. Letter of March 21, 1865.

8. D. P. Conyngham, *op. cit.,* p. 266.

9. *Ibid.,* 313. Captain Conyngham relates that in this instance he was able to shame the men into rescuing a part of the furniture.

0. G. W. Nichols, *op. cit.,* p. 140.

. Y. Snowdon, *op. cit.,* II, 801. From carefully collected testimony of a citizen's committee under the chairmanship of ex-chancellor J. P. Carroll. Little can be found concerning Carroll except that he was the author of "Historical Collections of South Carolina." The committee published its report in May 1866. More than 60 depositions and statements in writing from as many dependable citizens were placed in the committee's hands.

. Sherman to Halleck, December 24, 1864. *Memoirs,* II, 227.

. James G. Gibbes, *Who Burnt Columbia?* (Newberry, S.C., 1902), p. 98, from the deposition of C. F. Jackson. This witness doubtless saw units of the Fifteenth Corps because Sherman makes the positive statement that "the Seventeenth Corps did not enter the city at all." See *Memoirs,* II, 281–282.

. See *Memoirs,* II, 284–286.

. J. G. Gibbes, *op. cit.,* p. 96, from Gibbes's own sworn statement as to what he knew and saw in Columbia on February 17, 1865.

. *Ibid.,* p. 92. From the sworn statement of John McKenzie.

Joseph LeConte, *'Ware Sherman: A Three Months Personal Experience in the Last Days of the Confederacy* (Berkeley, 1937), pp.

141–142. LeConte was professor of chemistry at South Carolina Col lege, and during the period the college was closed he was consultin chemist for the Confederate States Nitre and Mining Bureau.

48. McCarter's Journal, II, 73–74. McCarter was prominent enough i Columbia to be a member of the citizen's committee which calle on Sherman the morning following the fire.

49. C. W. Wills, *op. cit.*, p. 350.

50. D. P. Conyngham, *op. cit.*, pp. 330–332. Sherman mentions in h *Memoirs*, II, 279–280, that the Lady Superioress asked his protectior claiming that she had taught Minnie Sherman at a convent school i Brown County, Ohio. Sherman refers to the convent as operated b the Sisters of Charity. In Y. Snowden, *op. cit.*, p. 806, it is referred t as the Ursuline Convent, and its head was properly called Mothe Superior rather than Lady Superioress.

51. [Major] S. M. H. Byers, *With Fire and Sword* (New York, 1911), 169. Byers was the adjutant of the Fifth Iowa Infantry, and he w one of the Union officers freed by Sherman's troops at Columbia. H was the author of the words to the song "Sherman's March to th Sea," which he presented to Sherman in Columbia. Sherman attache Byers to his staff for the remainder of the campaign. *Memoirs*, 1 282–283.

52. McCarter's Journal, X, 85.

53. M. P. Andrews, *op. cit.*, p. 258. From the story of the destruction Columbia by Madame S. Sosnowski, a Polish woman who was teacher at Barhamville College, two miles north of Columbia.

54. D. P. Conyngham, *op. cit.*, pp. 332–333.

55. Y. Snowden, *op. cit.*, II, 810.

56. *Idem.* See William Gilmore Simm's account of the burning of Colu bia in J. G. Gibbes, *op. cit.*, pp. 35–36. Simms describes the exte of Dr. Gibbes's valuable collections, particularly original South Car lina correspondence of the Revolution. Gibbes compiled and edit three volumes of documents which were also destroyed. There we collections of paintings, engravings and relics.

57. From the account of James G. Gibbes to *The Philadelphia Tim* published September 20, 1880, in J. G. Gibbes, *op. cit.*, p. 11.

58. Mrs. Joseph E. Johnston to Miss Louise Wigfall, February 19, 18 in Mrs. D. Giraud Wright, *A Southern Girl in '61* (New York, 190 p. 229.

59. McCarter's Journal, II, 80. McCarter was a member of the citize committee.

60. *Ibid.*, pp. 78–79.

61. J. G. Gibbes, *op. cit.*, p. 16. From Gibbes's own statement. He s the cattle in question and states that his brother was in charge them.

62. Y. Snowden, *op. cit.*, II, 809, quoting the committee report. Porti

of this report are also to be found in J. G. Gibbes, *op. cit.*, p. 126 ff.

63. G. W. Nichols, *op. cit.*, p. 222. Major James A. Connolly also noticed the improved conduct of Sherman's soldiers and mentioned it in his letters of March 12 and March 21, 1865, to his wife. See "Letters of Major [James A.] Connolly," pp. 379–381.

64. Manning Force Ferguson, "Marching Across Carolina," in *Sketches of War History 1861–1865,* published by the Loyal Legion of the United States (6 vols., Cincinnati, 1888–1906), I, p. 16. General Force commanded the First Brigade, Third Division, Seventeenth Army Corps.

65. G. W. Pepper, *op. cit.*, pp. 342–343. Captain Pepper reproduces General Slocum's order in full. It is stated by one writer, at least, that this attitude on the part of Sherman's army was of short duration. The Federal troops expected to receive a welcome from North Carolina's Union-loving citizens, but soon learned that North Carolina was still too sympathetic toward the Confederacy. Sherman then released his vandals to wreck the countryside, particularly around Fayetteville. Rev. J. L. Underwood (compiler), *The Women of the Confederacy* (New York and Washington, 1906), pp. 175–177, quoting Cornelia P. Spencer's *Last Ninety Days of the War,* pp. 214–215.

Bibliography

Primary Materials

Manuscripts

Autograph Draft of W. T. Sherman Memoirs. Copies of letters to military officers prepared for, but not included in *Memoirs.* Division of Manuscripts, Library of Congress.

Confederate State Papers, Miscellaneous, 1862–1865, Division of Manuscripts, Library of Congress.

Diary of Captain Wimer Bedford, Division of Manuscripts, Library of Congress.

The Diary of Edmund Ruffin, 1856–1865, 14 vols., Division of Manuscripts, Library of Congress.

Diary of William Owner, December 20, 1860, to May 12, 1867, 9 vols., Division of Manuscripts, Library of Congress.

McCarter's Journal, 1860–1866, 2 vols., Division of Manuscripts, Library of Congress.

Papers of Rufus Mead, Jr., May 25, 1861, to May 3, 1865, Division of Manuscripts, Library of Congress.

The W. T. Sherman Papers, 88 vols., Division of Manuscripts, Library of Congress.

Newspapers

Augusta Chronicle & Sentinel, 1864–1865.
Charleston Daily Courier, 1864–1865.
Canton (Mississippi) *American Citizen*, 1864–1865.
Canton (Mississippi) *Tri-Weekly Citizen*, 1864–1865.
Mobile Daily Advertiser and Register, 1864–1865.
Mobile Daily Tribune, 1864–1865.
Montgomery Daily Advertiser, 1864–1865.
Richmond Daily Dispatch, 1864–1865.

Memoirs, Diaries and Correspondence

Alcorn, James L. "Letters of James Lusk Alcorn," edited by P. L. Rainwater, *Journal of Southern History*. Baton Rouge, 1935—, III (1937), pp. 196–209.

Andrews, Eliza Frances. *The War-Time Journal of a Georgia Girl 1864–1865*. New York: D. Appleton and Company, 1908.

Belknap, Charles E. "Recollections of a Bummer." Military Order of the Loyal Legion of the United States. Commandery of the District of Columbia. War Papers 28. Prepared by Companion Charles E. Belknap and Read at the Stated Meeting of January 5, 1898, Washington, 1898.

Blackford, Susan Leigh (compiler). *Letters from Lee's Army*. New York: Charles Scribner's Sons, 1947.

Byers, S. H. M. *With Fire and Sword*. New York: The Neale Publishing Company, 1911.

Cate, Wirt Armistead (ed.). *Two Soldiers; The Campaign Diaries of Thomas J. Key, C.S.A., December 7, 1863–May 17, 1865 and Robert J. Campbell, U.S.A., January 1, 1864–July 21, 1864.* Chapel Hill: The University of North Carolina Press, 1938.

Chambers, William Pitt. "My Journal," in *Publications of the Mississippi State Historical Society*, Centenary Series. Jackson, 1916–1925), V (1925), pp. 227–386.

[Connolly, James A.]. "Diary of Major James A. Connolly," in *Illinois State Historical Society Publications*. Springfield, 1900–1942, No. 35 (1928), pp. 384–438.

[————]. "Major Connolly's Letters to His Wife, 1862–1865," in *Illinois Historical Society Publications*. Springfield, 1900–1942, No. 35 (1928), pp. 217–383.

Conyngham, David P. *Sherman's March Through the South with Sketches and Incidents of the Campaign*. New York: Sheldon and Company, 1865.

Cox, Jacob D. *The March to the Sea, Franklin and Nashville*. New York: Charles Scribner's Sons, 1882.

Dawson, Francis W. *Reminiscences of Confederate Service, 1861–1865*. Charleston, S. C.: The News and Courier Book Presses, 1882.

Erickson, Edgar L. (ed.). "With Grant at Vicksburg. From the Civil War Diary of Captain Charles E. Wilcox," *Journal of the Illinois State Historical Society*, Vol. XXX (April 1937–January 1938).

Fitch, Michael H. *Echoes of the Civil War as I Hear Them*. New York: R. F. Fenno & Company, 1905.

Force, Manning Ferguson. "Marching Across Carolina," *Sketches of War History, 1861–1865. Papers Read before the Ohio Commandery of the Military Order of the Loyal Legions of the United States, 1883–1908*. 6 vols. Cincinnati: Robert Clarke & Co., 1888–1908.

Gilpin, E. N. "The Last Campaign—A Cavalryman's Journal." Reprint from the *Journal of U. S. Cavalry Association*. Washington: 1888—, Vol. 18, No. 68 (April 1908).

Grant, Ulysses S. *Personal Memoirs*. 2 vols. New York: Charles L. Webster & Company, 1885.

Hedley, Fenwick Y. *Marching Through Georgia. Pen Pictures of Everyday Life in General Sherman's Army from the Beginning of the Atlanta Campaign until the Close of the War*. Chicago: Donohue, Henneberry & Co., 1890.

Hinkley, Julian Wisner. *A Narrative of Service with the Third Wisconsin Infantry*. Wisconsin History Commission, Original Papers No. 7. Madison: Democrat Printing Co., State Printers, 1912.

Hitchcock, Henry. *Marching with Sherman, Passages from Letters and Campaign Diaries of Henry Hitchcock*. Edited by M. A. DeWolfe Howe. New Haven: Yale University Press, 1927.

Johnston, Joseph E. *Narrative of Military Operations, Directed During the Late War Between the States*. New York: D. Appleton and Company, 1874.

Jones, Jenkins Lloyd. *An Artilleryman's Diary*. Wisconsin History Commission, Original Papers No. 8. Madison: Democrat Printing Co., State Printers, 1914.

LeConte, Joseph. *'Ware Sherman: A Three Months Personal Experience in the Last Days of the Confederacy*. Berkeley: University of California Press, 1937.

Lee, Stephen Dill. "Sherman's Meridian Expedition and Sooby Smith's Raid to West Point," *Southern Historical Society Papers*. Richmond, 1876–1930, VIII (1880), pp. 49–61.

Lunt, Dolly Sumner (Mrs. Thomas Burge). *A Woman's Wartime Journal; An Account of the Passage Over a Georgia Plantation of Sherman's Army on the March to the Sea, as Recorded in the Diary of* ————. Macon: The J. W. Burke Co., 1927.

Nichols, George Ward. *The Story of the Great March, from the Diary of a Staff Officer*. New York: Harper & Brothers, 1865.

Pepper, George W. *Personal Recollections of Sherman's Campaign in Georgia and the Carolinas*. Zanesville, Ohio: Published by Hugh Dunne, 1866.

Perry, Henry Fales. *History of the Thirty-eighth Indiana Volunteer Infantry*. Palo Alto, California: F. A. Stuart, Printer, 1906.

Porter, David D. *Incidents and Anecdotes of the Civil War*. New York: D. Appleton and Co., 1865.

Sharland, George. *Knapsack Notes of General Sherman's Grand Campaign Through the Empire State of the South*. Springfield, Ill.: Johnson & Bradford, Printers, 1865.

[Sherman, William T.]. *Memoirs of General William T. Sherman* by himself. 2 vols. New York: D. Appleton and Company, 1875.

[————]. *The Home Letters of General Sherman*. Edited by M. A. DeWolfe Howe. New York: Charles Scribner's Sons, 1909.

[————]. *The Sherman Letters.* Edited by Rachel Thorndyke. New York: Charles Scribner's Sons, 1894.

Stevenson, Benjamin F. *Letters from the Army.* Cincinnati: W. E. Dibble & Co., 1884.

Upson, Theodore F. *With Sherman to the Sea; the Civil War Reminiscences of Theodore F. Upson.* Edited by Oscar Osburne Winther. Baton Rouge: Louisiana State University Press, 1943.

Wills, Charles W. *Army Life of an Illinois Soldier, Including a Day by Day Record of Sherman's March to the Sea, Letters and Diary of the Late Charles W. Wills.* Compiled and published by his sister. Washington: Globe Printing Company, 1905.

Wright, [Mrs.] D. Giraud. *A Southern Girl in '61; the War Time Memoirs of a Confederate Senator's Daughter.* New York: Doubleday, Page & Company, 1905.

Other Printed Sources

Badeau, Adam. *Military History of Ulysses S. Grant from April, 1861, to April, 1865.* 3 vols. New York: D. Appleton and Company, 1885.

Bowman, Samuel M., and Richard B. Irwin. *Sherman and His Campaigns.* New York: Charles B. Richardson, 1865.

Boyd, David French. "General W. T. Sherman as a College President." Reprint from *The American College.* New York: 1909–1910, II (April 1910).

Boynton, Henry Van Ness. *Sherman's Historical Raid, The Memoirs in the Light of the Record; A Review Based upon Compilations from the Files of the War Office.* Cincinnati: Wilstach, Baldwin & Co., 1875.

Confederate Records of the State of Georgia. Compiled and published under authority of the Legislature by Allen D. Chandler. 6 vols. Atlanta: C. P. Byrd, State Printer, 1909–1911.

Gibbes, James G. *Who Burnt Columbia?* Newberry, S. C.: Elbert H. Aull Company, 1902.

Greene, Joseph I. *The Living Thoughts of Clausewitz.* The Living Thoughts Library. New York: Longmans, Green and Co., 1943.

Guemsey, Alfred H., and Henry M. Alden. *Harper's Pictorial History of the Great Rebellion*. New York: Harper & Brothers, 1868.

Jordan, Thomas, and J. P. Pryor. *The Campaigns of Lieut.-General Forrest and Forrest's Cavalry*. New York: Blalock & Company, 1868.

Lossing, Benson J. *The Pictorial Field Book of the Civil War in the United States of America*. 3 vols. Hartford: Thomas Belknap, Publisher, no date.

Morton, John Watson. *The Artillery of Nathan Bedford Forrest's Cavalry*. Nashville and Dallas: The Publishing House of the M. E. Church, South, Smith & Lamar, Agents, 1909.

Richardson, Albert D. *The Secret Service; The Field, The Dungeon, and the Escape*. Hartford: American Publishing Company, 1866.

Roman, Alfred. *The Military Operations of General Beauregard in the War between the States, 1861 to 1865*. 2 vols. New York: Harper & Brothers, 1884.

Trowbridge, John T. *A Picture of the Desolated States and the Work of Restoration, 1865–1868*. Hartford: Published by L. Stebbins, 1868.

Vattel, Emmerich de. *The Law of Nations . . .* (Translated from the French). Northampton, Mass.: Simeon Buckner, Publisher, 1820.

The War of the Rebellion: A Compilation of the Official Records of the Union and Confederate Armies. 129 vols. and index. Washington: Government Printing Office, 1890–1901.

Secondary Materials

Andrews, Matthew Page (compiler). *The Women of the South in War Times*. Baltimore: Norman, Remmington Company, 1924.

Avery, Isaac Wheeler. *The History of the State of Georgia from 1850 to 1881, Embracing the Three Important Epochs: The Decade before the War of 1861–1865; the War; the Period of Reconstruction, with Portraits of the Leading Men of This Era*. New York: Brown & Derby, Publishers, 1881.

———. "Atlanta, Its History and Advantages," *City of Atlanta—A Descriptive, Historical and Industrial Review of the Gateway City of the South.* Being the World's Fair Series on Great American Cities. Louisville, Ky.: The Inter-State Publishing Company, 1892–1893.

Bassett, John Spencer. *A Short History of the United States, 1492–1929.* Revised edition. New York: The Macmillan Company, 1935.

Battey, George Magruder, Jr. *A History of Rome and Floyd County State of Georgia United States of America Including Numerous Incidents of More Than Local Interest 1540–1922.* Vol. I. Atlanta: The Webb and Vary Company, 1922. Reprinted Atlanta: Cherokee Publishing Company, 1969.

Bettersworth, John K. *Confederate Mississippi. The People and Policies of a Cotton State in Wartime.* University Station, Baton Rouge, La.: Louisiana State University Press, 1943.

Burne, Alfred H., *Lee, Grant and Sherman.* New York: Charles Scribner's Sons, 1939.

Dictionary of American Biography. Edited by Allen Johnson and Dumas Malone. 21 vols. and index. New York: Charles Scribner's Sons, 1928–1944.

Garner, James Wilford. *Reconstruction in Mississippi.* New York: The Macmillan Company, 1901.

Gorham, George C. *Life and Public Services of Edwin M. Stanton.* Boston and New York: Houghton Mifflin Company, 1899.

Gray, Tom S. "The March to the Sea," *Georgia Historical Quarterly.* Savannah, 1917—   ), XIV (1930), pp. 111–138.

Halleck, Henry Wager. *International Law or, Rules Regulating the Intercourse of States in Peace and War.* New York: D. Van Nostrand, 1861.

Horn, Stanley F. *The Army of Tennessee; A Military History.* Indianapolis: The Bobbs-Merrill Company, 1941.

Johnston, William Preston. *The Life of Gen. Albert Sidney Johnston, Embracing His Services in the Armies of the United States, The Republic of Texas, and the Confederate States.* New York: D. Appleton and Company, 1879.

Kirkland, Thomas J., and Robert M. Kennedy. *Historic Camden.* 2 vols. Columbia, S.C.: The State Company, 1926.

Lewis, Lloyd. *Sherman, Fighting Prophet.* New York: Harcourt Brace and Company, 1932.

Mitchell, Ella. *History of Washington County.* Atlanta: Byrd Printing Co., 1924.

Phillips, Ulrich B. *The Life of Robert Toombs.* New York: The Macmillan Company, 1913.

Polk, William M. *Leonidas Polk, Bishop and General.* 2 vols. New York: Longmans, Green and Co., 1915.

Pollard, Edward A. *Southern History of the War.* 2 vols. New York: Charles B. Richardson, 1866.

Rhodes, James Ford. *History of the United States from the Compromise of 1850.* 8 vols. New York: The Macmillan Company, 1904–1919.

Sheppard, Eric William. *Bedford Forrest, the Confederacy's Greatest Cavalryman.* New York: L. MacVeagh, The Dial Press, 1930.

Snowden, Yates (ed.). *History of South Carolina.* 5 vols. Chicago and New York: The Lewis Publishing Company, 1920.

Temple, Sarah Blackwell Gober. *The First Hundred Years; A Short History of Cobb County in Georgia.* Atlanta: Walter W. Brown Publishing Company, 1935.

Underwood, J. L. (compiler). *The Women of the Confederacy.* Washington and New York: The Neale Publishing Company, 1906.

Wiley, Bell Irvin. *The Life of Johnny Reb, the Common Soldier of the Confederacy.* Indianapolis: The Bobbs-Merrill Company, 1943.

Wyeth, John Allen. *Life of General Nathan Bedford Forrest.* New York: Harper & Brothers, 1899.

Index

Fonda, Col. John G., 100

Food, taken by Union troops, 90, 111–13, 134–37, 146, 159–61; destruction by Sherman's forces, 91–92, 98–99, 118, 121, 123; starvation in Miss., 101–02; relief for civilians, 102, 134–35, 202

Foraging by Union troops, 153–55, 159–72, 176–77, 197, 201

Force, Gen. Manning F., 203

Forrest, Gen. Nathan B., 59, 88, 112, 117, 219(9–11)

Fort Corcoran, 20

Fort Donelson, 42, 44, 48

Fort Henry, 42, 44

Fort McAllister, 180

Fort Pickering, 56

Fort Sumter, 8, 15

Foster, Gen. Ira R., 173, 233(19)

Foster, Gen. John S., 180

Fourteenth Army Corps, 144, 155–56, 161–63, 172–73, 175–76, 178, 180, 192

Fremont, Gen. J. C., 27

Fullerton, Maj. Hugh, 100

Gallisonville, S.C., 193

Garrard, Gen. Kenner, 138, 139

Gay, Mary A. H., 134

General Orders No. 100, xii

George, Gen. J. Z., 100

Georgetown, S.C., 187

Georgia, march to sea, 80–83, 153–83, 221(8), 224(35); Sherman in northern Ga., 137–47, 189; Roswell Factory prisoners, 138–40; march to Atlanta, 147–49, destruction of Atlanta, 150–52, 155: defenseless, 156–57; destruction of

state buildings, 174–5; estimate of damage to, 181

Gibbes, James G., 198, 201, 246 (56)

Gibbes, Robert W., 201

Goldsboro, N.C., 185, 186

Gordon, Ga., 177

Grahamville, S.C., 193

Grant, Gen. Ulysses S., 21, 205; tacit approval of Sherman's policies, xiii; war activities, 42, 49, 53; at Shiloh, 44–45, 51; attacked by press, 45–48, 217 (14); base at Corinth, 50–53, 55–56; relations with Sherman, 53–54, 57–58, 64, 217(9), 218(23), 219(8), 221(9); and Sherman's war tactics, 67, 69–72, 74–76; and Sherman in Miss., 87–90, 96–98, 101–02, 107–11, 116, 156; order against pillaging, 108–09; and Sherman's march through S.C., 184, 186

Grave looting, 152

Greenville, Miss., 113, 114

Gresham, Gen. W. Q., 125

Grierson, Gen. B. H., 99

Griffith, Maj. Patrick, 136

Guerillas, 44, 50, 55, 57–65, 138, 143, 220(20), 230(107); Sherman's response to, 63–65, 69, 75, 142, 176; definition, 219–20(14)

Halleck, Gen. Henry W., 55, 181, 215(38), 217(7,14), 228(89); Sherman's superior officer, 34–5, 37, 39–40, 44–47; base at Corinth, 49–52; General in Chief, 53, 54; on international